The Barque
of Saviors

BOOKS BY RUSSELL DRUMM

In the Slick of the Cricket

The Barque of Saviors

The Barque of Saviors

EAGLE'S PASSAGE FROM

THE NAZI NAVY TO

THE U.S. COAST GUARD

RUSSELL DRUMM

Houghton Mifflin Company

BOSTON   NEW YORK   2001

Library of Congress Cataloging-in-Publication Data is available.
ISBN 0-395-98367-3

Book design by Anne Chalmers
Typefaces: Janson Text, OptiLord Swash

Printed in the United States of America

QUM 10 9 8 7 6 5 4 3 2 1

The line drawings are by Jeff Fisher.
The sail-setting illustration on page 24 is by Jason Biondo.

For Russell Malcolm Drumm

and Reta Hitchings Drumm,

who taught me to love life

He rises by lifting others.

— Robert Green Ingersoll

Acknowledgments

I WOULD first like to express my gratitude to the greater Coast Guard family for giving me the opportunity to experience the esprit that allows a perennially underfunded and often underappreciated organization to perform its many duties so well.

My thanks to Coast Guard historians Dr. Robert Browning and Scott Price. As for *Eagle* herself, let's have three cheers for the cadets, enlisted complement, and officers of the barque. There is much that she taught me. I offer my heartfelt thanks to former *Eagle* captains Paul Welling, David V. V. Wood, Patrick Stillman, Don Grosse, and Robert Papp and to current captain Ivan Luke; to lieutenant commanders Keith Curran and Cathy Tobias; to bosuns Keith Raisch, Doug Cooper, Rick Ramos, and Rick Birch; to petty officers Tracy Allen, Kelly Nixon, and Matt Welch; and to BM3 Greg Giggi. Thank you, Robert LaFond; I know our discussions were not easy.

There are two individuals without whom I could not have written this book. Karl Dillmann, *Eagle*'s square-rigger sailor, raconteur, and teacher extraordinaire, showed me a thousand reasons that this story should be told. The nation owes a great debt to Petty Officer Dillmann for helping to shape a few thousand Coast Guard officers over the past decade. And I extend my heartfelt thanks to Tido Holtkamp, a proud American who served on the barque as a German naval cadet in 1944 under the flag of the Third Reich. Mr. Holtkamp's honest recollections of Germany's darkest hours and his invaluable translation skills have thrown light into long-forgotten corners of *Eagle*'s history.

Detlev Zimmerman, who now serves with the U.S. Coast Guard Auxiliary, was a cadet on *Horst Wessel* in 1943 before joining Germany's

U-boat fleet. Mr. Zimmerman's translations and vivid recollections of World War II were extremely helpful to me. Thanks to my neighbor, Lynette Widder, a German scholar, who helped translate.

I have tried not to overstate *Eagle*'s German past, but it would have been wrong to ignore it. She is the product of a great German ship-building tradition, though she sailed under the German flag for just ten of her sixty-five years. Of course the decade from 1936 to 1946 was a hellish time, and the barque was lucky to survive it. I must thank the people of Blohm & Voss, the shipyard that built her, for their help.

And for their enlightening correspondence from across the At-lantic, I am sincerely grateful to Peter Jepsen, Otto Schlenzka, Ludwig Brenner, Gunther Tiegs, Otto Piepenhagen, Herman Adamowicz, Brigitte Jacobs, Siegfried Stiller, Karl Tadey, Hans-Joachim Meinke, Fritz Hugo, Karl Lederer, Marion Niemann, Willie Starck, Werner Fistler, Ludwig Brenner, Jürgen Gumprich, Karl Bethke, Heinrich Gutbier, Herbert Jander, and Paul Zock. Herbert Böhm, a fine journal-ist from Hamburg, deserves my special thanks for the research he so generously shared.

The only thing a writer with an idea really needs is a believer other than himself. I have been blessed with three. My very able agent, Emma Sweeney of Harold Ober Associates, recognized where I was going and deftly parted the seas. Elaine Pfefferblit, Houghton Mifflin's editor extraordinaire, led the way with a firm, guiding hand. Peg An-derson, manuscript editor, fine-tuned the prose and saw the manuscript through production. And thank you, Bill Henderson of Pushcart Press, for encouraging me to write books way back when.

Prologue ⌒

IT WAS on the deck of Coast Guard Patrol Boat 41934 on the night of July 17, 1996, that I realized the necessity of writing this book. Three of the boat's crew members were struggling to lift aboard the body of a young woman, one of the 230 victims of TWA Flight 800. Much more lifting would be required before the sun rose again off Moriches, Long Island.

As a reporter for a local newspaper, I watched my job shrink to insignificance as our boat and others like it moved through the wreckage. I did not have to be there, but the young Coast Guard men and women retrieving bodies and hoping against all reason for survivors did. The manner in which they went about their work was a story that needed telling.

I was no stranger to the Coast Guard, having had a working relationship with my hometown station and having written a number of stories over the years about scary Coast Guard rescues of yachtsmen and fishermen in the northwest Atlantic. They were stories of heroism plain and simple, but they seemed to blurt from the page, incongruous among the routine drug arrests, meeting announcements, and posturing letters to the editor. Except within the shrinking fishing community, drowning in giant seas appears to have gone out of fashion, to be a primal throwback, something like being eaten alive. The flares in the night sky, the ropes and floats of rescue, seem primitive, like leeches applied to the sick. The general public translates such stories into fiction, our repository for acts too selfless to fathom. The professionalism I was witnessing on the Montauk station's 41-footer, though familiar to me, was of another age—it had roots. That quality is old but strong, spawned long ago on vulnerable, wind-driven ships, but it continues to breathe today.

Two weeks earlier I had been aboard the barque *Eagle*, the Coast Guard Academy's training ship, as she moved down the Elbe River from the city of Hamburg. The cadet training cruise that summer had included a visit to the old Hanseatic port on the occasion of the barque's sixtieth birthday. In June of 1936 she had been christened *Horst Wessel* in honor of a Nazi martyr and put into service as a training ship for naval officers of the Third Reich. Adolf Hitler had attended the christening. Now, having been claimed and renamed by the Coast Guard after the war, *Eagle* trains rescuers.

There is good in the world and evil, heroes and villains, and a whole lot in between. There are ways to fall and ways to rise, to sink and to remain afloat. *The Barque of Saviors* is about falling and rising and staying afloat.

A few apologies. First, to those who are expecting a chanty-filled, "blow-ye-winds-hi-ho" profile of a sailing ship: *Eagle* is, indeed, a noble square-rigger, heir to one of the great shipbuilding traditions, but this book is more about her people and their worlds—Germans during one of the darkest periods in history and Americans ever since—and about the world of one man in particular. I apologize to the thousands of Coast Guard folks, active, retired, and passed over the bar, whose stories I was unable to tell. Finally, to readers who will confront nautical jargon for the first time: although I'm proud to have been called shipmate, I cannot claim to be part of the Coast Guard's extended family. I have, however, made an attempt to record its ancient language, and I include a glossary of nautical terms in the book's after section.

The Barque
of Saviors

Eagle *flies under the red, white, and blue.*
(Courtesy of U.S. Coast Guard)

1 UNDER WAY

Eagle shoulders large seas, her sails white against a bruise of clouds. Her masts sketch giant arcs as she rolls. Small, yellow shapes — the crew in rain gear high in the rigging — streak across a blackening sky. *Eagle's* bowsprit, holding the feet of four triangular jibs, points skyward, then down into a trough. Her sharp cutwater slices the large, cold swells lifting her 1,800 tons smoothly and deliberately, as only a 300-foot sailing ship can slice them. The t'gallants, the topgallant sails just set, have encouraged a stiff northeast breeze to heel us to 12 degrees, according to the brass clinometer mounted on the pilothouse. The deck is a hillside.

Eagle's beam is just 39 feet. She is yachty, with a sexy, rounded tumblehome, the type of stern called a champagne counter, which invites the waves of a following sea to lift it rather than crash down upon it. The teak fo'c'sle deck is 12 feet above the water, although today the bow watchman standing next to the ship's bell is riding 20 feet heavenward toward a lingering morning moon as the crests of waves pass under him. Then he drops into the troughs within easy reach of the geyser slices that peel with a roar from beneath the eagle eye of the barque's golden figurehead. Whistling low, the steel cable stays and shrouds supporting the masts withstand tremendous forces of wind and swell. Mainmast and foremast each rise nearly 150 feet above the sea. Their entire suit of ten square sails, plus the headsails and staysails and the mizzenmast's split spanker, total 21,350 square feet. When the sails are filled by a 30-knot wind such as this, they generate the power of 10,000 horses.

We left New London, Connecticut, yesterday, May 1, slipping past the black whalebacks of nuclear submarines at Groton en route to the Pacific Ocean via the Panama Canal. Officer candidate trainees, many from the Coast Guard's enlisted ranks, will depart at the former Rodman Naval Station on the west side of the Panama Canal and be replaced by the first-phase cadets of the United States Coast Guard Academy's class of 2001. The training ship will then head up the West Coast to Oregon. The cadets will spend five weeks on board learning basic seamanship, navigation, quartermastering, engine-room protocol, and watch-standing. The other half of their class will replace them in August. All are third-class cadets, sophomores, and have been aboard before only for a few days during the summer preceding their first year. But in that brief time most cadets begin their transformation. I've witnessed this process twice, once in 1994 under Captain Patrick Stillman and again in 1996, when Captain Robert Papp took command. Papp is to be relieved on July 3 in San Francisco by Captain Ivan Luke, who will join us at Guantanamo Bay, Cuba, and observe until we reach Panama. These three men, like 60 percent of all Coast Guard officers since 1946 and hundreds of German naval officers and sailors for ten years before that, began their careers as will the class of 2001 — with a mental rearrangement.

The change begins when an eighteen-year-old steps onto the deck of this sailing ship, onto what before had been distant horizon dressing: pretty and perhaps vaguely evocative of a lost era. With the ship still tied to the dock, the new cadet steps aboard and confronts the overwhelming power predicted by the masts and rigging. Large constructs are brought out of storage like antique furniture from the collective attic. They are muscled across slippery decks, down to where the stomach turns, and arranged among long shadows. Then, all at once, the teenager grasps that the towering steel masts with their crucifix yards, the taut cable shrouds, and the miles of coiled rope are meant to receive and harness an awesome force. These young men and (since 1976) women, who may never have given much thought to the wind, now sense the truth behind its invisibility. They begin to understand that they've come aboard with insufficient fears. Some realize faster than others that this is the point; that wild fear can and must be harnessed like the wind. It follows that humor, however nervous, is the first yoke to be applied. "Herculean," an adjective that fits the ship, is cut down and proudly shrugged off as "herky." The word is an active part of *Eagle* vocabulary, as is "pucker factor," the ship's standard measure of fear, based on the relative constriction of the anal sphincter. Today the pucker factor is low, despite the bad weather conditions. Only the more experienced hands are aloft. For them, climbing about the labyrinth of cable and line and handling a few acres of sail in a 30-knot blow is just another day at work. Yet there is fear nearby, or the ghost of it.

Here, off the Rhode Island coast, *Eagle* passes — all sails set, sleek, like the slipper of a goddess, with her golden eagle figurehead and a bone in her teeth — almost directly over the rusting bones of U-Boat 853. On this cold May 2, it has been fifty-five years and four days since Moby Dick, the name given U-853 by her pursuers, died right here on the ocean floor with all hands. It was Nazi Germany's final military defeat. The histories of this sailing ship and of the fallen submarine are tightly interwoven, like the lay of the long ropes coiled and hanging from *Eagle*'s brass belaying pins.

At the end of World War II, Germany had three nearly identical steel sailing ships, which had trained naval officers and petty officers, many of whom were bound for the U-boat service. One of the trainers was scuttled by her crew in the Baltic a few days before Admiral Karl Dönitz, Hitler's successor as head of state, surrendered. The other two were seized by the Royal Marines soon after. In bomb-gutted Bremerhaven, on May 15, 1946, after three months of repair and refitting, *Horst Wessel* was recommissioned as the U.S. Coast Guard Cutter *Eagle*. (A cutter is any Coast Guard vessel 65 feet or more in length and with accommodations for the crew to live on board.)

Though older than the cadets, I too came aboard innocent, a newspaper reporter who liked the idea of sailing ships but had only a basic knowledge of them. From time to time I'd seen the barque under sail on the horizon and seen it closer when she anchored in Montauk's Fort Pond Bay, a magnificent visitor whose people and purpose were unknown to me. A vow to one day go aboard took twenty years to realize. The academy's public affairs office suffered the likes of me on occasion and granted my request to join the ship for a leg of the cadet summer cruise in 1994.

Because of the perception that Coasties practice a lost art out somewhere at sea — and because they are also the cursed fish police to some of the very people who depend on their skills, I found the Montauk Coast Guard Station to be an outpost, cheerful enough within, but nevertheless a place apart. At the time I was unaware of any connection between the station's people and the barque that graced the horizon from time to time. And I was assured by the station's commanding senior chief, Ed Michels, that there was no connection. An excellent leader, well liked by his people and the community, he admitted that the last pangs of romance with the sea had been beaten out of him years before within the cramped bulkheads of dozens of "afloat assignments." He knew of my fascination with the barque and seemed to delight in telling me how *Eagle* squandered the Coast Guard's perennially limited resources. She was the officers' yacht and had nothing to do with "real" operations. Worst of all, she was a sailboat, bigger perhaps, but of the same species that was the bane of the SAR (Search and Rescue) stations' summers because of the sailboat crews' frequent lack of judgment. But then came the day when Chief Ed Michels approached me to say that his father, a man who had captained a charter fishing boat most of his life, was dying, and if I was going to New London, could I get this one particular poster of *Eagle* under sail, heeled, with a bone in her teeth. He wanted to put it by his father's bed. I complied.

I'm sure that although he'd never been aboard *Eagle*, Chief Michels knew far better than I that the immediate mesmerizing grace of her lines camouflages an immense strength that takes time to appreciate. It means learning enough to see the invisible tissue that grows among people, between the past and the present, the quick and the dead, the animate and its opposite. I've learned that the wind driving her is invisible just to prove that such tissue exists today. In '94 I watched a man who was about to be transferred from his *Eagle* billet sitting alone on a bench in the middle of the night looking up at the ship, moved to tears at the mating of form and function as she lay dockside in Baltimore's Inner Harbor. His fellow petty officers had taken him out, and he was drunk, crying, blubbering, and repeating over and over to the ship: "You beautiful girl, you beautiful fucking girl."

Michels liked to praise the superiority of engines, but in the process he protested wind too much. Motisola Howard, the meteorologist on this trip, can tell you that wind results from variations in temperature and barometric pressure, but after twenty-five years in the Coast Guard the chief knew that it all boiled down to the earth's turning, the spinning of todays into tomorrows. Wind is time passing. *Eagle* was built herky because some of it passes very hard. Like the Cape Horners she was designed after, she was made to withstand extreme weather but also to avoid another tragedy of the kind Germany suffered in 1933, when the trainer *Niobe* sank with the loss of sixty-four young men.

Even on sunny days, the northwest Atlantic in early May still holds the gunmetal of winter. The green color and the creatures of the Gulf Stream have not yet arrived. Cod and other bottom dwellers dominate the waters. On the bottom, the early spring lobsters are hard and black, their molting not begun. Traps baited with bunker and skate are set on the sea bottom all along the coasts of eastern Long Island and southern New England.

Below us, among the lobster traps, Moby Dick settles into the sand, sloughing metal. If ocean swells could reach down 17 fathoms, they would rinse the olive Thames and Connecticut river silt from the sandy bed to reveal white quartz, pink granite, and purple garnet grains. The same glacial sands drape the shoulders of Nantucket, Martha's Vineyard, Block Island, Narragansett, and Montauk, the islands and points of land that are the head and footstones of Moby's grave. The U-boat's last victim, the collier *Black Point*, rests nearby. Fourteen miles to the west, within the same cemetery, the skeleton of HMS *Culloden* lies where she ran aground when her pursuit of French ships during the American Revolution was interrupted by a violent winter storm. In Gardiner's Bay, near where we anchored last night, the wooden submarine *Turtle* was blown apart by Royal Navy guns during the War of 1812. *Turtle*'s captain, Joshua Penny, and the nine men who turned the sub's screw oar" by hand, failed in their attempt to attach explosives to the frigate *Superb* and paid the price. Two victims of Kaiser Wilhelm's U-boats are on the bottom near the Race, which connects Block Island and Long Island sounds. Fishing boats, too numerous to count, molder on this bottom. U-853 sits upright, with ragged depth-charge holes above the forward crew quarters and on the starboard side of the engine room. Over the years sport divers have taken souvenirs, including bones. In 1960 an anonymous German crewman was buried in Newport with full U.S. military honors after a diver brought his skeleton ashore from the conning tower. The West German government was outraged, as were the local clergy and a number of retired U.S. Navy officers.

The funeral illustrates a central fact of life: soldiers and sailors kill their enemy counterparts for an entire panoply of reasons — always noble, always heinous, according to the two-way mirrors of war. Then, when the shooting stops, they are often able to welcome their former foes as members of a larger fraternity, leaving it to heaven to cast blame, to wreak vengeance. Of course, they draw a distinction between war — to professionals a natural occurrence to be endured like a hurricane — and crimes against humanity, which are indefensible. The distinction can be obvious or subtle, but the inevitability of storms, be they man-made or heaven-sent, cannot be argued. Nor can the existence of the rescuers among us, the very few who are called to save the innocents from the maelstrom and even, as I've witnessed, to escort the drowned back from the sea.

Perhaps on the moral plane, *Eagle*'s is a rags-to-riches story, but it is not altogether simple. The barque that trained sailors for the doomed Third Reich is also the product of a maritime culture that created the master race of sailing ships. Should you wish to build a steel barque today, Lloyds of London will provide the insurance only if she is built to this ship's 1936 specifications, which are still the state of the art. Trial and tragic error went into the design, perfecting in steel the square-rigger technology that evolved in wood and hemp over centuries. Today *Eagle* lifts hearts and frees souls as she soars under sail, yet she will never escape her strange and fateful ties to *Unterseeboote* — submarines — and to their drowned crews, many of whom trained on this ship and her two sisters. She is a school of paradox, and I've become one of her students, with much to learn.

2 DREAMSHEETS

MOBY DICK was dead. She had fallen hard, and now oil, black fossil blood, crept from the U-boat and spread along the sand bottom of Block Island Sound. The oil called to the ancient nostrils of lobsters and crabs — the delicious reddish brown and white crabs with the vise grip and the spider crabs that wear a light pink armor beneath their olive-drab covering of algae.

Crustacean-to-oil is the oldest of animal magnetisms; knowing this, lobstermen used to weight their pots with ballast bricks soaked in oil as an enticement to complement the bait. During the war they used kerosene because the preferred fish oil, of crushed and rendered mossbunker, had become too expensive. The finer bunker oil, squeezed at the nearby Promised Land plant from the immense schools of menhaden seined from the sound, was being used to smooth the paint of ships and the mechanisms of millions of guns.

Helmut Frömsdorf, the U-boat's captain, had miscalculated or, more likely, at twenty-four, had thrown caution to the winds. It was the moon-made wind in this case, the ebb east into and flow west out of Long Island Sound, where his submarine should not have gone. It was much too late for such a dangerous mission. The heart of the Third Reich had stopped beating in a Berlin bunker less than a week before, but the end had been there to see ever since the Allies fought their way ashore at Normandy the previous June.

Before Normandy, U-853 was one of a number of subs sent out to track the weather approaching the Atlantic coast of Europe. The weather was seen as the key to predicting when the inevitable invasion would occur. For months the submarine ducked and dodged her pursu-

Captain Robert Papp speaks to an informal gathering in the waist, 1996. (Russell Drumm)

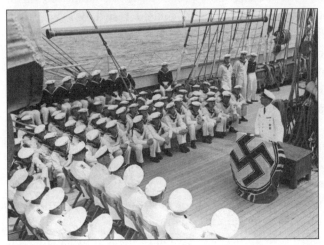

Captain August Thiele addresses his crew, 1937. (Collection of Herbert Böhm)

ers, surfacing only to transmit reports and recharge batteries. But her enemy's presence was ever-increasing, even in the mid-Atlantic between Newfoundland and the Azores, U-853's assigned hunting and forecasting grounds.

Lieutenant Commander Helmut Sommer was the skipper; the six-foot ten-inch Frömsdorf was his executive officer. They both had taken part in the *Baubelehrung* — literally, construction teaching — a word without an English equivalent. It means the building of a ship in the presence, and under the scrutiny, of its captain and most of the crew. The word bears the added assumption that an almost mystical bonding takes place during the process, making ship, captain, and crew one entity.

Sommer and Frömsdorf had missed the glory years of the submarine war, the "happy time" that had begun with eight U-boats in early 1942 as Operation Drumbeat, *Paukenschlag* — the start of the war with the United States. Back then oil tankers and freighters silhouetted against the lights of American coastal cities were perfect targets. The U-boaters listened to jazz on the radio. They could hear "Deep in the Heart of Texas," "Chattanooga Choo-Choo," and "I Got It Bad and That Ain't Good." The wolf packs had dominated for four years, sending 10 million tons of Allied ships, along with their men and supplies, to the bottom. Twelve hundred ships were sunk in 1942 alone. In March of 1943, when U-853 came off the ways in Kiel, the U-boat fleet sank three-quarters of a million tons of shipping. Then the tide turned. By late June, when U-853 was commissioned on the banks of the Weser River in Bremen, the German wolves had begun to lose the battle of the Atlantic. New technology, code breaking, and tactics destroyed 40 percent of the entire U-boat force the very next month. By the end of 1943, 237 U-boats had perished.

Twenty-one were sunk in April of 1944 alone, the month Sommer set out from Lorient in occupied France on U-853's first patrol, without benefit of the new device called a *Snorkel*, a Dutch invention that came too late for most of the boats. With it, batteries could be recharged and air delivered to oxygen-deprived men while they were submerged. Without it, the U-boats had to surface, a vulnerability the Allies' hunter-killer groups of small aircraft carriers, destroyers, and corvettes were exploiting with increasing success. It was not possible to retro-fit U-853 with a snorkel before she left Lorient. She would have to surface to breathe. To make matters worse, the Allies' radar and sonar had improved. Every weather broadcast betrayed the U-boat's position. Each, therefore, was followed by a mad dash to a new location.

On May 25, far out in the Atlantic, U-853 had a shot at the *Queen Mary*, but the opportunity was lost to the *Queen*'s great speed. The U-boat surfaced in the liner's disappearing wake and was attacked almost immediately by Swordfish aircraft catapulted from the merchant ships *Ancylus* and *MacKendrick*. Captain Sommer stayed on the surface and fired on the planes with the boat's 20- and 37-millimeter antiaircraft guns. Then she dove. Six destroyers and the aircraft carrier *Croatan*, an American hunter-killer group that had been tracking the submarine for weeks, found her again on June 15. She dove, but the hunters, knowing she must surface, kept up the search for seventy-two hours with ship's radar and from the air. So dogged was the pursuit that the men of the *Croatan* group saw Ahab in their commander, John Vest, with U-853 as Moby Dick. During the same four days the sub was dubbed *Der Seiltänzer* — Tightrope Walker — by the forty-eight crewmen cramped and breathing the batteries' acid fumes within her pressure hull. Sommer was a skillful commander, but with each desperate breath and submergence, his crew must have feared that the sea saw them as playing at sinking, daring the bottom so far below. More even than their fight with the enemy, the foundation of their fear was the fall to the bottom and the effortless crush of the sea's embrace. They prayed Sommer could keep his balance.

When they heard "Alaaarm!" the crew ran forward in the stale air to weight the bow and speed their downward escape. It's not hard to imagine that through the thin steel bulkheads, the sound of the ballast tanks, inhaling to dive and exhaling to surface, became that of a giant creature dying. The sound mocked the crew's own difficult breathing. On June 18, *Croatan* intercepted a weather forecast from U-853; the carrier's high-frequency direction finder put her thirty miles away. Eleven minutes later, fighter planes were strafing the sub, killing two of her gunners and the meteorologist. Shrapnel tore into Captain Sommer on the bridge. Though hit in the stomach, head, and arms, he remained standing and took Moby Dick down just as Avenger bombers arrived to finish her off. Ahab's sonar searched for her well into the Bay of Biscay before breaking off the chase, certain that the sub had been sunk.

⌒

BEFORE dawn between June 8 and 10, a young helmsman named Detlev Zimmermann left the port of Bordeaux on his first U-boat assignment. His time aboard would be short. The Resistance was everywhere on the docks of the French port, and although the sub left under quiet battery power, British dive bombers found her on the surface just after dawn. Zimmerman and four others were on bridge watch when the bomber dove like a gannet after a school of herring and made a direct hit on the foredeck. The boat sank with all hands except for the men on the bridge.

Zimmermann cannot recall the U-boat's number today. If he could, he would know where the doomed submarine was built, for the number identified the yard that built it: Deutsche Werke at Kiel, A. C. Weser in Bremen, Blohm & Voss in Hamburg. Such details aren't important until later in one's life, when the adrenaline that kept all the numbers from running together has long ago been spent. For Zimmerman, it all happened so fast: growing up on the farm in Pomerania on the Baltic coast, then learning that his father, a farmer, and two of his uncles had died on the Russian front. He joined the Kriegsmarine and, like many a U-boater, learned basic seamanship on the beautiful white-hulled sailing ship *Horst Wessel*. The steel barque had been built seven years earlier at Blohm & Voss, a yard renowned for its powerful, wind-driven cargo ships, as well as *Horst Wessel* and her nearly identical sisters, *Gorch Fock*, *Albert Leo Schlageter*, and *Mircea*, and later for its U-boats and for the battleship *Bismarck*.

Horst Wessel was named for an early follower of Adolf Hitler, a student who grew up on a street named Judenstrasse in a part of Berlin whose residents tended to favor the teachings of Karl Marx. His father, Dr. Ludwig Wessel, was a decorated veteran of World War I and a Lutheran pastor. Political debate during the turmoil that followed Germany's humiliating defeat in 1918 and the Depression took the form of brutal street battles among members of dozens of organizations seeking to fill the leadership void. Young Horst moved restlessly from one nationalist, anticommunist group to the other, more often fighting than pursuing his university studies, much to his mother's dismay. He finally found a home with the Sturmabteilung, the S.A., a group that accepted the theories of Adolf Hitler. In Berlin the organization was divided into units called *Stürme* — "storms." Horst was a handsome young man, tall, blond, and strong, and the brown uniform pants and shirts of the S.A. fit him well. A musician, he had a gift for leadership and was fond of a fight. In May of 1929 he was chosen to lead the cell known as Sturm V. Horst Wessel had just one flaw that the S.A. leaders worried about. Her name was Erna Jaenicke, a.k.a. Lucy of Alexanderplatz, a penniless prostitute whom he'd rescued from a beating by one of her johns. He'd found her in a seedy part of Berlin, to which he had moved in order to better understand the feelings of the working class, for as a middle-class child he had had little contact with workers. Horst and Erna moved in together. She quit the street and worked as a seamstress. The S.A. leaders overlooked this scandal because "Die Fahne Hoch," the song Horst had written, was fast becoming its anthem.

> Make way, make way, here come the brown battalions!
> Make way, make way, the storm troop men are here!
> Upon the swastika the millions look with longing.
> The days of freedom and of bread are here!

Albrecht "Ali" Hohler, a convicted murderer who had affiliated himself with the Red Front Fighters, a communist group, was not impressed by Wessel. A big man, with arms covered with tattoos and with a large tattoo of a girl on his chest, he was Erna Jaenicke's former lover. In February of 1930, on a tip that Wessel was at home with Erna and one of her girlfriends, Hohler showed up with a pistol. He shot Horst in the mouth and fled. It took Wessel nine days to die. Joseph Goebbels, Hitler's able propaganda minister, came to his bedside. It was not long before a martyr was born. "How high Horst Wessel towers over Jesus of Nazareth," as one Nazi newspaper put it. Hohler was killed. Streets were renamed Horst Wessel, and a ship. The "Horst Wessel Lied," as his song was known, became the Nazi anthem, and Germany's second national anthem after "Deutschland über Alles." All this in honor of a death that was far from the result of ideology. The killing that elevated Horst Wessel to such a vaunted place in the Nazi pantheon was the act of a jealous lover.

Detlev Zimmermann served aboard *Horst Wessel* in February of 1943. After leaving the barque, he went to artillery school on the old battleship *Schlesien* and to submarine school on beautiful Lake Constance in southern Germany. Then, suddenly, it seemed, he was desperately treading water in the Bay of Biscay as his shipmates descended to the bottom.

Today he lives in my hometown at the eastern tip of Long Island, fourteen miles from the grave of Moby Dick. He has lived there for thirty years. During the summer months, he teaches seamanship to recreational boaters with the U.S. Coast Guard Auxiliary. His wife, Ruth, from a small town in East Prussia, tends a neat garden. High on a bluff near their home, facing south, are the thick concrete shells of two artillery-fire control bunkers. At the beginning of the war their slit-eyed windows were made to look innocent with a cozy shingle façade and summer-cottage sashes and sills. Curtains were drawn as though for shade, to hide the telescopes that searched for U-boats, ready to guide the fire of Montauk's hidden 16-inch naval guns. Absorbed into the background now, dozens of such sentinels remain, searching the past from atop the bluffs of nearby Gardiner's, Plum, and Great Gull islands, as well as on Montauk and, farther east on Block Island, overlooking the grave of U-853.

Over two thousand miles away and more than half a century ago, Zimmermann and the rest of his watch were picked up by a German escort ship. He went by bus back to Germany and then on to Trondheim, Norway, and U-Boat 815, known to the crew as *Schwarze Hand*, Black Hand. Her insignia was a black mailed fist rising from the sea with a broken ship in its grip. At the same time, in the Norwegian port of Stavanger, U-853, with her prancing horse insignia, waited for her next assignment. It had taken more than two weeks for the sub to sneak back through the phalanx of hunter-destroyers, dive bombers, and mines that all but cut off her return to Lorient. Frömsdorf, who had taken command from the wounded Sommer, was good at keeping the boat hidden beneath thermoclines of denser, colder water, which blocked the enemy's sonar reception. The boat arrived in Lorient on July 4 and underwent repairs. She was to have been fitted with a snorkel, but again there was no time. By early August of 1944, the invading armies had fanned out from Normandy and surrounded France's German-held Atlantic ports, including Lorient.

U-853 left Lorient for Norway on August 27 under commander Günter Kuhnke, of the tenth U-boat flotilla. She was the last U-boat to make it out of port. Helmut Frömsdorf was promoted to the official command of U-853, though with the unofficial foreboding of Sommer, who considered his former first officer incautious and overly ambitious. Frömsdorf had spent his last day in Germany with his sister, Helga. Before leaving for the train station, the newly promoted captain stopped to wind the family's 150-year-old grandfather clock. Because of his height, he was the only one who could do so without using a stool. On the last turn of the key, the clock's spring broke. Brother and sister drove to the station in silence.

U-853 finally got her snorkel at the Blohm & Voss yard in Hamburg before proceeding to Norway. U-boats were being sunk at a terrible rate. One hundred fifty-nine went to the bottom with all hands between July of 1944, when U-853 returned to Lorient, and February 24, 1945, when she left on patrol from Stavanger. Miraculously, Frömsdorf was able to navigate through the minefields that surrounded the port. The boat entered the Atlantic, where she hunted convoys for a month. Frömsdorf never broke radio silence. Four other U-boats that left with her did use their radios and were quickly sunk.

On April 1, Frömsdorf was ordered to the American coast on what must have seemed a futile mission. He was bound for the waters off Boston. If the pickings proved slim there, he was instructed to prowl around the busy ports of Halifax, Nova Scotia, or New York. The crewmen listening to the radio while on the surface heard "Rum and Coca-Cola" and "Swinging on a Star." The boat was moving down the New England coast on May 1, the day Hamburg radio announced the death of Adolf Hitler. The words were preceded by a movement of Anton Bruckner's Seventh Symphony, played as a dirge. There was a long drum roll, and then a sonorous voice: "In his operational headquarters, our führer, fighting to his last breath against Bolshevism, died for Germany this afternoon in the Reich Chancellery. On April 30, the führer appointed Grand Admiral Karl Dönitz as his heir. The grand admiral, heir to the führer, now speaks to the German people."

Dönitz told them that he intended to continue the fight against "the advancing Bolshevik enemy" and against the Americans and British as long as they impeded Germany's stand against the spread of Bolshevism. "God will not forsake us after so much suffering and sacrifice."

Three days later, Dönitz, whose earlier requests for more submarines might have changed the course of the war had they been granted, ordered the few left to cease fire. As Germany's new head of state, he surrendered to English forces on May 5. The next day he issued a second communiqué to the remaining U-boats:

My U-boat men, six years of war lie behind you. You have fought like lions. An overwhelming material superiority has driven us into a tight corner from which it is no longer possible to continue the war. Unbeaten and unblemished, you lay down your arms after a heroic fight without parallel. We proudly remember our fallen comrades who gave their lives for führer and Fatherland. Comrades, preserve that spirit in which you have fought so long and so gallantly for the sake of the future of the Fatherland. Long live Germany."

The battle for the Atlantic had killed 28,000 of the 39,000 enlisted in the submarine service. There is no record that U-853, with its crew of fifty-five, received the cease-fire order, which was never acknowledged.

Frömsdorf had his boat at periscope depth east of Block Island on the day Dönitz issued the order. He was in only 80 feet of water, which was especially dangerous because Newport, Rhode Island, only 10 miles away, was home to a number of destroyers. He then entered Block Island Sound, the heavily guarded entrance to the larger Long Island Sound, the route to the busy ports of Newport, New London, and New York.

Frömsdorf found the small collier *Black Point* five miles southeast of Point Judith and made a decision the more cautious Sommer would not have made because of the shallow water and the proximity of American warships. Years later Sommer's wife said her husband had urged his young replacement to play it safe. The wounded captain feared that with the war already lost, the young man's rash ambition would put the lives of his young crew at risk.

At 5:55 in the afternoon, a torpedo designed to home in on propeller noise found the *Black Point* and tore off her stern section. The collier sank with twelve of her crew. A Yugoslav freighter witnessed the attack and transmitted a warning. The U.S. Coast Guard frigate *Moberly* and two Navy destroyer escorts, *Amick* and *Atherton*, were stationed off Cape Cod. They steamed the 30 miles to the scene, searching the depths with sonar to block the sub's escape to the east. By nightfall U-853 was lying low with engines off, but the bottom was only 100 feet below the surface, and at 8:14 P.M. *Atherton*'s sonar found its target.

Moby Dick was creeping along the bottom due east toward the open sea. *Atherton* let go thirteen depth charges set with magnetic fuses that would go off only if they hit metal. The sixth one exploded.

All manner of prayers and promises were surely made by the Tightrope Walker's crew as the rain of depth charges began. If only the boat could walk this one last wire. Keep her footing as she had the other times. After so many close, claustrophobic escapes, this silent, battery-powered reprise was balanced yet again upon the very nerves — spliced together and stretched to the limit — of her fifty-five crewmen.

Atherton followed up with smaller depth bombs called hedgehogs. Air bubbles, oil, splintered wood, a mattress, and a life jacket came to the surface. Seven destroyers now formed a line to cut off all escape. U-853 was trapped. *Atherton* made a run and dropped another thirteen depth charges. More oil and bubbles, another life jacket, a pillow, and a wooden flagstaff surfaced.

Still, Moby Dick continued to creep eastward at four knots. *Moberly* discovered the slow escape when she moved in to take over from *Atherton*, which had been damaged by her own charges in the shallow water. *Moberly*'s run resulted in similar damages, and the attack was suspended for an hour. Had the U-boat been able to run, this would have been the time to do it.

She had succeeded in sneaking 4,000 yards east of the original attack to 71 degrees, 27 minutes west longitude. But it was here, where the tide's more violent gusts roil around the morainal boulders of Block Island, that Captain Frömsdorf's squandered caution set sail in the tidal wind and escaped out of reach entirely. The clock could not be rewound.

Frömsdorf had told his mother that his boat was leaving on a most important mission from which he would not return. And he did not. His foolhardy attack on the *Black Point* in shallow water at war's end can be considered important only if his dreams of glory had been warped by defeat into a mission known only to him: the smuggling of wasted German pride via suicide into an afterlife of his own design. The ambitions of soldiers and sailors are meant to be the opposite: unselfish, clearly stated, and self-serving only if they benefit the group. Documents known today as dreamsheets are requests to a higher authority for the next assignment, the most preferred followed by alternatives in order of desirability. In a broader sense, and in the full spectrum of possibilities, a dreamsheet might be a formal request for an admiral's billet or a quick, prayerful chit begging for survival. Like a will, it can be rewritten quickly. And what of the fifty-four men who perished with Frömsdorf on the broken U-853? Navy divers entered her soon after the sinking. One sailor whose body had floated to the hatch just below the bridge was brought to the surface. Today, as *Eagle* passes over his grave, I can imagine his end:

He had been surprised by the water's cold, but not by its impatience. He had foreseen the rising flood more times than he could possibly count in the seconds he had left, so many times that his panic seemed a mere formality — and then his first breath of water and the list of people, beginning with his mother, he'd promised himself so many times to remember. Then he forgot his own name. And he was stomping around the capstan of the Horst Wessel *to weigh anchor with the others. The accordion player was sitting on top of the capstan as usual, but the boys were singing the "Horst Wessel Lied" — strange, because they never sang that song:*

Die Fahne hoch! Die Reihen dicht geschlossen.
S.A. marschiert mit ruhig festem schritt . . .

Raise the banner! Stand rank on rank together.
Storm troopers march, with steady, quiet tread . . .

The panicked treading continuing now underwater toward a diminishing pocket of air, the capstan in his mind turning, the anchor rising from the mud now to an old Berlin song:

The lamp cleaner is my father . . .

And then to the funny alphabet song to help turn the capstan with the lazy accordion player getting a free ride on top. Going right to the letter Q:

Quietsch is the sound of screwing underwater . . .

He was high on the ship's royal yard and the ship was heeled in a powerful wind. He was bent over the yard trying to grab the sail that was his mother's dress when he was small and he lost his grip and fell. The lightning jolt of fear left when he felt himself floating, not falling, up and away from the yard, the three masts, and her most beautifully shaped white hull like the slipper of a goddess, die Lorelei, *with a golden eagle below her bowsprit until she was very small and distant and moving away under full sail with a bone in her teeth.*

When the sun rose on May 6, it found a smooth lake of oil over a mile in diameter on the surface of the sea. Upon it floated escape lungs, empty life rafts, deck planking, the captain's cap, and the top of a chart table that identified the submarine: U-853.

A few divers have gone broke searching for the fortune in mercury, jewels, and U.S. currency rumored to have been taken from American Express vaults when the Germans entered Paris and eventually placed on U-853. There was, in fact, testimony at the Nuremberg war crimes trials that travelers' checks had been welded inside artillery shells and put on the submarine. These were never found, but nonetheless and not surprisingly, the rumor grew that U-853 was to have been Hitler's escape to South America, one of a thousand such escapes. Black spawn on the wind.

The war that ended in May 1945 is now rust and thick concrete. The brick chimney that never did lead to a fireplace is still attached to the Montauk bunker, but the cedar shingles are gone. The peaked roof blew off years ago. It is now just a thick, gray box with two floors, a basement and the observation floor, connected by a steel ladder. The gray interior walls of the bunker light up at sunrise through the narrow ribbon windows. The concrete is perpetually damp and smells even in the driest months, as though the salt rain of a sixty-year-old storm is pooled within. When the sun finds the west wall it explodes in a rainbow of serpentine graffiti shapes and the more legible words "I love krack" in black letters. There are the half-burned sticks and coals of several campfires. A filthy matted sleeping bag. The torn and rain-bleached pages of a magazine featuring a self-made hermaphrodite with large bosoms, a penis, and a 900 number to get in touch.

At least twice a year, Zimmermann's beautiful white-hulled *Horst Wessel,* long since rechristened *Eagle,* passes the bunker on her way around Montauk Point leaving the Thames River and, months later, returning. She passes by Moby Dick's grave on the way home before proceeding up the Thames past the nuclear submarines-in-progress at the Electric Boat yard in Groton to her dock at the Coast Guard Academy.

3 *The Yellow Satinwood Berth*

May 4, 1999

"Now! On the fore, on the main, set lower and upper topsails!"

"Uppers and lowers, aye!" A centuries-old litany of commands is shouted the length of the ship, starting from the bridge, along the waist, repeated to the fo'c'sle deck, and echoed back in acknowledgment. The weather is miserable; the ship is 100 miles off Barnegat Bay, New Jersey, heading south in a pea-soup fog, the sun fighting its way through like the promise of Panama, our destination so far away. A confused sea is summoning "technicolor yawns" from the sick crew members in the waist, while word spreads about what the bow watch on the four-to-eight discovered: the Coast Guard shield that *Eagle*'s figurehead holds in its talons was split in half by waves on the way around Montauk Point in the night. It was brand new, expensive Italian gold leaf over teak. I think it's the port side of the shield that's gone. *Semper* is there, but *Paratus* might be missing. Always without the Ready. We won't know for sure until someone climbs under the bowsprit and takes a closer look. The boatswain's mates who attached the shield to the figurehead are not happy because the bosun, Rick Ramos, is not happy. He's pissed off because the old shield cannot be found below in the bosun's hole and because it's his job to tell Captain Bob Papp what happened, and the captain's displeasure is sure to flow back downhill.

The crew is short by about fifty people. On board are forty-five officer candidates, in addition to *Eagle*'s thirty-five "permanent" enlisted crew, eight officers, a five-man navy contingent from the USS *Constitution* — Old Ironsides — and five civilians, including Colonel Charles García, retired from the air force, who has brought an urn with the

Seaman Greg LaFond on the mainmast crosstrees. (Roger Archibald)

combined ashes of his uncle, a navy admiral, and his uncle's wife, who are to join the waters of the Caribbean somewhere between Cuba and Panama.

"Lay out headsail downhauls. Man your lower sheets!" The general order to set sails is broken down into its subtler components by the mast captains. Coils of line are thrown off brass belaying pins. Line is faked out fast and taken up by dozens of hands.

"Lay aloft. Ungasket the lower topsail gear." One and two at a time, foremast and mainmast hands swing onto the windward ratlines from the fo'c'sle deck and from the pin rail in the waist, respectively. The soles of black combat boots step onto the lower ratlines and ascend the web from where the massive steel rigging screws called bottles tie the masts' thick cable shrouds to the hull. Once they've positioned themselves along the Flemish horses — the footropes below the upper topsail yards — the hands will loose the gaskets, the narrow strips of Dacron and line that hold the furled sail to the yard, and wait for the order to "let fall."

Back on deck, Greg Giggi, who was recently assigned to the foremast from the mizzen, anticipates the setting of the upper topsails, the next sails in order. He begins by making an offer — an *offer* — to a group of officer candidate trainees: "Those who want to go aloft . . . ," but he's overheard by the boatswain's mate–mast captain, who interrupts: "Those who *want* to go aloft? *Would like* to go? Lay aloft, goddammit!" Despite the weak and raspy nature of the commanding voice, the trainees jump to the wooden chest that holds the climbing belts. Earlier, the mast captain complained of postnasal drip, a sure sign, he said, of an approaching upper respiratory infection. It explained the rasp as well as the uncharacteristic fit of pique, especially as it was aimed at Giggi, whom the irritable petty officer likes and expects great things of. Seaman Giggi is a stocky blond bear whose arm wears a tattoo of an anchor adorned with the face of a fox. Though chastened, he thinks to remind one of the candidates climbing that the shrouds are the handholds, the vertical standing rigging made of steel cable, not the horizontal ratlines made of poly line.

"On deck!" bellows one of the hands on the lower topsail yard so that those 70 feet below can hear above the wind's growing whistle, the engine-room blowers aft, and the galley fans forward. The fans blow the essence of fried onions into the air, where it is welcomed by the hungry and not by the seasick. A freshening northwest wind takes the smell of the all-American burger topping over the leeward, port, side, mixing first with a final few cigarette exhalations before the butts follow and the work starts in earnest. "Lower topsail's in its gear," shouts the yard. "Aye!" the deck responds in the grated soprano of the acting main mast captain, Kelly Nixon.

"On the fore, on the main, let fall!" The command from Bosun Rick Ramos, standing with feet set wide on the bridge, is answered immediately by a chorus of "Sheet home!"

"Heave!" shout the line captains closest to the belaying pins. "Ho!" answer their crews. "Heave-ho, heave-ho," and the two-stroke human engines pull the lower topsail clews down to the main yards on both masts. "Ease the clewlines and bluntlines, let 'em run." The lower topsails fill. Aft on the quarterdeck, the mizzenmast team sets the lower spanker. Main and mizzen staysails are started by their own heaving teams and then roar aloft on the cable stays as the wind takes over. The

sound of their steel-ring hanks riding on the cable is that of swords being unsheathed. "That's well, main topmast staysail. Belay!" The rhyth-
mic exchanges of the "rope chokers" overlap as they squat for traction,
their feet adjusting to the roll of a six-foot sea and the heeling deck as
the sails are stretched and *Eagle* gets a taste of the wind.

"Man your upper topsail gear!" Those aloft, including the officer
candidates, who proceeded there most gingerly, are in place; they signal
their readiness to let the upper topsail fall. *"Let fall! Sheet home! Walk
away with the halyard!"* The setting of the upper topsails is the juice. It
takes the most muscle to set them, but when they are finally filled, in a
wind over 20 knots, the ship acts like a thoroughbred given rein. The
electricity spreads through the lines and rigging, completing a circuit
and lighting up the crew.

Eagle is a three-masted barque with a raised poop deck aft, with its
mizzenmast, and a raised fo'c'sle deck forward, home to the foremast.
The mainmast towers above the more expansive and sheltered waist in
the middle.

The foremast and mainmast actually consist of a lower mast and
a separate topgallant, or *t'gallant*, mast. The lower mast carries the
yards for its three square sails, and the topmast carries the t'gallant
and royal yards. The two mast sections overlap and are joined at the
doublings. A platform called the crosstrees supports the t'gallant mast's
separate shrouds. *Eagle*'s t'gallant masts were designed so that they
can be housed — slid into a lower position alongside the partner masts.
The housing and stepping procedures — or "evolutions" — are dangerous work. It was common on wooden sailing ships to drop or house
topmasts to lower the center of gravity in a bad storm. This is not
done on *Eagle*. Her upper masts are housed only to allow her to fit
under bridges whose spans are lower than 147.3 feet. Originally the
ship needed to squeeze under the bridges that spanned the Kiel Canal,
which was built in the nineteenth century to shorten the distance between the Baltic and the North Sea.

The mizzenmast has three fore-and-aft sails. The lower two of
these are gaff-rigged in a typically German design called a split spanker.
The smaller, topmost sail is affectionately known as the "turbo hanky."
The sails on the foremast and mainmast are square-rigged. Each mast

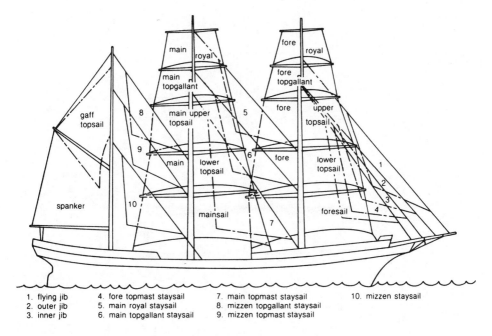

Eagle's sail plan. (Courtesy of U.S. Coast Guard)

1. flying jib	4. fore topmast staysail	7. main topmast staysail	10. mizzen staysail
2. outer jib	5. main royal staysail	8. mizzen topgallant staysail	
3. inner jib	6. main topgallant staysail	9. mizzen topmast staysail	

carries five square sails supported by hollow steel horizontal spars, or yards. The Germans designed the three upper yards of this ship and of the grain- and guano-hauling ships she was modeled on so that they could be dropped closer to the deck when not in use. Like lowering the topmasts on a wooden ship in a storm, lowering the heavy yards, and thus the ship's center of gravity, reduces a ship's rolling in heavy seas. Because of this arrangement, the three uppermost sails — the upper topsails, t'gallants, and royals — are set by hauling their yards upward into position. The lower topsails, mainsail course, and foresail are hauled downward when set.

Of the three movable yards, those that carry the upper topsails are the heaviest. When one is raised, fifty people "walk away" with the halyard, each marching in step and pulling a section of line the 50-foot length of the waist, dropping it, and circling back to clap on to another section. "Stomp together! Wake up the late bunks!" shouts Tracy Allen, a whip-thin Texan, *Eagle*'s outgoing mainmast captain, inspiring the

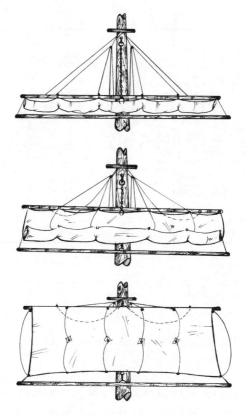

Setting the upper topsail.

crew with the sadistic thought of rousing the unfortunate twelve-to-four watch asleep below.

The newer members of the crew are hauling on the lines as directed without the faintest idea where they lead or what they do. In all, nearly two hundred lines rise from the pin and fife rails on the deck through a maze of blocks and fairleads. Shana Morris, one of the officer candidates, a former parachuting fighter of wildfires, widens her eyes and screws her face into a question mark when she's told that identifying the lines while feeling her way down the pin rail blindfolded will be part of the program. Justin LaMountain, a veteran deckie with a Crescent wrench growing from among green leaves tattooed on his wrist, tells her about the upper topmast halyard she's just finished hauling, explaining that the square sails of the upper topsail yards on both masts, as well as the t'gallant and royal yards above them, are sheeted home first. That is, their bottom corners, or clews, are pulled down to the yards below. These sails are stretched into action as their own movable yards are hauled upward into position. The lower topsails and mainsails, also called courses — "We'll set them now," LaMountain tells her — are bent onto fixed yards and clewed down into position "like a window shade." Shana's face remains screwed up but shows the start of a smile.

Higher spirits are emerging from the chrysalis of second-day offshore depression as *Eagle* heels and gains speed with her big courses set and now her "top-hamper," the t'gallants and royals, so high aloft it hurts one's neck to watch them blossom. The galley slaves have cranked up their CD player and are getting jiggy with it as the noon meal approaches completion. Those aloft continue to overhaul the sails, adjusting the slack of the buntlines, which run in parallel down the face of a square sail and control it when the sail is set or doused.

"See how the sail takes its natural shape and floats when slack is left in the buntlines. See the catenary in the buntline, the belly in the sail. The belly should be in the center of the ship." Boatswain's Mate First Class Karl Dillmann dispenses the rudiments of sail trim to his foremast squad, his meaty hands sculpting a picture for them. The ship's most experienced sailor, Karl is here, there, and everywhere, easing lines, grabbing a few bodies to heave around on a lift, a clewline, the tack jigger. Now he's forming up his people to adjust the upper and lower foremast yards. Kelly Nixon, his counterpart on the mainmast, is doing the same.

Meanwhile, Lynn Hensen, the helmsman of this particular watch, is communing with the father of modern fluid dynamics, keeping a close eye on the windward leech of the t'gallants, which she maintains just on the plus side of luffing. It's *Eagle*'s best point of sail. In the mid-1700s, Daniel Bernoulli lent his name to a principle that had been put to work long before his time. He determined that it was the low pressure created on the back of a sail that pulls the ship forward when the wind approaches it at a right angle, on its beam, as it does today, or forward of that. Other factors are at work when the wind is abaft the beam, that is, coming from behind the ship. To get the wind to attack the leading edge of square sails at the most advantageous angle, the yards can be moved from being braced square, their position when the wind is coming from behind, to a position known as "braced sharp," turned so that they are nearly parallel with the keel of the ship. As the ship sails closer to the wind, the yards are braced sharper, which is done using the lines known as braces. Once sails are set, the bracing is harder to do. Ideally, each of the yards would have at least ten people hauling around on its brace to move the thousands of pounds of steel spar and wind-filled Dacron to the desired angle. And, ideally, the yards would all be braced at once.

Today, because of our small crew, the yards are trimmed two at a time. "'Vast hauling starboard. That's well, uppers and lowers. Take the slack out of port, handsomely! Pass the stopper and belay — keep what you got!" The line crews squat low against the strain. "Back easy," barks the line captain, asking his crew for enough line to check the stopper, a length of flat, braided line attached to a pad eye on the deck. The stopper is quickly wrapped, in two hitches, around the loaded line. It's meant to hold the strain if the team can't. "Stopper's holding, back easy." The line captain handles the loaded line as if it were nitroglycerin until he gets a wrap on the brass pin. "Back easy." The repeated order gets him enough for two more figure eights. "Up behind." The line is belayed. Hands will not be dragged through the block. The deckies drop the relaxed part of the brace, leaving one of their number to coil it and hang it on its pin. The waist is a turmoil of line, as though an animal had spilled its guts. "Now. Make up all lines. Secure from sail stations." Officer candidate Mitch Fulcher walks away, watching the blisters grow on the palms of his hands.

There are no motorized winches, no ways to cheat, so off-duty engine-room "snipes," quartermaster's mates, cooks, and even the doctor have helped the deck force with the lines. The relatively slow pace of the sail-setting evolution is the result of inexperience as well as the small crew. Much of the deck force is new to the job. *Eagle* has not sailed in months, and in that time she has lost a number of her more seasoned seamen and petty officers, who have moved on to other billets. However, most of the work aloft is being undertaken by veterans, so it's graceful. Their ascent into the rigging is unhalting, a classic ballet performed upon a vertical stage of ancient design. At times, in the right light, it can seem even older, a simian jungle gathering of mysterious purpose.

Eagle is meant to sail in blue water and big wind. When she's in port or progressing under engine power, the bosuns and bosun's mates I've met exhibit a certain anxiety and crankiness that is only partially explained by their great responsibility. The mood seems like that of a man trying to act carefree while putting off something important his wife has asked him to do. The ship will surely draw an equivalent emotion from her female petty officers. We may see it before this trip is done, because while *Eagle* has had a number of female officers, Kelly Nixon, as soon as she gets her stripe officially, will be the ship's first female boatswain's mate first class and mast captain. She is already showing signs of a disciplined attachment to sails and spars.

Eagle's current bosun, Rick Ramos, at times has difficulty camouflaging his impatience. At forty-three, he's an experienced man with smooth, gorillalike movements and eyes that miss nothing. He's now stalking the deck deep in what appears to be thought, but it could be withdrawal. He's been trying to regain his humor after breaking with tobacco. A cigarette used to follow automatically in the afterglow of sail stations, but over the winter he was forced to quit when pneumonia evolved into pleurisy and chest-cracking surgery. Ramos has twenty-eight years in the Coast Guard, five of them on *Eagle*, and he is torn between his love of the ship, that is, another physically demanding three-year tour on board, and the alternative of a comfortable preretirement assignment. From time to time he paints an idyll, which would be like

Foremast hands put their backs into it.
(Russell Drumm)

an assignment he once had in northern California with an 82-foot cutter and a small boat under his command. He lived in an old lighthouse with his family, and his son had a trout pond of his own. Ramos recreated the scene for me earlier in the day while twitching and scratching and sweating in *Eagle*'s waist. He was watching his people aloft, conferring with his mates Allen, Nixon, and Matt Welch, suggesting, "If I have to convene the fucking boards it ain't gonna be fun." They understood he meant to delegate to them the job of administering certain qualifying tests to the crew. "Aye," they said, smiling, as he was, the beauty of telling and being told what to do for the ship at least as mysterious and satisfying as any damned trout pond on the coast.

To me, this bosun emotion proves that *Baubelehrung*, the welding of human and boat, may continue well after a sailing ship has been built. Perhaps it's because a ship is never really done. She's always under construction, in a sense, via the ever-shifting set of her sails. Keith Raisch, the bosun during Captain Stillman's time, in 1994, spoke of how sailing ships "make" time — sculpting it out of green ocean currents and wind, using the sharp leech of sails — while engine-driven vessels "keep" time. He said that keeping time presupposed a schedule imposed from without, like the S.O.A. — speed of advance — that *Eagle* is required to keep between ports. If necessary, it's kept using the "iron wind" — engine power. Raisch disliked any such interference in the symbiosis of sea and sailing ship, an extreme position only if you accept the world as it was at the end of the twentieth century, which Raisch did not. Doug Cooper, Raisch's successor, was not so fixated, but he too, as the bosun of a sailing ship, bridled at windless imperatives. Cooper might as well have been tracing his family tree, pausing to admire each ancestor, as he explored every branch of *Eagle*'s rigging chart for me.

"On the plans, the bottles are called rigging screws, and that's probably what they were called in the old days," he said, explaining how the cable shrouds that support the masts, yards, and tons of wind tie into the hull. "Forged steel bars carry the load down through the [belaying] pin rail to really herky forged chain plates in the waterways [the steel gutters that take water from the weather deck and channel it overboard]. The chain plates connect to the hull plating and frames. *Eagle*'s chain plates, like much of the rig, are identical to *Peking*'s." He was referring to the most familiar of the "Flying P" ships of Hamburg's house of Laeisz, most of which were built at Blohm & Voss. "The post–World War II sailing ships have straps for chain plates that look pathetic alongside the Blohm & Voss version. We tension the shrouds by cranking until the bottles won't turn any more. Some modern rigging consultants peddle expensive tensiometers, and they work great in port. I scoff at them. It takes wind to tune a rig! The mast should be straight, and in the stiffest breeze the lee shrouds should not go slack. We tried a surveyor's transit to check the alignment of the masts and found it no more accurate than Dillmann's eye."

He meant the critical, discerning eye of Karl Dillmann, whom four *Eagle* captains have depended upon. It's an eye fixed on the ship, but it looks inward, too. There's much to see there, I think. If the inward gaze matches the outer, it is blue but perhaps deeper, not as warm. I'm not sure. It is the possibility of discovering what Karl Dillmann sees that has brought me back to the *Eagle*. He knows her miles of running and fixed rigging the way a surgeon knows the veins and sinews of the body. He moves about them like a powerful spider. And I've seen that spider charge as he climbs the 100 feet from the deck to the mainmast crosstrees over green cadets, even on the inboard side of ratlines.

I was on board in June of 1994, when *Eagle* was in the mid-Atlantic en route to Plymouth, England, via the Azores. She was free and flying after a stifling passage up the Potomac River to serve as backdrop to the commandant's change-of-command ceremony at the Coast Guard's headquarters in Washington. For a week after fleeing the Chesapeake, *Eagle* proceeded, windless, under engine power on her course across the ocean. The free-flowing wardroom conversation often returned to the captain's main concern — what he called the Coast Guard's gross identity crisis.

The crisis stems from its being a military service but attached not to the Department of Defense but to the Department of Transportation, which has very different priorities and budget. Also, the service's disparate missions made it hard for personnel to see the organization in a single light. Someone in the public affairs office once broke down the annual statistics, averaged them, and offered to the public a typical Coast Guard day:

Ninety large vessels are given port safety checks, the documents of 120 seamen are processed, 209 pounds of marijuana and 170 pounds of cocaine worth $9.2 million are seized, 120 boats are boarded during routine law enforcement patrols, 17 marine accidents are investigated, 64 commercial vessels are inspected, 14 lives are saved, 328 people in distress are assisted, $2,490,000 worth of property is preserved, 150 aids to navigation are serviced, and 176 illegal immigrants are interdicted.

New commandants tend to recreate the Coast Guard in their own image. Admiral J. William Kime, who took over in 1990, following the 1989 *Exxon Valdez* oil spill in Alaska, emphasized "M-Ops," operations of the Marine Safety Office, which also oversees pollution cleanup. The man he replaced, Admiral Paul Yost, led the Coast Guard during the Gulf War and ushered in an era of police operations. An *Eagle* lieutenant once told me that the Coast Guard changed missions like underwear, leaving the public, and its own people, confused as to its purpose.

Keeping the service in the public eye by making mayors and port cities' chambers of commerce happy reminds Congress of its budgetary needs. So *Eagle* is often used to go begging, in a sense — to look pretty for special events, activities usually seen by those on board as a form of prostitution that squanders valuable sailing time. I found the issue of *Eagle*'s identity — sailing ship or public relations tool? — to be touchy enough that it wasn't debated by her officers. But among the enlisted crew, the future of the ship, her very course, is a constant source of lively conjecture. It's discussed both openly and in whispers in a way that says *Eagle*'s heading and handling on any given day either validates her past and assures her future or does not. Cadets are oblivious to this issue for the most part. At first they are vague as to why they're at the "summer camp from hell," though they seem of one voice in stating that it was the everyday peacetime missions — search and rescue, pollution control, fisheries enforcement — that made them choose the Coast Guard over the army or navy.

I think Captain Patrick Stillman saw the Coast Guard as like himself — small, scrappy, able to prevail by having a morally superior sense of mission. The challenge, he said, was to instill the sense of service and duty in people in a society with a genius for avoiding responsibility. "It's always the system that's wrong. Well, we *are* the system and we must re-invent it," he told me on the quarterdeck one day when *Eagle* was still windless. "Tocqueville was right: individualism will kill us unless we're willing to serve the community. Otherwise we'll drown in the solitude of our own hearts." Stillman, as well as the other *Eagle* skippers I've met, believed that a core experience shared by Coast Guard officers and by as many of its noncoms and enlisted people as possible was needed more than ever now. *Eagle* continues to serve that purpose.

Stillman was infatuated with naval history even as a boy. He built models of *Thermopylae* and *Cutty Sark*. "We are married to English sea-manship, as were the Germans. How they did this," he said, looking up at the rigging, "we don't know really. We try to tie lines to the past, but with a sense of purpose, to breathe life into it, embrace change. What we refer to as romance — it is not the ships themselves but the disci-pline and sacrifice. A ship is nothing without her people. If this ship can provide the spark, the nature of the Coast Guard will burn on as an identifiable culture: doing your duty because it's your duty — no mar-ket mentality."

We had been hearing the ship's engine grind away for a week, but then wind occupied the mid-Atlantic like an invisible tsunami. We were descending from the apex of our great circle course, traveling just south of east. *Eagle* was flying between a series of low pressure systems spin-ning off the continent we'd left behind and a high sitting stationary over the Azores, where we were bound. She was carrying all her sails except for the course, or mainsail, which, with 40 knots of wind finding *Eagle* slightly abaft the beam, would have stolen wind from the driving fore course. The crew was giddy because the ship had been sailing near or at her hull speed of 17 knots through 8- to 10-foot seas and continued to do so, on the same tack, for days. At one point Eric Jordahl, a twenty-four-year-old seaman assigned to the foremast, talked down a third-class cadet who had frozen high up on the upper topsail yard. "What's endearing about this job is getting the crap beat out of you. Makes you feel alive," Jordahl said in mock complaint after stepping back on deck. He had studied jazz theory at the MacPhail Center for the Arts in Min-neapolis and said he appreciated that *Eagle*'s shrouds were all tuned to the same frequency — equal tension. "The ship is a huge stringed instrument. I'd like to bring my violin aboard, but the captain would make me play for his guests." He leaned in anticipation of the ship's roll and offered a cigarette to Seaman Amy Miller as she stepped off the lowest ratline on the foremast rigging, a dolphin tattoo leaping on her ankle. Angelic face, hard hands.

Lieutenant Eric Jones, a math teacher at the academy; Keith Raisch, the sailing master; and Karl Dillmann trimmed and retrimmed the sails. They had the yards "fanned," so from the deck, with the sun backlighting the sails, the rig looked like a luminous circular staircase, the uppermost royals braced to catch the apparent wind and each lower sail braced farther forward to receive the wind from its true quarter. The deck was a steep hillside. Six people, one on each side of *Eagle*'s three parallel wheels, were applying Norwegian steam, working hard. They were alert to the helmsman's every command. He had been given the freedom and responsibility to sail "full and by," keeping sails full and drawing but near, or by, the wind, that is, as close to the wind as the set of the sails permitted. Eric Jordahl had taken the helm and was elated as he watched the royal leeches, keeping them on the edge of luff, at the entire suit's maximum draw. Under the press of sail, the ship's bows peeled off tons of water in giant arcs. Broken waves were vibrant white, turquoise. The lee scuppers gushed seawater and the ocean's iodine perfume. Flying fish flew their short escort flights, ecstatic. Blue uniforms were salt-stained. The hands aloft on the mainmast crosstrees, practically lying on the windward side of the mast because of our heel, could hear, above the moan of shrouds, the bass roar of displacement each time the ship launched from the top of a swell into its trough. Captain Stillman stood on the leeward bridge wing at the bottom of the mountainside that was the deck. The shadows of *Eagle*'s square sails appeared as perfect silhouettes on the white-foam remains of waves the bow had cleaved. I heard Stillman say, "The good Lord has given us a gift today — awesome!"

He ordered the royals doused to reduce the ship's heel in search of an even better trim, but a royal buntline was hauled too soon. The extra belly in the sail pulled the yard away from the mast and left it swaying, its entire weight supported on line rather than its chain lift. The thud and ring of the hollow steel yard striking the steel mainmast resounded from one end of the ship to the other. The popping of the sail filling and spilling were rifle shots. Just below it, seven cadets and crew, sent aloft to furl the sail, hovered on the crosstrees, scared to death. Captain Stillman ordered the helm up a few degrees, a ballsy move in that much wind, but it pinned the recalcitrant yard to the mast.

And at this point Karl Dillmann assessed the situation and saved the day. He ascended from the deck, charging 100 feet to the trouble, climbing around and over others to get there. "On deck. Ease the buntlines," he bellowed. "Clew up!" the captain screamed, taking his cue from the sailor whose instincts he trusted beyond all others. "Heave, heave, heave!" The t'gallant spilled its wind. The rest of the sails, on the verge of backing, filled again as *Eagle* bore off. A cheer from the adrenalized seamen on the crosstrees. Cadets and crew were flushed, looking about at their shipmates and ship as though they'd landed on a new planet. Moments later pilot whales appeared off the port beam. The captain, moved by his ship's and his crew's performance, told those within earshot on the quarterdeck and above the roar of *Eagle*'s progress, "An organization seeking its roots has found them today."

Soon after, Karl recited Rudyard Kipling's "Mandalay" in mock rap style, to the great delight of his foremast crew, who beat out the funky rhythm on the pitching fo'c'sle deck.

> By the old Moulmein Pagoda, lookin' eastward to the sea,
> There's a Burma girl a-settin' and I know she thinks o' me;
> For the wind is in the palm-trees, and the temple-bells they say:
> "Come you back, you British soldier; come you back to Mandalay!"

⌒

ALL THIS happened a day after Dillmann told me about his knowledge of German, how he had begun speaking the language spontaneously as a child in a house on the Rhode Island coast where German had never been spoken before. "People said I spoke German in my sleep. I was speaking it in my sleep when I was in scout camp, and I'd never studied it at that point." He offered up this story cautiously as something he wished he could explain. I'd known him for about a month by then. We had spoken often enough that I knew vainglory did not fit this man with vise grips for hands, a lean, hard exterior, and a bark that cut through the cadets' lingering sloth when necessary, a man whose humor appeared when lives didn't hang in the balance. Dillmann's forearms are like Popeye's, but he has soft eyes, and the homy Rhode Island cadence of his voice speaks deep paradox, as do the fingers so thick from splicing they barely fit the keys of his accordion sweetly playing "for those in peril on the sea" during Sunday services. Five years have passed, and now he says this may be his last trip. He says he is thinking of retiring, and I sense he has reached a decision. His mother is sailing with us as far as Panama, which I take as a sign that his retirement is nigh.

Right now Karl is climbing aloft to help overhaul, and his mother says she is making a conscious effort not to watch, just as she did when he and his brother, David, climbed high up in the oak tree in the back yard when they were kids. He will miss being aloft. *Eagle* falls off the top of a swell, and her masts bow deeply to leeward as he reaches the futtock shrouds below the mainmast crosstrees. The trees are the small platform 100 feet off *Eagle's* deck where the topmast, with its sails and rigging, is fixed — to the mainmast and its three yards — like a bayonet to a gun barrel. The futtock shrouds are the path around the crosstrees to reach and work the uppermost sails. They include a short spiderweb of ratlines, a rope ladder that leaves the mainmast ratlines at a 45-degree angle. Dillmann moves effortlessly over the shrouds, hanging precariously, slothlike, for a few steps and handholds, up and around the underside of the crosstrees to gain the top. The climb is always made on the windward side of the ship. Under way, her heel makes it less vertical and thus easier, although experienced hands navigate the entire jungle of lines and spars with uniform ease. To the permanent deck crew, the futtock shrouds appear, on the ascent, not as a maze requiring thought but a path where the memory of muscle meets again the many, many hands and feet that have gone before on the same old weave.

That's why, when Greg LaFond fell the 100 feet from the mainmast crosstrees to his death on June 11, 1998, it shook the crew to its core. That morning *Eagle* had sailed through Drake's Passage between St. Thomas and Tortola, a thrilling run under full sail. The ship dropped anchor off St. John in the Virgin Islands, Captain Papp's favorite anchorage, one he'd discovered years before when he commanded the buoy tender *Papaw*. He'd used the anchorage the previous winter during a trip with a group of boot-camp graduates from the Coast Guard's training center in Cape May, New Jersey.

No one saw LaFond leave the mast. A cadet on deck in the waist heard a noise, metal on metal, and looked up to see him in midair facing the mast. His body was positioned as though he had been gaining or leaving the crosstrees via the futtock shrouds when he fell. Another crewman first saw a black shadow on the deck and looked up to see LaFond falling, his back facing the port side. He was falling feet first until they were snared by the ratlines above the mast's lower platform, causing him to flip. The back of his head hit the main yard hard. The blow brought his body upright again for a split second before he tumbled down the ratlines like a rag doll, one witness said, until his head hit the ship's steel gunwale. LaFond seemed to hang there for a moment, then bent at the waist to complete a final somersault into the Caribbean. The clanging of the metal clip on his climbing belt hitting the steel yards was the only sound that accompanied his fall, until the "Oh my God, oh my God," from a witness, followed by the man-overboard pipe, the splashes of people going in after him, and the alarm to general quarters.

At first only a shoe could be seen floating on the surface. Three cadets went over the side, found LaFond underwater, and brought him to the surface. They were joined by Boatswain's Mate First Class (BM1) Tracy Allen, the mainmast captain and LaFond's immediate boss. LaFond was placed on a litter and lifted back on board, where the ship's doctor, a corpsman, and Allen, also trained in emergency medicine, worked to save him. The injuries were too severe. He had suffered a badly fractured skull and a torn aorta. His eyes were fixed and dilated, and he was in full cardiac arrest. Attempts at resuscitation continued, however, as he was transferred to one of *Eagle*'s small boats, which had been launched as soon as man-overboard was piped. At 7 P.M., an hour after the fall, the small boat *Eagle II* was under way to Red Hook Harbor, where an ambulance waited. Greg LaFond was pronounced dead aboard a Coast Guard helicopter en route to Roosevelt Roads Hospital in Puerto Rico.

Except for the mournful return to New London last July, this is the ship's first passage since LaFond's fall. The captain alluded to it while speaking at morning muster in the waist yesterday, emphasizing the priority of safety. Most of this crew was aboard when he fell and took part in the investigation that followed. What disturbed the captain and crew most was that LaFond had fallen, not during one of *Eagle*'s cold and stormy passages but at anchor on a beautiful, sunny, and, at the time, windless day. I feel sure the pain of his death will return by degrees and minutes of latitude as we approach the Caribbean. Greg Giggi, one of LaFond's best friends, accompanied his body back to Raymond, New Hampshire, his hometown. Lynn Hensen, who served on *Eagle* last year, returned here from a station in Miami after Seaman Frank Conka, who blamed himself for the death, offered to trade billets. Conka, too, had been a close friend of LaFond's, a barracks mate back at the academy's enlisted quarters. He blamed himself because he had told LaFond he would go aloft with him to help tighten the main t'gallant shroud, as Petty Officer Allen had asked him to do earlier in the day. Fellow crewmen said Conka had difficulty getting beyond the incident and needed a change.

LaFond had been in trouble following his arrival on *Eagle* in late 1997, not too seriously by the standards of the outside world, but bothersome to those who had to pick up the slack for him. He was often late, indulged in skylarking aloft, and sometimes took shortcuts when assigned tasks. He was placed on performance probation in April of 1998. Two days before his fall, he was the subject of a captain's mast, a nonjudicial disciplinary hearing before the captain, for "gundecking" — not completing his assigned watch duties. LaFond asked Karl Dillmann to represent him at the hearing. He apologized to the captain for his poor performance and for being a burden to others. He was given extra duty and a fifty-dollar fine and was restricted to the ship for thirty days. He had not been allowed to take part in the swim call that morning. Nevertheless, his friends said he had not been despondent and seemed to have turned over a new leaf. After the disciplinary hearing, he told Captain Papp that he appreciated Papp's not giving up on him. Petty officers Allen and Dillmann said they had noticed a positive change.

Bitching, jokes, and more serious matters surface in particular places on the ship. One of these is the aircastle, the narrow space allocated for smoking. It's located forward on the weather deck between the galley and the shoulder-high bulwarks on both the port and starboard sides and just aft of the ladders leading up to the fo'c'sle deck. It was in the aircastle that I heard someone say that perhaps the fall was somehow owed the ship, an overdue sacrifice. It had been almost twenty years, an impressive interval, since Richard Coe was crushed by standing rigging in 1980. One of the pins that fasten the main t'gallant mast to the mainmast sheared during a housing evolution, and the shrouds collapsed on him.

Captain Papp has given me permission to use the quiet of the flag berth to read over letters and portions of the ship's old German logs that I've brought along, at least until Captain Luke joins the ship in Cuba; he will take over the berth. The logs tell the story of *Eagle*'s first ten years: the storms, visits by high-ranking officials, days of perfect sailing, and deaths. The entries are written in the graceful old-style German script, which Detlev Zimmermann, the former U-boater, has helped me translate. The fine loops and flourishes are like the intricate decorative knots that sailors tie, and they fasten this day to the same date more than fifty years ago; they might have been inscribed at this very desk.

I know the flag berth, for Captain Stillman assigned it to me for the passage across the Atlantic in '94. It adjoins the main cabin in the aftermost part of the ship, within the rounded tumblehome on the starboard side. The small berth's bed, chest of drawers, closets, bed stand, escritoire, and chair are made of rippling blond satinwood. It has a blue rug and bedspread and an adjoining head. In German days the head held a bathtub, since replaced by a rain locker, or shower. When not in use, the single chair is secured to the escritoire by brass clips. I felt honored and unworthy when shown the place I was to call home for three weeks. Stillman smiled and said he thought the desk would be useful, but later, as I picked myself up off the deck, still half asleep, I wondered if I hadn't detected a mischievous expression on his face as he accepted my thanks the day before. There was a large following sea. *Eagle*'s beautiful counter was simply doing what it was designed to do — lift the stern. An especially large wave combined with my bed's already steep incline from our starboard tack to launch me, fast asleep, into the air. The next morning no fewer than a dozen people, including the captain, asked me how I'd slept, all with the same knowing smile. The berth is a good place to visit, however. The sound of the sea passing along the hull is loud here, where, legend has it, Hitler napped. Except for the bathtub, this interior section has changed the least in sixty years. The words *auf* and *zu* — German for open and closed — remain inlaid in black letters on white porcelain on the sink's stainless steel drain fitting. The trip back in time is made easier in the blond satinwood berth, where the past rushes in and out in the same mysterious way the heave of the sea keeps dreams awake during our conscious hours.

4 SEGELSCHULSCHIFF HORST WESSEL

IN 1790, Treasury Secretary Alexander Hamilton urged that "ten boats for the collection of revenue" be built. The American penchant for smuggling, which had served us well prior to the Revolution, was then hampering trade — "especially in coffee, which is an article easily run, from the nature of its packages being generally imported in small bags," stated one report to Hamilton. Replace coffee with cocaine, and the report might have been written yesterday. With Hamilton's suggestion the Revenue Cutter Service was born. It was the golden age of sail. Lord Horatio Nelson would not be mortally wounded at Trafalgar for another fifteen years. Captain James Cook, whose ships, *Endeavor, Discovery,* and *Resolution* — the space shuttles of their day — took him to places Europeans had never dreamed of, had been killed by angry Hawaiians only eleven years earlier. Cook's lieutenant at the time was William Bligh, who, despite his infamous leadership problems, was considered the greatest navigator in the greatest navy in the world.

The U.S. Coast Guard today is an amalgam of five federal agencies formed at different times, from the Lighthouse Service in 1789 to the Bureau of Navigation and Steamboat Inspection in 1932. It now operates under the Department of Transportation except in wartime, when the navy directs its operations. One part of the identity crisis of which Captain Stillman spoke results from the Coast Guard's being the stepchild of unlikely bureaucracies. But it is also a military service with nonmilitary police powers. Still intact from its eighteenth-century Revenue Cutter Service beginnings is the authority of Coast Guard officers and petty officers to police civilians. The service is not bound by the policy of posse comitatus, which makes it illegal for the other military

The cutter Eagle *captures the French privateer* Bon Père, *1800.* (Painting by Wendell Minor, courtesy of U.S. Coast Guard)

branches to carry out police operations within the United States. Boarding teams may therefore halt and climb aboard any vessel, search if there is probable cause, and make arrests if federal laws appear to have been broken. Such laws include those that regulate fisheries, merchant vessel safety, marine pollution, and immigration. Coast Guard teams are on the front line in the war against drug smuggling. Ice patrol, maintenance of navigational aids, and, of course, search and rescue make up the Guard's humanitarian missions.

There have been a number of constants. One originated with the precursor Life Saving Service, whose crews operated small coastal stations and responded to shipwrecks in the worst of conditions, using rowed surfboats. Their motto, "You have to go out, but you don't have to come back," has survived. And, from the Revenue Cutter Service, so has another tradition: the organization never has been without a sailing ship. In the early days, of course, wind was the only source of power, but later it was deemed that no other kind of training could teach the requisite skills and humility needed for a career at sea.

The Coast Guard has had seven ships named *Eagle*, including this one. The first sailed out of Georgia in 1792 as one of the Revenue Service's first ten cutters. The second *Eagle*, a 187-ton vessel, 58 feet in length, bedeviled the French fleet during the undeclared naval war with France and captured five armed French vessels in the West Indies between 1798 and 1800. At the start of the War of 1812, the third *Eagle*, a schooner-rigged cutter armed with four four-pound cannons, took part in a dramatic action in Long Island Sound, where she had been given the job of protecting American shipping from the British. While escorting the sloop *Susan* out of New Haven, *Eagle* came up against the British eighteen-gun brig *Dispatch*. *Eagle*'s captain, Frederick Lee, unable to outsail the *Dispatch*, headed for Negros Head on the north shore of eastern Long Island and beached *Eagle* beneath a bluff. The crew removed two of the four-pound guns and two smaller ones and hauled them to the top of the bluff in an effort to defend their cutter. The *Dispatch* closed in and attempted to drive the Americans from the bluff. When this failed, they shifted their attack to the *Eagle*. The men on the beach beat back the British throughout the night. The story goes that when the wadding for their muzzle-loaded cannon ran out, they ripped out the pages of *Eagle*'s log and rammed them home with the powder and shot. When the shot was gone, they scavenged the enemy's spent balls from the ground and fired them back. The cutter was finally taken the next day.

The fourth and fifth *Eagle*s, each about 80 feet long with a 19-foot beam, were built on the Baltimore clipper design. Cutters in the early 1800s intercepted contraband and rescued people in distress, as they do today. The record shows that Frederick Lee, the skipper of the third *Eagle*, also commanded the fourth and that he and his crew were commended for a daring rescue off Montauk Point. The sixth *Eagle* was commissioned in 1925. She was stationed at New London and later at Charleston, South Carolina. In both places she was given the thankless, near-impossible task of keeping rumrunners from offloading during Prohibition; she was rammed and slightly damaged by a "black," as the stealth smugglers were known. She was decommissioned in the early 1930s. *Horst Wessel* became the seventh *Eagle*.

Formal cadet training began in May of 1877 aboard the topsail schooner *J. C. Dobbin*. Navigation and seamanship were the only subjects taught during her cruises between the States and Bermuda. Academic courses were added to the curriculum when *Dobbin* put into

New Bedford, Massachusetts, during the winter months. *Dobbin* was re-placed by the 106-foot barque *Chase* in 1878. By 1900 the floating acad-emy had changed its wintering location to Arundel Cove near Balti-more. *Chase* was converted to a barracks ship in 1907 and was replaced at sea by *Bancroft,* a former Naval Academy trainer. *Alexander Hamilton,* the second vessel to be named for the founder of the Revenue Cutter Service, was formerly the gunboat *Vicksburg,* which served in China in 1898. She became the Coast Guard training ship in 1921 and remained so until after the academy moved from Maryland to New London in 1930. From then until the United States entered World War II, smaller sailing craft were used for seamanship training, including the two-masted fishing schooner *J. C. Dobbin II* and the 65-foot schooner yacht *Curlew.*

The 185-foot, three-masted schooner *Atlantis,* given to the Coast Guard by Gerard B. Lambert, set the record for a transatlantic crossing in 1943 while serving as the academy trainer with Miles Imlay, the man who would be the present *Eagle*'s second American captain, at the helm. Ed Lowe, an electrician's mate on *Atlantis* during her record run, re-members the ship doing over 21 knots off Block Island. The entire en-gineering department had to be shut down because the rail was sub-merged and the boilers were being starved of water. The lifeboats on the leeward side had to be brought up on deck; they were skipping on the surface of the sea. Lowe said, "We should not have been out there because the U-boats were there." Lowe was also the electrician on *Danmark,* the full-rigged Danish ship that happened to be in Flor-ida when Germany invaded Denmark. Captain Knud Hanson offered her to the Coast Guard to help train the thousands of officers needed in the war effort. From January 1942 to September 1945 *Danmark* sailed under the American flag. Because of his experience under sail, limited though it was, Lowe was chosen to be part of Commander Gordon McGowan's "advance precommissioning" ten-man team that traveled to Germany to claim *Horst Wessel* as a spoil of war. As we shall see, *Eagle*'s history nearly came to an end on her initial transatlantic crossing.

Beginning with that trip in 1946, most of her annual cruises have been to distant shores. She returned to Europe often during the '50s and '60s, usually with a cutter escort. In 1994, the year I first came aboard, Captain Stillman took *Eagle* from New London to Baltimore; Washington, D.C.; Ponta Delgada in the Azores; Plymouth, England; and, after I left the ship, to Rouen, France; Bermuda; Newport, Rhode Island; and back to New London. The previous year, the cadet cruise included calls in Ireland, Portugal, Spain, Madeira, and Bermuda. The leadership has kept the belief that blue water is where the old wind lives under the ancient guiding stars. Long, uninterrupted ocean passages — it takes three weeks to sail to Europe — assure the necessary training focus. Nor does it hurt to make future officers more worldly and familiar with their counterparts abroad by visiting foreign ports of call. It's all about navigation, after all, moral as well as celestial — which brings us to the summer cruise of 1996.

That summer *Eagle* called at Dublin, Amsterdam, Hamburg and Rostock in Germany, St. Petersburg, Helsinki, London and Portsmouth, Ponta Delgada, and Bermuda. *Eagle* returned to Hamburg on the occasion of her sixtieth birthday. When I think of Hamburg I see Tracy Allen at a dockside stall wearing our German liaison officer's cap sideways on his head and drinking beer out of a horn from a Viking's helmet. I see young girls, some of them very beautiful, selling themselves on the Reeperbahn, the archipelago of shops, bars, and whores once lighted by gas lamps, and now, a century or so later, by neon. "The money is hot in my pocket, the ship leaves tomorrow, so tonight your price is not so high," goes the old Reeperbahn song. And I see a proud Adolf Hitler standing just below the bowsprit of the ship at her christening.

I can still see the strange light after midnight on July 2 at the top of Denmark, 57 degrees latitude. It was 0130. Unable to sleep, I went topside, where I was met by a silver-blue mackerel sky off the port side to the west and a full moon periodically covered by small puffy clouds to starboard. Sunlight and moonlight in the middle of the night. *Eagle* was nearing the north end of Denmark in a dome of nautical twilight.

"Up here, the difference between day and night is the turn of a log page," Captain Papp observed, just above a whisper, as he passed me slowly. His unseen approach from his quarters via the companionway to the afterdeck surprised the watch. "Captain on the bridge!" Quick attention, a salute, then the watch sank back to a kind of meditative state imposed by the black silhouettes of sails aloft against silvers, golds, metallic blue, and a rolling sea. The colors were somehow reflective of the events of the previous thirty-six hours — and of the last sixty years. We were sailing under headsails, the fore course, lower and upper topsails, and t'gallants in 10 knots of wind from the west and northwest as we neared the Skagerrak, the channel between Denmark and Norway. Bosun Doug Cooper had the conn. He told me, again in hushed tones inspired by the light, that he expected to wear onto a starboard tack and turn south into the greater Baltic by morning. I wondered how many times the ship had left the Elbe River, sailed north, and prepared for the Skagerrak in just this light.

On the previous day, July 1, as we left the Elbe, birth canal of many great ships, including this one, the wind was blowing a cold 40 knots. By the afternoon it had dropped out — gone to sleep, as the Germans say — but for a while, in some of the cadets, the pale green of inexperience blended with the pea green of sickness. The group had flown from the United States to Hamburg to meet the ship and to replace the cadets who had brought *Eagle* across the ocean. Most were sophomores, third-class cadets, with experienced "firsty" seniors mixed in.

The usual nausea of getting under way seemed a special kind of mourning sickness, a subtle mix of birth and death pains. The suffering cadets did not at that moment care about the complex history they were part of. What's the saying about mal de mer? "At first you're afraid you're dying, and then you're afraid you're not." The stricken, clipped to the ship's bulwarks by safety belts, knelt as though in supplication to the world's greater agonies. I was sure the captain would fill them in on *Eagle*'s past during the trip, show them the video he had been given by Blohm & Voss.

When the cadets first brought their sea bags aboard, they could not have understood that the old German men, conservatively dressed in suits and ties, a few accompanied by their wives, some wearing vests against the colder-than-usual June wind, were their predecessors. A few had traveled across Germany to meet the ship, whose scheduled arrival had been advertised by a veterans' association. They walked slowly along the pier, looking up at *Eagle*'s yards, which invaded the space above the walk despite having been braced sharp to avoid street lights at docking. The wind blew southwest off the Elbe into the streets of Hamburg and put a light strain on the barque's white braided hawsers.

Across the river, the cranes of Blohm & Voss bowed to the horizon. The men were spotted immediately by the captain and those members of the crew who awaited them.

Captain Papp, in welcome, told the men that their eyes gave them away. "Your eyes are nineteen years old," he said. They brought forth their photographs and black hat ribbons with the inscription *Segelschulschiff Horst Wessel* in gold letters Their eyes shone with the misty triumph of recaptured youth. Rejoining the ship had erased the years like dust blown away in a gale. Until their feet touched the deck, the photos and ribbons had been their only way back. They wore delirious smiles, and their eyes followed the grandsons and granddaughters of their former enemy as the young people came aboard and sought their berths.

Captain Bob Papp, a tall man with kind but commanding eyes and a shaved head, was gracious. He invited the old sailors aft to his cabin, settled them on couches. A bottle of Cutty Sark appeared, and coffee. Laughing, the Germans said they had never been in that part of the ship, with its walnut bulkheads, blond satinwood berth, paintings, and bronze ceiling lamps. Karl Dillmann translated for them:

"We were told, The captain is here, the officers here, the noncommissioned officers here, seamen here, then twenty-six miles of nothing and then you," one of the men told the captain, laughing, his hands dividing the ship into hierarchical sections from stern to stem. The captain told his guests that he felt like an adopted child who researches to find his real parents. "I feel a part of the ship and want to know her roots." He was referring, of course, to the living roots of seamanship. He told them that viewing the tape the day before was like watching the birth of his child. Everyone understood that he was speaking of the delivery of the ship herself, not of the gore that attends every birth, and certainly not of this one's gruesome legacy.

A video copy of the four-minute black-and-white newsreel, beautifully produced in the Leni Riefenstahl tradition, had been shown to about twenty-five of *Eagle*'s officers and crew the day before at Blohm & Voss. The screening was the finale of a tour of the very place where the ship was built in the old stretch-keel-and-riveted-steel tradition. The birthplace was the top of the ways on which the ship was launched on June 13, 1936. The video showed the same location, but with a crowd of thousands, some watching from high on the cranes and scaffolds that towered above the reviewing stand as Grand Admiral Erich Raeder climbed the stairs to the christening platform with Adolf Hitler at his side.

"We are very proud to be here today," Captain Papp said to his visitors. "She is a beautiful girl. We're always thankful that she's made of good German steel. Many times in storms, we thank heaven for Blohm & Voss. And we take pride in the way America has taken care of her." After toasts, the captain led the way to the wardroom to show a copy of the video he had been given, a gift from the shipyard.

The month before the christening, Hitler had ordered the occupation of the Rhineland and declared sovereignty over the territory that had been stripped from Germany under the terms of the Versailles Treaty. Neither England nor France reacted to his action, as they were obliged to according to the separate Locarno Treaty. In July of 1936, Hitler pledged to support Franco's revolt in Spain and committed the Condor Legion of the German Luftwaffe, which would annihilate the town of Guernica. The die was cast.

June 13 was a fine summer day. Horst Wessel's mother was introduced by Rudolf Hess after a speech to the throng that had gathered for the event. Flags bearing the crooked cross of the National Socialist party waved below the platform where Hess stood, with *Horst Wessel's* majestic cutwater and bowsprit rising above his head and Hitler looking on from behind him. Neither the anchors nor the eagle figurehead, with the swastika in its talons, had been placed.

"Mein führer," Hess began in slow, impassioned German, "fellow German men and women. This ship shall bear the name of the fighter and poet at the forefront of the German revolution, Horst Wessel, just as her sister ship bears the name of the soldier and poet at the forefront of the great war at sea, Gorch Fock. Thus, the two sailing school ships of our navy bear the names of fighters and poets for the same idea, of men who gave their lives for this idea. The idea is Deutschland! The mother of Horst Wessel will now christen the ship."

With that, the martyr's mother smashed the champagne bottle upon the Krupp steel of the ship's bow, the echo resounding through the hushed yard.

"Sieg Heil! Sieg Heil! Sieg Heil!" Hess shouted into the mi-

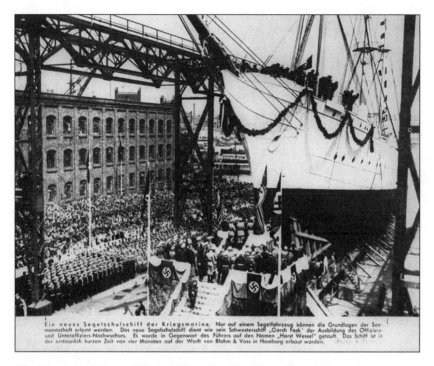

Ein neues Segelschulschiff der Kriegsmarine. Nur auf einem Segelfahrzeug können die Grundlagen der Seemannschaft erlernt werden. Das neue Segelschulschiff dient wie sein Schwesterschiff „Gorch Fock" der Ausbildung des Offiziers- und Unteroffiziers-Nachwuchses. Es wurde in Gegenwart des Führers auf den Namen „Horst Wessel" getauft. Das Schiff ist in der erstaunlich kurzen Zeit von vier Monaten auf der Werft von Blohm & Voss in Hamburg erbaut worden.

The barque is christened Horst Wessel *in Hamburg, June 13, 1936.* (Courtesy of U.S. Coast Guard)

crophone, his arm outstretched in salute, his voice joined and then drowned out by the crowd as the ship began her backward descent on the ways toward the Elbe. On the video's sound track, the launching was accompanied by the "Horst Wessel Lied."

As we watched in the wardroom, Hitler strutted toward the reviewing stand, and the wife of one of our visitors let out a long, wounded sigh. Her husband clicked his tongue. And when the newsreel ended with the *Hitlergruss,* a maelstrom of emotions swirled invisibly but palpably above the captain's table. The Germans were uncomfortably aware that their younger hosts were studying their reaction. Their expressions seemed to say, "You cannot possibly know the entirety of it — the humiliation, the surrendered pride, the lasting confusion of having risen and then fallen so fast like a large broken wave still retreating from the beach." So when they thanked the captain, sincerely, it was for celebrating their youth and the ship, but also for bringing to mind things they thought he was unable to see. The ship's first four captains stood nearby in framed photographs, gifts from one of the guests, iron crosses at their necks and hats at rakish angles. It was the rakish angle, the pride, that had been taken away from these men. This was what the *Horst Wessel* veterans thought the American captain could not see, though I think he did. Sadly, the Coast Guard is familiar with pride unsung.

I was reminded of what Gordon McGowan had written about preparing the barque, after her capture, to sail from Germany with no budget. Getting ready with no money was and is the familiar Coast Guard task. McGowan's expert scavengers were able to find most of what was needed for refitting the ship, including new manila line, in the secret caches and underground stores of a burrowing, defeated Germany. The line was run through blocks and reeved into leechlines, buntlines, and braces. McGowan admitted he had not been square-rigged enough to know that the virgin manila was too full of coil — what sailors call memory — so that when the first orders to set sail rang out, the line, remembering the peace of its coiled hibernation, snarled and tangled. Rick Ramos, who was a seaman on *Eagle* beginning in 1979 under Captain Paul Welling and later under Captain Martin Moynihan, recalled that at the time *Eagle* had not switched to the softer, synthetic Roblon rope used today. When a coil of new manila was needed, Bosun Richard T. (Red) Shannon would order it out of the bosun's hole and have it tied to *Eagle*'s taffrail and towed, with a fat knot on its bitter end for drag, until it lost its memory.

In the wardroom on the day the Germans visited, it occurred to me that some memories are easier to lose than others. There are those that won't go comfortably through the blocks and fairleads of the present. Just as a ship floats when her weight is equal to that of the water she displaces, we remain buoyant so long as the weight of our works is no more than the displacement of our days. But what if our dunnage includes the mass of murder upon murder? Then, even though the rigging is filled with youth, with innocent skylarking, and even though a sailor has earned the right to cock his hat just so, his ship may sink or go aground, as, in fact, *Horst Wessel* did.

When Captain McGowan found *Horst Wessel* in February of 1946, she was high and dry on the banks of the Weser River, listing to port, stained, and stripped of her rigging. Her rudder had been damaged in a bombing raid. Surrounded by the gutted buildings of Bremerhaven, a small, half-starved crew lived on board. Because of the gravity of duty, August Thiele, Kurt Weyher, Martin Kretchmar, Peter Ernst Eiffe, and Berthold Schnibbe, *Horst Wessel*'s five commanding officers from 1936 to 1945, might share the blame. The ship herself should not, although the suck of the Nazi maelstrom runs so deep that for some, even fifty years later, the logic that a ship's elements — wood, rope, and steel — and the ship herself cannot be evil is still suspect. The ghost of *Horst Wessel* presents the Volkswagen paradox: how some lasting examples of Germany's genius for engineering and efficiency remain coupled with the memory of well-oiled evil.

One of the ship's enduring stories, possibly apocryphal, is that Captain Carl Bowman, *Eagle*'s fourth skipper, changed the ship's mizzen rig from the classic German split spanker to a single fore-and-aft sail as part of a general retreat from all things Teutonic. In the 1950s there were enough sailors around who knew the difference that a split spanker would make. The swastikas disembarked over a number of years. *Horst Wessel*'s eagle figurehead, painted gold as it is now, but much larger, had flown beneath the bowsprit clutching a swastika. That shield departed early. The machine parts with their swastika stamps left the ship one by one as they were replaced. The final piece to depart was "Elmer," the old 800-horsepower Maschinenfabrik Augsburg-Nürnberg (M.A.N.) engine, which was traded for *Eagle*'s more powerful Caterpillar in 1982. After a complaint from a visitor in the 1980s, a plaque bearing the ship's original name was banished from the head of stairs leading to the mess deck to a bulkhead farther below in the petty officers' lounge.

The Coast Guard has resisted expunging all traces of the ship's past in deference to her, something that is perhaps difficult for terrestrial types to understand. From time to time, during the eternal polishing of brass, small screws are backed out and the plate bearing "U.S.C.G.C. *Eagle*" is removed from the circular brass facing on the first of her three wheels, to reveal the words "Segelschulschiff *Horst Wessel*," which are then polished. A week before leaving New London for Panama, I received a photograph from Germany showing Hitler on board. I know where he walked. I decided to leave the picture at home.

The sea has always required rumor and superstition to explain what science and faith cannot. This ship has far more fertile ground than most for superstition to grow. Legend has Hitler napping in the flag cabin, smashing a crystal glass against the cabin's bulkhead following a toast. But up until the day before we left New London there was no proof that Hitler had actually been on board. For one thing, the records of Blohm & Voss were destroyed when the Elbe flooded in the 1960s. Other sources deliver a trickle of often painful information. Hamburg's city museum now tells of how slaves from the Neuengamme camp were used to build submarines at Blohm & Voss, though several years after *Horst Wessel* was christened. Slave labor and then a flood . . .

Eagle's recent captains have not shied from the past. Captains Stillman and Papp, in particular, have made use of it. Bob Papp saw fit to hang, temporarily, the portraits of *Horst Wessel*'s commanding officers in their dress uniforms, with caps raked, in the *Schlossgarten* (castle garden), the short passageway to the captain's quarters and the flag cabin beyond. The ship's original port anchor was lost in a collision with the Philippine SS *José Abad Santos* in Chesapeake Bay in January of 1967. *Eagle* now has one American and one German anchor.

The visiting *Horst Wessel* veterans were impressed with the condition of *Eagle* and with her young crew. I could see the old men reaching with their eyes: Did the captain understand that the young very often have more in common with the structural elements of a ship than with the motives for building her? The ship was the trees, not the forest. The captain's hospitality communicated to the elderly Germans that he knew this to be as true of young soldiers and sailors today as it was in their time. They remained on board for the day and were joined in the afternoon by a group of old-timers who sang German sea songs accompanied by an accordion, then "Lili Marlene" and "Rose Marie," in the waist with cadets joining in. The import of the moment seemed to dawn on all of them during the singing of "Rose Marie," when the time-worn faces of the visitors registered their delight in the voices of the female cadets. It was evidence of how many times the world had turned. The captain noted in a quiet aside that the ship was the old men's youth, and they realized she would soon be sailing away forever. "Rose Marie" was a capstan song for hoisting a very deep anchor.

Karl Dillmann and the young German liaison officer continued to follow the men around, translating. Memories flowed. But in the ward-room after the video, the liaison officer stopped spinning German into English as an old man spoke: "I'm eighty years old. In Germany nobody knows the value of the ship's story. They teach it wrong. The Prussian values of order, duty, discipline, cleanliness, are all gone." At that point the younger German stopped translating, angered at what he presumed was going to be a defense of the Third Reich, and walked away, leaving the old man equally angry. The old scar was bared again. For the young lieutenant, I think, it ran right up into the immediate future of more Turks immigrating to Germany, some living in freight containers along the Hamburg docks.

He may have misinterpreted the old man. After all, order, disci-pline, and duty are values that continue to be hammered into resistant minds on board the ship. It was the evil purposes to which the Prussian strengths had been put that halted the translation, for they had caused the Prussian baby to be thrown out with the Nazi bathwater for genera-tions, and not just in Germany. Captain Papp saw this loss very clearly. The ratio of applicants to available positions at the Coast Guard Acad-emy is far greater than at the other military academies. The required discipline seems to be more acceptable in a nonbellicose service, but cadets still bridle at it. Captain Stillman told me that as popular as the Coast Guard's "humanitarian mission" had become, it remained an enormous challenge to breathe life into the all-but-dead notion of duty. To do so demanded wind, lots of it, and open sea. The danger was that this was becoming less appreciated by the "Nintendo generation," as Bosun Raisch called those of all stripes with a blind faith in electronics, satellites, and computers.

As the old men left the ship, one of them offered the captain the traditional German sailor's handshake, which began like any other. Then he held his palm up, and showed the captain how to hold his palm above the extended salutation, leaving about five inches of space be-tween. The gesture meant, "May there always be at least a hand's width of water beneath your keel." It looked like something out of *Star Trek*.

We left Hamburg the next day.

5 DILLMANN'S EYE

MY HANDS smelled of glue on that cruise around the top of Denmark in 1996. I'd been in the sail locker talking to Karl as he patched and sewed a torn headsail on an industrial Adler machine bolted securely to the deck. Now, three years later, my fingers are glued together as I again help him with a sail. Earlier, on deck, he got his deckies to spread the sail out in the waist so he could "trim off the dead stuff," the ragged edge of the tear, with a hot knife. "We'll pay it right into the machine after it's taped." One of the hands remarked on Karl's boots — shiny black, very well worn boondockers — as he stretched across the sail. "July 1971. Had 'em ever since. I'm the original owner, too. Had 'em resoled, though," Karl said with a chuckle. The seaman's apprentice looked back at the boots and computed the years as Karl continued cutting the dead stuff.

The sail locker, the quiet center of *Eagle*, is located deep on the third deck, down a narrow passageway past the ship's store and some female berthing. Situated just beyond the bosun's hole, it is filled with shackles, pad eyes, and the smells of cauterized twine, oil, and metal shavings from the adjoining machine shop. The locker is wide athwartships, as wide as the ship, but it's narrow fore and aft, and the folded and shelved sails stacked on both sides give the place the feel of a library. Deep coils of brown virgin Roblon sit on the deck.

Karl loves this place. The ship surrounds him here. He's made the mending of sails part of his job because it's an art integral to the ship and because, for him, sewing and mulling go hand in hand. They became synchronous years ago. He spreads glue to support his patch, and I hold the section of flying jib so the Adler can bite. It's a "walking foot" ma-

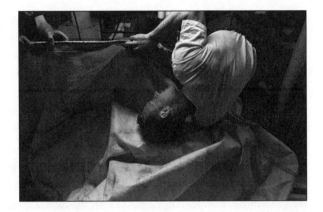

Karl Dillmann mends a tear in one of the head-sails. (Doug Kuntz)

chine, meant for heavy cloth. With a strong guiding hand and a light touch on the foot control, the Adler marches the Dacron along, pressed between a pressure plate and the feed dog, all in synch with the needle. Karl knows the gales that tore each of the older sails: the backup courses and t'gallants and the heavier storm sails folded on the shelves. He knows where the ship was when the storms hit. The patches and stitches are proud battle scars, a few of which he has told me of already.

He also knows the history of this sewing machine, as he knows the history of so many things. He says it was scavenged for *Eagle* from the *Tamoroa*, an old 205-foot ocean tug, which, he says, reminds him of the *Bibb*, his first Coast Guard assignment. *Tamoroa*'s dramatic rescue of downed helicopter pilots was chronicled in Sebastian Junger's book *The Perfect Storm*. The *Bibb* now lies on the bottom off Key West, scuttled to make an artificial reef to attract fish for sport fishermen. I can see we're going the long way round to the *Bibb* via the machine's clacking and the old English rhythms of Karl's Rhode Island tongue.

"I have seven Singers at home. Two treadles, one that was my great-aunt's that still has its bill of sale in the drawer, and I have my mother's aunt's first machine, one they got in 1929, and then I got a portable one, and I have an old commercial Singer that I picked up. I try to give up sewing, but I can't. This one's very herky," he says, bending over the black humped back of the ship's machine to eye the stitch. "You could sew your fingers right to the sail. They'd have to cut them off. Wouldn't want to hurt the sail." He laughed. He'd sewn clothes as a boy. "And I made Spartan armor out of dog food cans. Coffee cans and dog food cans, those big Alpos — cut 'em lengthwise and then hammered 'em flat." The *r* in Karl's "Spartan" is as flat as the cans, just as "great-aunt" is "great-ont." "I finally got my father to buy three feet of aluminum, and I hammered out Roman breastplates and back plates and took old ski-boot straps, thongs, and used that for fastening with buckles and rivets."

Karl tells how he later learned the architecture of clothing, figuring out where the seams would have to be to give a piece of wool the look of a colonial soldier's coat. Forebears on both sides of his family fought in the Revolution. When he was very young he slopped around in his dad's old Marine Corps herringbone shirt, and it seemed to follow that he served in the Marines for four years beginning in 1972. Served in the Philippines. "I had forty-two men, eight crews serving weapons; M-60 machine gun, mortars. I could do all the logistics and aim eight mortars in my head. Drop 'em down through the trees. Good-lookin' uniform too." The Adler guides his recollections away from the Philippines and toward the more comfortable Marine Corps dress uniform, the blue pants. He has showed me a photo of himself as a young man in the dress uniform standing with his girlfriend in a long gown. The picture was taken in the early '70s before they left for a formal event. They're still together, unmarried, in the difficult way of couples who must endure long separations. "She's prettier now than she was then," he says.

"They don't make them like that anymore. They were real wool, doeskin flannel, looked like doeskin dyed blue," he says of the dress trousers. "It's soft. They still fit, but I couldn't get the jacket buttoned anymore. It's from being out here. Even my Coast Guard uniforms I've outgrown in the upper body just from all the pullin' and stuff." He stops talking for a few minutes of serious sewing back and forth across the patch, a rattling tug of war to position the heavy storm Dacron of the jib. "I have Dad's blues. His blues didn't have pockets. That was before the days they had pockets. I like the green uniform. I particularly like the old wool. We had gabardine, but I like the flannel."

Karl stayed in the Marine Corps reserves while using up his Veterans Administration money at the University of Rhode Island. For a time he went tub-trawling for cod. He would bait hundreds of hooks on shore, hang the hooks over the lip of halved whiskey barrels, their leaders trailing, and lay the coils of main line carefully so it would pay out of the boat evenly when set. Fishing is always an option, if not necessarily a good one, for those who grow up on the Rhode Island coast. Karl says his mother tended a string of lobster pots from a dory when she was young, before she married Karl's father. "She was the first woman in Rhode Island to have a lobster license. That was during the war. She would set them early in the morning, row the dory out the river and through the surf, and then go to her teaching job."

Clackety, clackety goes the Adler. "Shit," says Karl, burning his finger on the overheated needle. "I decided time was flying by and I was going nowhere, so I joined the Coast Guard. My dad's uncle was in the navy, and my grandmother's uncle, John Hazard Knowles, was in for forty years, all fighting sail, battle of Mobile Bay in 1864. My grandfather's brother Theobolt was a gunner's mate on the *Olympia*, and he had orders on the USS *Maine*, was supposed to meet it on February 15, 1898, down at New Orleans, but she got diverted to Havana. So I don't know if he went to Mardi Gras or not, but the *Maine* didn't meet him there. I always wanted to go to sea. I didn't think I could get on a merchant ship. Coast Guard indoctrination was different for people with military experience." And that was a good thing, he says. "Might not have done it if I'd had to start at boot camp. It was humiliating enough to drop from E-6 to E-3 and to spend the next fifteen years taking orders from guys ten years younger." This is the first time I've seen this, or any other, chip on Karl's shoulder.

"My first assignment was the *Bibb*. George Mortimer Bibb was the seventeenth secretary of the Treasury. That was a good, seaworthy ship. A 327-foot steamship, built about the same time as this one," Karl says, extending his foot to adjust for *Eagle*'s roll. "*Bibb* was oil-fired. She burned bunker C. They could get her going pretty good, 23 knots," his "they" being the engine-room snipes; as a weather-deckie boatswain's mate, he makes the distinction. Karl takes me back to a long patrol on *Bibb* during which the crew fought a fire aboard a fishing boat for four hours 200 miles off the New England coast, and then, 375 miles off the coast of Halifax, responded to a mayday from a dismasted sailboat. Captain David Van Voorhees Wood, who took command of *Eagle* a few years later, was the *Bibb's* commanding officer (CO) at the time. "The guy in the sailboat was a journalist floating in the Gulf Stream. We hailed him: 'We are here to assist you.' He said, 'Oh, I'm all right.' Grass was growing on his bottom, there was rope in his screw, and his sails were in shreds. He was dazed. He and his dog were just surviving. The captain said, 'How would you like to come over for breakfast?' We wanted to get home. I was missing my friend's wedding. The guy said he had left Miami bound for Bermuda. 'Would you like to see a chart?' we asked, to prove how far off course he was. We sewed his sails, built a new mast out of shoring [timbers], and gave him clean fuel. The machine shop made a new shear pin for his wheel. We had to tow him anyway. Turned him over to the cutter *Cape Henlopen*. They got the credit."

"*Bibb* was in the North Atlantic mostly when I was aboard," Karl went on, "although we did blockade Colombia for a couple of months doing drug ops. Traditionally she had done the North Atlantic, a lot of convoy patrols during the war. She was at the battle of North Africa at Casablanca when we landed troops. She was Coast Guard then, under the navy, but she was always Coast Guard. The navy would've liked to have her because she was better than theirs, much heavier, faster, more seaworthy." And, speaking of Casablanca, he tells me that in the movie, when the Nazis and the Free French fight a duel in song at Rick's place, it was to have been the "Horst Wessel Song" versus the "Marseillaise," but when Warner Brothers learned that the Nazi anthem was under copyright, it was replaced by "Wacht am Rhein" (Watch on the Rhine). Karl sings a verse of "Wacht am Rhein," his good voice accompanied by the machine's percussion — until "Shit!" when the needle overheats again. Karl rethreads the bobbin. After his two years on *Bibb*, *Eagle* was at the top of his dreamsheet. "I put in for *Eagle* but didn't get her right away. I went to two small-boat stations — Menemsha on Martha's Vineyard for two and a half years and Fire Island for about a year."

He joined *Eagle* in 1989 as a first-class boatswain's mate under Captain David Wood. He had always been fascinated by sailing ships. Growing up in Rhode Island, he never had a boat with a motor. "I've never been much for the twentieth century. In our town we still have the Yankee accent, eighteenth-century English, but there's so many outsiders now that they make a joke of it, you know." After serving on *Eagle* for six years, Karl met the captain of the German trainer *Gorch Fock II.* "Captain von Schnurbein and I seemed to hit it off all right, and he invited me to sail back to Germany with him. The Coast Guard would only let me do the last leg, but at least they let me go. What I learned in five minutes of sail stations was phenomenal. You've done this a hundred times, and all of a sudden you see somebody do the same thing differently and you see it worked to perfection. The routine is different, the goal is different. It was the same on the first *Gorch Fock* in 1935, and it was the same in the Kaiserliche Marine [Imperial German Navy] sixty years earlier. They haven't changed the routine. They have traditions. We talk about traditions, I don't think we really have very many. We change things constantly. We have different goals. We try to expose the cadets to as many aspects of going to sea as possible, and in a pretty short period of time. So the mess cook will stand watch on the bridge, stand helm watch, lookout watch, and engine-room watch, and work with the DCs [damage control crew], and help the bosun's mates chip paint, learn how to tie some knots.

"If you read the old logs, the German cadets trained as soldiers first, just like they do today. They crawl under machine-gun fire and everything else, and when they're full-fledged soldiers then they go to sea for two months, and they're just seamen. They stand watch as seamen. It doesn't matter what they're going to be. While on the sailing ship, they're not allowed on the bridge as helm and lookout. They're not allowed in the engine room. They never do navigation. They just learn seamanship. They will learn to splice wire and everything else following the traditions of the old German navy. And they observe their traditions religiously, even if it's the coffee break at three o'clock in the afternoon on Thursday. They have what they call seaman's Sunday, and it's a really nice, refined coffee hour where everybody from seaman to captain is going to sit out on deck and have a fine cup of coffee and nice pastry and enjoy life. On the other hand, it's just as stratified as ever. When it comes time to get back in your peer group, the crew is still forward, the cadets are in the middle, the officers are still back.

"There's a strong petty officers' corps. They really run the ship. The cadets and nonrates come in and salute the junior petty officers and request permission to speak and do this and that. But that's like the Marine Corps. I had forty-two men back then. The longer I stay in the service, the less responsibility I have," Karl says with a half laugh.

I know from my previous time aboard that Dillmann brought back from the *Gorch Fock II* a knowledge of old German riggings and techniques, which he has passed on to *Eagle*. He also brought back a certain less definable feeling, which he conveys to the crew via story and example. "It's funny. I felt in awe of those guys," Karl says of the German sailors. "I didn't want to tell them — they would think I was whacked — but I think they felt it too. German sailors have told me I'm one of them. I've always been interested in the German navy. When I was three, I played I was a U-boat commander. U-853 sank only five miles from my house, between Point Judith and Block Island."

⁓

NOW, in the summer of 1999, Karl is due to take the servicewide exam he must pass to rise from his BM1, E-6 status to chief boatswain's mate. It's his fourth try. He left *Eagle* in '95 and joined the buoy tender *Bittersweet*, in part to get the diversity of experience the Coast Guard likes in its chief boatswains. The following year, leave from *Bittersweet* was arranged so that he could join *Eagle* for her visit to Germany. "The XO [executive officer] requested my services. He knew I really wanted to come. My German's okay. I know the terminology and history of the German navy." But this didn't go over particularly well on *Bittersweet*, an example of how a strong, special attachment to *Eagle* can block a career path. It's said in the aircastle that those who have sacrificed their careers to *Eagle*, those who have elected or been encouraged to stay aboard to maintain continuity, have been "fidded" by the service; a fid is a tapered spike used in splicing, but the verb form implies a different use.

On the other hand, when Karl approached *Eagle* at the dock in Amsterdam, where he met the ship for her anniversary return to Hamburg, he was given three cheers by cadets and deck crew. The present crew knows that he's about to make his fourth attempt at the servicewide, and they're pulling for him. It makes no logical sense to them that he has failed before, except that these days the questions may be weighted toward "human relations" — which Karl manages well without memorizing doctrine — as much as basic seamanship. Karl may see an underlying logic to his coming up short thus far and draw solace from it. Over the clacking of the Adler that day in the sail locker in 1996, he made a strange and oblique reference to his slow climb through the ranks. Or did he mean another sort of ascent?

"Maybe if I come back in a higher capacity, I could do more. I'm happy I moved forward" — to the *Bittersweet*, I think he meant. "My attitude is more positive. It's like running a farm. You have to run it for a few years to know what to expect. When you hear people whine, you know they don't see the whole picture, they've lost sight of the mission. It's the love of the ship, the love of the sea. I imagine a German sailor in 1943 had the same spirit. I think we always come back for more — mostly character development, spiritual development. The body is not important, the spirit needs a medium. You come back to exorcise the bad traits out of yourself. We tend to make the same mistakes over and over, working toward a higher plane. Seven deadly sins, seven virtues, habits all. By staying on the same ship, you're seeing people come and go. It's sometimes boring to hear the same complaints, but you're not surprised by the things you see them do, their everyday complaints, the same complaints over the last two thousand years."

At various times on deck back in '94, and in the sail locker, instructing cadets in the art of making baggywrinkle — the lengths of line whose fibers are freed to create a fluffy boa wrapping for the stays to protect sails from chafing — Karl footnoted our trip from Hamburg around the top of Denmark, through the Skagerrak and the Kattegat to the Baltic. Many hands and Karl's stories made light work of the monotonous off-duty times. He spoke about the friendly old links between Hamburg and England, about the British royal family's German roots, about the German houses of Hanover and Battenburg, a name that was anglicized to Mountbatten. How Queen Victoria had given her grandson, Kaiser Wilhelm, Mount Kilimanjaro as a birthday gift.

While the Adler chugged away, Karl's super-fingers holding a sail in place, he spoke of the Hanseatic League and the herring trade that first bound it, of the similarities in the languages of Denmark, the

Karl makes a crane line fast to a shroud. (Russell Drumm)

Frisian Islands, Norway, and England. He named various parts of the ship in the different tongues — starboard, *Steuerbord, stuurbord* — to reveal shared roots. He said the Skagerrak had been heavily mined during World War II, as it had been in the 1918 war. One time Count Felix von Luckner, known as Seeteufel — Sea Devil — piled on sail in order to add heel to his full-rigged ship *Seeadler,* the better to skim over the mines. But the rigging froze, fixing the course all the way to Iceland until a thaw allowed a new tack. Karl respected von Luckner, the son of an aristocratic cavalry officer in a long line of cavalry officers, who nevertheless decided to run away to sea. He got his nickname by bedeviling Allied merchant ships the old-fashioned way; his vessel would appear as a pretty sailing ship before showing the German imperial colors and her guns. He would claim his prize and then, as she sank, entertain her officers with fine wines and civilized conversation.

Now, five years later, in the never-changing sail locker, we begin to fold the repaired jib with the help of a few of the four-to-eight watch who have wandered in. The sail crackles and barks its resistance. Karl brings up von Luckner again. Tells how he had once commanded the *Niobe*, which was built as the Danish cargo schooner *Morten Jensen* in 1913. The ship saw duty in World War I and was seized by Germany. After the armistice von Luckner purchased her and had her rerigged as a jack-assed barque and outfitted to be an oceangoing yacht. She was less stable in her new incarnation in part because of the new square-rigging aloft. Von Luckner's yachting dreams died for lack of money, so he sold the rerigged ship to the government as a naval trainer. On July 26, 1932, *Niobe* was knocked down by a white squall; sixty-nine young cadets and crew drowned within sight of land. The tragedy prepared the ground for a new class of sailing ship and the birth of Hitler's Kriegsmarine.

Karl says suddenly, "I'll probably pass it, now that I don't care anymore." But I know he does care.

6 Hemp and Flax

A sun/cloud mix. Blue skies at last. *Eagle* is on the same starboard tack 200 miles off Delaware. *"Now! Reveille, reveille. Heave out, trice up, lash and stow, lash and stow. It is now 0600. Reveille, reveille."* Deckies are swabbing as they do each morning. Salsa music and the smell of frying bacon pour from the galley. I awoke early enough this morning to watch my dreams slip back into their lairs like eels into coral, unrushed by *Eagle's* rude awakening pipe on the PA system. The *Now!* — short for "Now hear this" — precedes all pipes, an attention getter and constant reminder of what time it really is. I've come forward from my berth in officer's country for coffee in the crew lounge one deck down in the fo'c'sle, where the pot is an eternal caffeine fountain. The pot aft in the wardroom gets shoal in the latter part of the four-to-eight watch and doesn't begin its steady flow again until the subsistence specialists start preparing the officers' breakfast at 0630.

Except for those with late bunks (the twelve-to-four watch), the crew has heaved out. The tricing up, lashing, and stowing went by the boards beginning in 1976. The hammocks were replaced by pipe racks, which are more comfortable for the most part, except in heavy weather, when the tendency of a free-swinging hammock to remain relatively plumb would be welcome. For this reason, the captain and bosun keep hammocks and the bulkhead fittings for them in their quarters.

Two crewmen from northern states in the chow line are hectoring Brian Hanum, "Bama," a big southern boy with Weimaraner-blue eyes, demanding that he pronounce "butt" once again.

"Butt, butt," he says, and the way he's able to loose-lip the *b*-sound

*Gravity is not just a good idea;
it's the law.* (Russell Drumm)

and drawl the one-syllable word is, to the Yankees, a great early-morning discovery, a hilarious cultural artifact, and they won't let go of it. They pronounce it to show Bama the correct way and he *butts* back, until the back-and-forth *butts*, northern and southern, sound like a tired engine trying to start. All because the sleepy Bama noticed that the number-10 can serving as an ashtray now sports a handwritten "butt can" sign to identify and encourage its use. The American spoken on *Eagle* is New England and southern for the most part, as it is throughout the Coast Guard, with West Coast mixed in. The littoral states are well represented, which is not surprising. The lingua franca, however, is the Coast Guard dialect of militarese: American of whichever sort happens to be in the speaker's mouth, generously sprinkled with common military acronyms and abbreviations, with the addition of ancient nautical terms. "Ya'll 'vast chippin' and baggywrinklin' and get into your trops. And I want to see gig lines like lines of longitude," has stuck in my head. The petty officer was saying, "All of you may now stop chipping paint and making chafing gear. Please change into your tropical blue uniforms and take care to align your shirt buttons with your pants fly."

For fourteen years, sailing orders flowed from the quarterdeck in the strong accents of Boston. The voice was that of Red Shannon, a short, stocky man with the look and manner of a quick and crafty leprechaun, the same man who straightened the memory out of new manila by towing it behind the ship. Shannon likes to spin a yarn. His love affair with *Eagle* — he calls her Liebchen — began in 1957, when, as a young quartermaster, he sailed on a few trips from New London to the Coast Guard shipyard at Curtis Bay, Maryland. His sailor's instincts first came to life along the docks and bulkheads of the port of Boston, where the older language of wind and sea mixed freely with Irish and Italian English. Red's family lived a few blocks from Hingham Harbor, where he sailed catboats and wood pussies as a boy and worked in local boatyards. There were occasional trips to visit the *Constitution* at the Charlestown Navy Yard with its huge rope walk, where miles and miles of manila were laid in the old days. As on Hamburg's Reeperbahn (rope walk), rope was made by first twisting hemp fiber left to right to spin the yarn, then twisting the yarn right to left to form a strand, then twisting the strands left to right to lay the rope. Shannon remembers waiting, as a boy, for the *Saturday Evening Post* to hit the stands with the latest installment of C. S. Forester's Horatio Hornblower series, and he recalls seeing people collecting money in cans down by the docks for the merchant seamen rescued from ships torpedoed by U-boats. He sailed at Tabor Academy, where he got to know the 72-foot *Tabor Boy*, a yawl, and the *Edlu*, which nearly won the Newport-to-Bermuda race in 1938. In the early part of the war, the Coast Guard painted over *Edlu*'s varnished mahogany hull with navy gray so she would blend with sea and sky while on patrol as part of the "Corsair Fleet," the picket line of sailing craft that served as lookouts for U-boats.

Following Pearl Harbor, it became clear by the light of the burning oil tankers that the Atlantic coast was naked of defenses. A man named Alfred Stanford, an advertising executive and yachtsman, was commodore of the Cruising Club of America at the time. He reasoned that sailing vessels could be used as lookouts because they could remain on station for long periods without any engine sound telegraphing their presence to submarines. The navy rejected the idea, but President Franklin Roosevelt, a bit of a sailor himself, gave the go-ahead to do it anyway. The donated craft were lightly armed and carried radios and equipment for listening underwater. Most of the fleet was retired in the fall of 1944 after the tide had turned against the U-boats, although the records of the 112-foot picket schooner *Valor* show that her crew listened underwater as U-853 was crushed by depth charges on the last day of the war.

Today, Shannon, who retired from the Coast Guard in 1987, is master of *Sea Cloud*, a beautiful four-masted barque built in 1931 in Kiel at the Friedrich Krupp Germaniawerft as a wedding gift for Marjorie Merriweather Post. In January of 1942 the heiress donated the ship — which her husband, Edward F. Hutton, had originally christened *Black Hussar* — to the war effort. At the Curtis Bay Coast Guard yard, the barque was stripped of her masts and brightwork and given a five-inch gun forward and depth charges. Painted gray, she became a Coast Guard weather frigate on the Greenland patrol of ships attempting to protect the supply convoys bound for Europe. Shannon said *Sea Cloud* radioed her weather report at noon every day. "The U-boats would surface to hear the report themselves. The crews waved to each other. She was never torpedoed because the Germans recognized her for what she was, a beautiful German-built ship. Her replacement was a destroyer and was sunk almost immediately." After the war, *Sea Cloud*'s masts, sails, and glorious hardware were replaced, and she has sailed ever since.

Shannon enlisted in the Coast Guard in 1953. His first billet was aboard a weather ship out of Miami, and from there he went to a buoy tender, an old boat kept alive from the days of the Lighthouse Service. In Greece for two years he served on a ship that assailed the Continent with Voice of America programs. On board he met academy graduates and chiefs who had sailed on *Eagle*, and it was then he filed his first dreamsheet requests for a billet on her. *Eagle* remained at the top of his dreamsheet for ten years, while he was assigned to weather duty aboard the cutters *Winnebago* and *Bering Strait* and buoy tender billets in Honolulu and Maine.

The bosun's job on *Eagle* opened up in 1974. Shannon, by then a warrant first lieutenant, joined the ship in Norfolk. In an attempt to standardize the training of seamen and watch officers, the captain, James Irwin, designated Shannon sailing master, the first time a bosun was given that responsibility. Two future *Eagle* skippers, David Wood and Don Grosse, were lieutenants on board at the time. Until Shannon was given the job, the sailing of the ship was overseen by deck officers. Usually the operations officer got the job by default, but this failed to provide the desired continuity. Deck officers served only half a summer and were often replaced by someone with a different approach; the ship's handling was subject to more interpretation in those days.

When Shannon came aboard, the reputation of *Eagle's* fourth American captain, Carl Bowman, as a great square-rigged sailor was part of *Eagle* lore. Bowman had compiled a rough manual of ship-handling techniques, some of which had been passed directly from the German crew. *Eagle* also had inherited two German seamanship books. Since then Bowman's pages have been added to and refined by a number of apostles through the years, including Shannon, to create the bible known today as "*Eagle* Seamanship." Bowman is best remembered for replacing *Eagle's* German-style split spanker on the mizzenmast with a single sail, a configuration that was more common on American barques. Although it didn't work very well on *Eagle*, it remained that way for nearly forty years. The original split spanker made it easier to reduce weather helm, compensation the helmsman must make when the wind's pressure on the bow and stern is uneven. Because the split spanker is actually two separate sails, it permits a finer tuning of the balance between headsails and mizzensails by adding or subtracting just enough sail area. The single spanker, though easier for the deck force to handle, was often too overbearing when set. One of *Eagle's* enduring rumors is that Bowman, a veteran of World War II, chose the single spanker to change the barque's distinctly Teutonic look, but apparently that was not his motive. When Captain Paul Welling, *Eagle's* sixteenth commanding officer, asked Bowman about this rumor, Bowman told him the change had merely been an attempt to make life easier for his deckies. The spanker reverted to the German model under Captain Wood in the late '80s.

Shannon was witness to a great many changes. In the 1950s, *Eagle* still had the German admiralty–pattern anchor on the port side, the kind commonly seen in tattoos, which was brought up on deck with a mechanism for quick release. That anchor was lost in the collision and replaced with an American-made version. The anchor on the starboard side is still the original 850-pound stockless German one. Sails and line were made of natural fibers in Shannon's day; the sails were made of flax as in the German years. Sun and weather turned the flax sails charcoal gray, which contrasted with the barque's white hull and gave her a more sinister look in early German photographs. The rope was manila, except for the smaller line used for buntlines, leechlines, and clewlines. "For that we had nylon line left over from the war," Shannon told me. "It was towing line for gliders — surplus. It came in big rolls. It's what was used on *Eagle* throughout the '40s and '50s. The nylon was tightly laid and had a wire heart, a wire that ran through the middle of it that was the communication between the glider and the tow plane. It wouldn't wear out. We had some tightly laid Italian hemp we used for the lifts, where there was heavy strain. When we ran out of it, we went back to regular manila. Manila was good because there was no waste. You could downgrade it as it wore, use it in places where there was less strain, and finally as chafing gear, baggywrinkle." Manila was still in use when Shannon left in 1987, but by then it had become difficult to get the right size. "A lot of time you'd order three-and-a-half-inch-circumference manila, and get four."

Shannon told me that stabilized Dacron replaced the traditional flax sails in the '70s, and I recalled the sardonic chuckles on the quarterdeck twenty years after the change, when Bosun Keith Raisch gave the order: "Fill the sky with stabilized Dacron." The flax was usually purchased in Belfast, Northern Ireland, where the linen mills were. The sails themselves were cut and sewn in the academy's sail loft by the trainer *Danmark*'s sailmaker, who stayed on in New London when his ship returned home after the war. Shannon told me that sixteen-ounce flax was used on the larger, lower sails, and lighter material for the upper sails. The flax was heavy when wet, making it difficult for those aloft trying to fist it up to the yards in a squall.

The first suit of sixteen-ounce stabilized Dacron was lighter but tended to blow out at the clews. Vern Vermott, the sailmaker at the time, went to see Colin Ratsey, owner of a big sail loft on City Island in New York City. Generations earlier, the Ratsey family's company, on the Isle of Wight, made sails for the Royal Navy, including Horatio Nelson's *Victory*. Colin's uncle, George Ratsey, had donated his yacht *Zaida* to the same wartime picket fleet that *Edlu* sailed in. *Zaida* was known as Coast Guard Reserve Vessel 3070 while on U-boat patrol. In the winter of '42, *Zaida* and her crew were caught in back-to-back northeasters and blown from southern New England to North Carolina before being found. The search was front-page news along the coast. Ratsey showed Vermott how to reinforce the clews with synthetic webbing, but there have been other problems trying to force synthetic materials on a ship from a presynthetic world.

"The stuff doesn't give like natural fiber," Shannon said, "and a lot of reproductions [of wooden sailing ships] have had their yards and masts torn up, while with the old flax, if you get in a hurricane it'll blow out. You still have your masts and rigging." Dacron also breaks down eventually from the sun's ultraviolet rays. *Eagle*'s Dacron sails have generally been made by companies that supply the modern yachting world with designs that are very different from those of traditional square sails. The ropes that add strength to the head and feet of these modern sails are either hidden inside the sewn folds, the tabling, or are replaced by layers of cloth glued together. In Shannon's time, *Eagle*'s sails were made the traditional way, with external bolt ropes at the heads and feet, with only the wire at the leeches sewn into the tabling.

Today the ship is wearing two headsails, a staysail, and upper topsails made the old-fashioned way, with external boltropes. The clew rings, head earings, and other hardware to which the lines are bent are attached as they are on traditional square sails. The advantage, Shannon explained, is that when sails tear in a blow — and the synthetic will usually tear before damaging a steel yard — the hardware is left intact. The sail can be more easily repaired. *Eagle* used to build sails the way they were built on the old German freight carriers: the Coast Guard's sailmaker would make the basic sail, and the boatswain's mates would attach the boltropes and hardware during the winter months. This was cheaper than having the sailmaker do it, because making the attachments is the most labor-intensive part of the process. In addition, the mates learned the art so that they could do it while under way. The new sails, drawing perfectly today and standing out brilliant white against their yellowing neighbors, were made by Nathaniel Wilson, a former second-class boatswain's mate on *Eagle.*

"*Eagle* had switched over to modern sails for a couple of years when I came aboard in 1972," Wilson told me. "But all the other sails in the sail locker were from *Horst Wessel:* hand-sewn flax and still in use. I was a seaman/sailmaker. Worked for the academy's sailmaker, Vermott, and was sent to the Ratsey and Lapthorn loft at City Island. Ratsey was using heavy webbing to strengthen the edges, particularly the leech, of sails." Later Wilson became convinced that the new-style sails being made for yachts were not up to the demands of square sails, or of any sails on larger vessels. Bosun Ramos agrees and has lobbied for a return to traditional sails. "It's come full circle. Now it's back to the technology of the German steel ships," Wilson says. "Sails are an extension of the rig. They hold the yards in place. They are the standing rigging for the yards once they are braced into position. When you rely on cloth for this, it stresses and eventually distorts. Then the yards are not parallel. Flax was not as strong as synthetic, but with external boltropes, the load was on the ropes, not the sails. With the hardware attached to the ropes, even sails made of modern cloth last longer." Wilson said he saw the light during a race against *Gorch Fock II* from Cowes, on the Isle of Wight, to Kiel Bay in 1972 in over 40 knots of wind. Nearly all of *Eagle*'s sails blew out. "I knew that something wasn't right."

Since that time Wilson has founded a sailmaking business in Boothbay Harbor, Maine, and he is now making sixteen more sails for *Eagle* with external boltropes and using Oceanus cloth, a blend of two types of Dacron: a short-fiber spun yarn, and a long-filament yarn. The short fiber gives it the feel of flax, the filament gives it strength. A complete suit, all twenty-two sails, for a total of 21,350 square feet of cloth, would cost about $150,000 today. *Eagle* hasn't had the budget for a whole suit since her last trip to the Pacific in 1987, on the occasion of Australia's bicentennial. Her previous suit was purchased for the Bicentennial Fourth of July celebration in New York Harbor, when she was reunited with her Blohm & Voss sisters *Sagres II,* the former *Albert Leo Schlageter; Tovarisch,* originally *Gorch Fock; Mircea* of Romania; and Germany's *Gorch Fock II,* the barque made by Blohm & Voss in 1958.

David V. V. Wood, Karl Dillmann's CO on the *Bibb* and *Eagle*'s

Eagle *minus her bowsprit after a collision with the freighter* José Abad Santos, *January 1967.* (Courtesy of U.S. Coast Guard)

nineteenth captain, said that he too experienced an epiphany during the Cowes-to-Kiel race in '72, when he was a lieutenant on *Eagle*. Besides Captain McGowan, Wood is the only *Eagle* skipper not to have graduated from the Coast Guard Academy. "I was an English major at Amherst and got into the Coast Guard through the OCS [officer candidate school] program in 1962. I had intentions of being an English professor, but marriage and the Berlin crisis in '61 delayed that, so I joined the Coast Guard and found that I liked driving ships. I got out in '65 and started a master of arts teaching degree at Harvard, but I had two kids by then and no income. I went back to active duty in July of '66 as executive officer of the buoy tender cum research vessel *Spar* out of Bristol, Rhode Island. Fifteen days later we left for a three-month oceanographic survey of the Norwegian Sea. My wife was not pleased. But we're still married, with five grandchildren." Wood did become an

English teacher after all, at the Coast Guard Academy, during which time he sailed on *Eagle* under captains Harold (Hap) Paulsen and Edward Cassidy, the skipper during the race to Kiel.

Wood's experience in the race brought home to him the importance of sail training. The American Sail Training Association (ASTA) was getting under way at about that time. (Wood lent his time to the organization after retiring from the Coast Guard and is now its interim director.) Borrowing from a venerable European model, American sail training starts with the premise best expressed — if a bit angrily — by the renowned Alan Villiers, author of *The Way of a Ship*, when speaking about the British Outward Bound program of the early 1950s: "The aim of [sail training] is to undo the harm done by the taming effect of so much of what passes for education in the great democracies in the mid-twentieth century, where the emphasis so often is on finding somehow the equipment to furnish youth with a safe job, regardless of the pallid stamp of mediocrity and uniformity which are imparted in the process."

Beginning in 1974, just about the time Shannon came aboard as bosun, the barque's overall condition was given a hard look by the Coast Guard command. The inspection was prompted in part by the changes being made belowdecks to accommodate women, who joined the ship's company for the first time in Miami during the Bicentennial summer. A separate female berthing area was created two decks down, along with a separate head, from space that had been a larger sail locker. The female accommodations were the first of a number of "compartmentalizations" of this "first deck" and of the cavernous space on the second deck where cadets ate and slept. Shannon said that wear and corrosion of steel bulkheading and deck were observed during construction of the female quarters. Safety concerns were also prompted by a slew of maritime accidents involving sailing vessels in 1979 and by the sinking, in October of 1978, of the *Cuyahoga*, a 125-foot gunboat from Prohibition days that was serving as a training ship for Coast Guard officer candidates. She turned in front of a collier in the Potomac River, was hit, and sank. Because her hull was not compartmentalized, she went down like a stone, killing thirteen people.

It was decided that *Eagle* should undergo a major refitting over the winter months of the next four years at the Curtis Bay shipyard. Shannon was given command during these extended visits. Most of the hull's riveted and butt-welded steel plates were found to be in good shape, but some frames and decking needed replacement. When the original teak weather deck, deeply rutted by the wooden soles of German boots, was pulled up, the thin-gauge steel of the underdeck was found to be badly corroded. *Eagle* sailed for two summers without a teak deck while sections of the steel were being replaced. Shannon said it came as a somewhat shocking surprise to find that it was the teak decking that provided the ship's "stiffening," the longitudinal strength that gives the transverse beams their integrity. "Without the teak you could feel that steel deck warp in a good seaway, and that was half-inch steel." *Eagle* got her new teak deck in stages. The job was completed in 1984.

Even after *Eagle* reached the States in August of 1946, she continued her strange relationship with submarines by spending her first winter undergoing repairs at General Dynamics' Electric Boat yard, across the Thames River in New London from the academy; the yard has been responsible for building most of the navy's submarines. When Shannon first came on board in 1957, the ship was laid up every winter, taken out of commission. Throughout the 1950s and '60s and for most of the '70s, *Eagle* maintained only a skeleton crew, comprising a chief boatswain, a chief engineman, and three first-class boatswain's mates, who were the riggers for each mast in charge of maintenance. The one lowly seaman was so much in demand "that you'd have captains fighting over him," according to Shannon. Because of the small size of the permanent crew, the academy cadets, the Coast Guard's future officers, actually got more time aboard the barque back then and had more basic seamanship training early in their careers.

John F. Kennedy was *Eagle*'s chief boatswain's mate from 1955 to 1958 and again from '61 to '64. That's John Francis Kennedy. "During the winter I'd have three deck hands and three BM1's. They'd send cadets down every day. They learned how to use their hands. The work was part of their seamanship training. I'd muster them on the dock, thirty of them. The BM1's would turn 'em to. Then we'd get thirty more in the afternoon." At the time, the cadets still had the joy of stomping around the forward capstan, which, though it no longer hoisted *Eagle*'s anchors, was used to sway stuff aloft on the foremast —

usually the heavy flax sails. Kennedy recalled that en route to Scandinavia in 1958, *Eagle* was forced to heave to off the Shetland Islands to bend on ten sails to replace the ones that had blown out in a gale. The cadets had to march around the capstan in that ancient tight circle, leaning into the resistant capstan bars, a privilege denied them when the capstan was finally removed.

The two John F. Kennedys met on board in August of 1962. Because the president was a sailor, *Eagle* put on quite a show, as the chief boatswain's mate remembers. "Cadets were standing fingertip to fingertip on the yards. The president was piped aboard with ruffles and flourishes, and as he stood in the waist the cadets slid down the backstays and mustered in formation. He was flabbergasted. He gave a speech in the waist and then told the captain he wanted to meet the crew. We were mustered on the fo'c'sle deck, the deckies on the starboard side. The guy next to me was John Paul Jones, my BM1, and next to him was Robert Louis Stevenson, a yeoman. The president loved it. He was easy to talk to. He said to me, 'Tell me, Chief, ever had any trouble with that name?' I said, 'No, sir.'" Three months later President Kennedy was killed. John Francis named his son John Fitzgerald. Procedures on Board the *Eagle* changed, and dangerous skylarking was banned. Gripping the backstays and sliding the hundred feet to the deck was no longer condoned — in fact, except for Kennedy's visit, it had not been since 1959, when Mike Greely fell to his death while attempting to hand-over-hand his way up the mainstay to the maintop.

Don Grosse, who was *Eagle*'s commanding officer before Captain Papp, grew up among dairy farms in Wisconsin "without a clue to the outside world, but with a terminal case of wanderlust." He received appointments to both the Coast Guard and the air force academies. He studied the cover pictures of the two catalogs. The air force featured the campus chapel framed by the majestic Rockies, with dogwood in flower in the foreground; the Coast Guard's photo was of *Eagle* under full sail, and he made his choice. "I never saw saltwater until I got to the academy." He graduated in '69 and was assigned to the *Yakutat*, an old World War II seaplane tender. It had serviced the surveillance aircraft that accompanied troop and supply convoys and watched for U-boats. The ship still had her torpedo mounts and depth-charge racks.

"I desperately wanted an exciting assignment after graduation but had to settle for an aging cutter out of New Bedford performing lowly ocean station duties. To my delight, the ship was selected to be the first destroyer-sized U.S. ship to be turned over to the Vietnamese. Nixon was Vietnamizing everything so we could get out of there. I was sent to Berlitz class to learn Vietnamese. The *Yakutat* spent one year on "market time" patrol — blockading the Vietnam coastline against gun smuggling and other Vietcong activities. We provided lots of gunfire support for navy riverine forces and Seal units along the coast. Every month, 10 percent of the U.S. crew would be sent home and replaced by South Vietnamese personnel. In the end, there were only ten of us aboard a totally Vietnamese-manned Coast Guard cutter. I was first lieutenant and gunnery officer. For the most part we were not in danger, but once we had to tie up alongside an anchored navy LST to help extinguish a raging fire on board. Naturally, the local VC took the opportunity to overrun the navy swift-boat base. It was an interesting twenty-four hours of round-the-clock artillery support and shipboard firefighting."

After the *Yakutat* was turned over to the Vietnamese navy (she escaped to Guam in the last days of the war with a couple thousand refugees), Grosse was ordered to the cutter *Active* out of Portsmouth, New Hampshire, and then in '72 was assigned to teach seamanship and navigation at the academy. During the summer he served as a lieutenant navigator on *Eagle*. There followed a master's degree in civil engineering and ten years of erecting loran (radio navigation) antennas all over the world. He found his way back to sea aboard the cutters *Jarvis, Vigorous*, and *Boutwell* before taking command of *Eagle* in 1995. At this writing, Captain Grosse, now retired from the Coast Guard, is driving ships filled with grain and other food to Third World nations.

⌒

IN THE middle of the Vietnam War, the Coast Guard was transferred from the Department of the Treasury to Transportation. Its military operations were overseen by the navy. Neither of these changes soothed the Guard's identity crisis. It was decided that a new uniform might help. Admiral Chester Bender suggested replacing the enlisted men's navy-style bell-bottom dungarees with what came to be known as "Bender blues," straight-legged cotton trousers with matching shirts and baseball-type caps in place of the traditional white navy round covers. Officers climbed out of their khakis, identical to the navy uniform but for the patches and devices, and into their own version of Bender blues. The change was complete by 1975.

Shannon explained that the academy was small before the "Vietnamese thing." Cadets had a lot of time on *Eagle*, but "as academia took over," their afternoon ship duties were curtailed. All the maritime and service academies were trying to be less like trade schools and provide a more well-rounded education. "The course load and extracurricular stuff has affected the amount of time on *Eagle*," Shannon said, and as a result, *Eagle*'s enlisted complement, which was made larger beginning in 1978, "has been the leveling process." Enlisted personnel have taken on the job of sailing and maintaining the ship as well as passing on basic seamanship skills to the cadets by example.

The cadets' transformation, which begins in the overwhelming presence of *Eagle*'s spars, continues during the first days under way, when, innocent of any insulting intent or disrespect, they don shorts during their time off and exercise in the waist, skipping rope, doing pushups and situps, oblivious to the seamen heaving on a line a few feet away. The petty officers are not amused — "Avast those goddamned pushups and haul around on that brace," I recall one suggesting. Nor are the cadets themselves amused after a few days, as the barque exacts her toll of real work. The disparity in worldview between future officers and the enlisted crew shrinks quickly, as intended. The style and manner of the latter are soon emulated. Blue baseball caps with *EAGLE* in gold letters are rolled and squared just so. Undress blues are clean, but become stained with the Stockholm tar used to slush *Eagle*'s wire ropes. From the deckies' belts hang hand-worked leather sheaths for their knives and marlinespikes, so that when they're aloft, tools don't fall onto shipmates far below. The sheaths are fixed again to their belts by long lanyards lovingly braided. Fingers thicken. Hands appear to hold lines even when they aren't, calluses and muscles having molded them to that purpose. The men keep their hair "high and tight." Most of the women wear theirs short; those with longer hair keep it pulled

The art of the splice is observed.
(Russell Drumm)

back as required. From behind, or from below as they climb aloft with plaited tresses, they could be young men 200 years ago, jacks with tarred and ribboned pigtails. They could be, and might as well be, because just hours into any trip, the experienced crew, like their predecessors, cease to think about time — a protective response to life aboard a sailing ship. The cadets have no such shell. They are often sick and confused, and they think of time — spent in the arms of a first love or the path to sweet release five weeks away — as a refuge. It is not. As the sails are set and the land sinks out of sight, *Eagle* sails back into a warped time via the precepts of celestial navigation and ancient tricks of wind and current. If she is allowed, she will sail past the comfort on shore, past Hitler, past Nelson, past Galileo, to a universe in which she again will be the center, a flat place over which all heavenly bodies parade. Far offshore, and in the absence of the polluting ground light of ten thousand malls, can be found a brilliant time, a time to be feared in the Old Testament sense, a time of amazement. Out here in blue water, she is the crucible.

Shannon was the bosun under Captain Ernst Cummings in 1984 during a race with a group of sailing ships from Bermuda to Halifax. *Eagle* was dueling it out with the Polish trainer *Dar Mlodziezy*, *Simón Bolívar* of Venezuela, and the smaller *Marques*, a 117-foot British barque. By 9 P.M. on June 2, about 70 miles from Bermuda, the wind had increased to 25 knots and Captain Cummings ordered that *Eagle's* t'gallants be put "in their gear," clewed up but not furled, and the mizzen gaff topsail doused, along with several staysails. A line of squalls had appeared on the radar 20 miles out. At 10:16 the deck watch went aloft to furl t'gallants. The seas had risen to more than 12 feet and continued to build. Suddenly *Eagle* was hit by a squall packing 70-knot winds. The force of impact pushed her so far onto her starboard side that her railing was underwater, the masts at a 50-degree angle from vertical. Headsails were blown away. Shannon ordered the helm down, "right full rudder," in order to fall off the wind. For two or three terrifying minutes, *Eagle* continued to sail forward, heeled over like a small yacht. More people were ordered to the wheels. The barque righted. The bad news came the next morning: the *Marques*, hit by a similar blast, had sunk in seconds. Eighteen of her crew were lost; nine survived.

Shannon said it takes at least a three-year tour on *Eagle* to develop "a well-trained, well-oriented" enlisted hand. These days training time is hastened by using the *Eagle* year-round, a schedule that began at Captain Paul Welling's strong suggestion in 1978. Before that time *Eagle* basically hibernated during the winter with her small crew and was put back in commission each spring. *Eagle's* commanding officer, who usually taught at the academy and oversaw the school's entire waterfront area, climbed on board for summer duty along with his officers and an added complement of enlisted people. Shannon said the system resulted in reinventing the wheel, training people from scratch at the start of each summer. Welling, along with his predecessor, Captain James Irwin, lobbied headquarters to make the *Eagle* commanding officer position a year-round billet and to consider only the Coast Guard's very best mariners for the job. They argued that *Eagle* had the largest complement of any cutter: between 200 and 225, counting officers, enlisted, and cadets. Welling warned that "the majority of officers and crew assigned during cadet cruises [had] little or no *Eagle* experience."

Welling became *Eagle*'s first "full-time" CO. He'd made his reputation commanding the cutter *Vigorous*, devising strategies for enforcing the country's fishing laws within the newly expanded jurisdiction, to 200 miles out from shore. *Vigorous* played hardball with foreign fishing boats and notched some big seizures of illegally harvested fish. *Vigorous*, a 210-foot cutter, was based in New London at the time. Welling took command of her in 1974, two years before the Magnuson Fishery Management and Conservation Act, also known as the 200-mile-limit law, took effect. Before then he had worked at the State Department for three years, with responsibilities for fisheries, pollution, and law-of-the-sea negotiations. He had started law school at nights and had a fair sense of what was happening with fisheries here and internationally. He explained that even before the Magnuson Act, the United States had claimed exclusive rights to *Homarus americanus*, the American lobster, on the continental shelf. "The coastal lobster industry had suffered from foreign fleets with midwater trawls that came through and carried away the lobster gear. That fall [of 1974] a more aggressive boarding posture was authorized. I was an aggressive captain. We would watch to see what was being done by studying the haul-back of the net to determine if they were bottom fishing. We boarded and would inspect them from keelson to top hamper. We seized five fishing vessels before any other Coast Guard cutter had seized any. The fines were up to $500,000. Sometimes, when they were hostile, I would bring *Vigorous* real close and unmask our 50-caliber machine gun." Welling came to *Eagle* with enough swat to convince his superiors that the trainer could be better used.

Since then, *Eagle* has remained in commission throughout the year. Her permanent crew (seamen assigned to *Eagle* serve a minimum of three years) grew slowly to today's forty. By the time Boatswain Shannon retired in 1987, *Eagle*'s commanding officer was able to give the ship his total attention with the help of a wardroom of mostly full-time officers. The ship's financial picture improved when responsibility for her budget, at Patrick Stillman's suggestion, was taken from the academy and given to the Coast Guard's Atlantic Area command. Welling, who retired from the Coast Guard as admiral in charge of Atlantic Area operations, attracted a faithful following of officers who sailed with him from 1976 to 1980. Captain Papp is probably the last of Welling's boys.

Shannon said that although the core family was small at times, *Eagle* had always been handed down like an heirloom from one generation to the next, from former ensigns to future captains, and on through a long line of seaman who left only to return as bosuns and bosun's mates. I remember Billy Lambert, an *Eagle* seaman in 1994 with shy, downcast eyes, who didn't climb into the rigging but glided there. His grandfather served on the ship when she was *Horst Wessel.* There have been a few like Billy who can trace their connection back to the German years. Commander Kathy Hamblett, in charge of port operations in Philadelphia at this writing, came to *Eagle* on temporary duty from an antidrug assignment in New Orleans. She sailed with the first group of female cadets in 1976. Her husband had joined *Eagle* six years earlier, and his father had gone aboard as a cadet upon her arrival from Germany in 1946. There are many sons who inherited *Eagle* from their fathers, a few from their mothers, and a handful who believe they were drawn to her by even stronger but less apparent bonds. "People who were into *Eagle* always seemed to gravitate back," said Shannon, "and people at headquarters would always move them aboard again. We were building a cadre of people who had been trained as cadets, came back as middle-grade officers who also taught professional studies at the academy, and returned as XOs and COs."

The cadre included women beginning with the academy's class of 1980, the first to graduate female ensigns. This was a great shock to nautical tradition. To the doubters it was nothing less than a portent of the next diluvial event; to the rest it was an overdue realignment of the spheres. Paul Welling, captain at the time, had his doubts: "My concern was the lack of sophistication among the male population. I knew that the women would be as eager as anyone, but those gals from the class of '80 had a tough time. There were psychologists, sociologists, brought on staff to help with the transition. In preparation for the cruise to Europe, we got four pages of instructions about unauthorized contact with the opposite sex. Eisenhower said he never wanted to see a memo longer than one page. You had to make reference to the instructions to see if you could grab a woman's hand who was falling overboard."

The catastrophes that superstition said would be spawned by jealousies between the ship and her female hands never materialized. Quite the contrary. "I kind of welcomed the inclusion of women," Shannon said. "To me it was a better operation. A lot of senior people didn't think they could handle the work, but I knew that most jobs take more than one person anyway, and the higher they went, the better they fit. Up there on the upper yards and around the crosstrees it's a tight squeeze for a lot of the football-player types to get around the backstays."

Commander Monyee Kazek, one of the first female cadets, remembers the fatigue. "I fell asleep practicing blind bowlines. I was yelled at by the captain for serving a sugarbowl of salt for his coffee, though it wasn't my fault. I visited Ralph and Alice [puked] regularly when the weather got rough, and I loved to watch the dolphins play in the bow wake when we were under sail. I loved climbing the rigging. Getting away from the people who were constantly yelling at me more than made up for any fear, that tightening coil low in the gut that I felt climbing to the highest yardarm. I even loved it when we storm-furled the sails at 0200. Surrounded by darkness, the black water, clouds hiding even a hint of light from the stars — only the decks lit up. *Eagle* rocking from side to side. Seeing water, then boat, then water below me, and wondering, if I fell, would I hit water, or boat. And if I fell in the water, would they find me in that blackness. With my sense of immortality, I was not so much afraid as thrilled."

Joanne McCaffrey, a classmate, at first thought the triple-decker bunks in the new female berthing area were a plus. These were the first racks the ship's crew had had. "We thought it was a good deal until the ship was under sail and heeled over. Then you would have to hang on to your rack to avoid rolling out. Not conducive to sleep. The guys all slept in hammocks. The hammocks would sway with the ship, cradling their occupants like babies." Kathy Hamblett described walking through the men's berthing area while on night rounds, "picking my way through the swinging mass of cocoons, timing my steps so as not to be taken out by one of the swinging sacks."

Shannon said the resistance to women was a generational thing for some of the senior officers, although he didn't know why. "There had been female officers, SPARs, in the Coast Guard during World War II. They went to navy OCS, not to the academy, and they stayed on shore, but they were officers."

To nautical purists, the women, referred to as females in the service, were the second blow in three years. The first was the orange stripe, which already graced (or cluttered, depending on one's point of view) the hulls of other Coast Guard cutters. It was painted on *Eagle*'s bow for the Bicentennial parade of sail in New York Harbor. Shannon said it was done to distinguish *Eagle* from her German sister ships, which had crossed the Atlantic for the parade and were also white. He thought of fashioning a stripe out of sailcloth that could be removed after the event. "The Stripe," which interrupts *Eagle*'s graceful sheer, but on the other hand identifies her as a Coast Guard cutter, was painted on and has remained. "This generated favorable publicity and money was put into her," Captain Welling said. "At the same time, adjustments had to be made to accommodate females. Their well-being, or lack of it, would have repercussions servicewide."

Commander Judy Keane was another of *Eagle*'s original female cadets. "The first night I went on board *Eagle*, she was in port in New London. For my first duty, I was told to stand at parade rest on the pier at the end of the brow and not let anyone on board. I was seventeen years old and had been in the Coast Guard for less than two months. As I stood there, an elderly gentleman who was obviously intoxicated came up to me and said, 'It's all your fault.' I stared straight ahead, wondering what he was talking about. I hoped he would just go away, but he persisted. 'You see that stripe on *Eagle*? It's all your fault that the Coast Guard put it there. *Eagle* used to be a beautiful sailing ship, but then women were admitted to the academy and the Coast Guard painted a racing stripe on *Eagle*.' He ranted and raved, and I continued to stare straight ahead until he left."

Our bosun, Rick Ramos, was a BM1 on *Eagle* when Shannon rejoined the ship in 1981 after a two-year hiatus. Ramos himself left on other assignments for nearly twenty years before coming back, leaving again, and then relieving Doug Cooper when he went to the buoy tender *Ida Lewis*. The ebb and flow of people is constant, as it is throughout the Coast Guard. *Eagle*, however, has the challenge of training a crew in all-but-lost arts and holding on to enough of them so that they can sail the barque safely and lead her cadets, officer candidates, and transient enlisted members. It falls to the bosun to worry about the amount of experience *Eagle* has in the bank, and these days Ramos is concerned because *Eagle* will lose a number of experienced hands in the next few months.

7 *Beware the Dark Force*

Thirty-four degrees 21 minutes north, 70 degrees 5 minutes west. Little wind. An order is given to brace the yards around three points on our starboard tack. The sun is out, but it won't last. Fifty-three years ago at this time on the same day, oil from U-853 made a smooth lake on the surface of Block Island Sound. Fifty-three years ago tomorrow, *Horst Wessel* received orders to lower her flags and pennants identifying her as a German naval vessel. Flags and pennants are also used as telltales on a sailing ship that show the direction of the wind. *Horst Wessel* would no longer need them.

This morning there's been plenty of off-duty talk about Guantanamo Bay, the Dominican Republic, the Windward Passage — "Gitmo," "the Dom-Rep," "the Windward" — and about "migrant ops" (migrant interdiction operations) in general. There is old-stomping-ground anticipation on board. A good share of the permanent crew, as well as a number of the officer candidates, participated, before joining *Eagle*, in the thankless job of stemming the flow of Cuban, Haitian, and even Chinese migrants who try to reach the United States through the Windward Passage, for which we're bound. Captain Papp was commanding the cutter *Forward* in the Caribbean in 1994 when President Clinton came within hours of ordering an invasion of Haiti. At the time the United States was returning Cuban boat people to Cuba, but Haiti's Jean-Bertrand Aristide would not allow intercepted Haitian migrants to be repatriated. Twenty thousand people were carried as deck cargo on U.S. cutters from Florida south through the Windward Passage to Guantanamo Bay, where they were held. The migrant camps at Gitmo

Deckhands "walk away" with the halyard. (Doug Kuntz)

were bursting at the seams. Clinton may have realized that it would not be politically acceptable to have the world see the United States return-ing Cubans to their homeland but not black Haitians. An invasion force was poised to force Aristide's government to accept the returnees. Haiti relented but continues to leak disaffected people.

The Coast Guard has been given the near-impossible task of clos-ing America's golden door while simultaneously saving those who foun-der on the yellow brick road to it. Deck chat reveals that quite a few on board have witnessed how, in the Windward Passage, the yearning to breathe free often becomes the yearning to breathe at all.

"Three dead Haitians were badly decomposed. We were going to put them in the reefer, but they were leaking fluids. Their fluids were all over the elevator. My very first job was to clean it up. It was a rude awakening. There's nothing like that stink. Now, even if I smell my own B.O. —"

Lynn Hensen was steering the ship yesterday toward the passage and recalling her first assignment. She was on the cutter *Seneca* out of

Boston on patrol in the Caribbean during the Able Summers, as the migrant ops of 1995 and '96 were called. She said that it was hard and frustrating to block the pursuit of happiness when you've been taught all your life that it's a god-given right — harder still to learn that it's not.

After the *Seneca*, Hensen came to *Eagle* on temporary assignment, then went on to a station in Miami for a year before trading billets with Greg LaFond's friend Frank Conka to get back to the ship. "The Cubans called us blue devils because of the uniform. We'd pull up to a disgusting boat — raw sewage, no cover, a tiny boat. They'd see us and wouldn't want to stop. Kept saying, 'Liberdad.' The sun alone would kill you. No water. What's hard is their family's waiting in Florida. The family calls press conferences for where they're supposed to show up. When they don't, we're the bad guys."

It's clear that morale can slump during migrant ops because the majority of the 35,000 active-duty Coast Guardsmen joined to be good guys. The service has been able to draw on the country's shallow reservoirs of idealism on the strength of its humanitarian mission. Last night Captain Papp and Dan Reynolds, the engineering officer, discussed current recruiting strategy in the wardroom after dinner. Except in the heaviest weather, there is usually food for thought in the wardroom, the location of the officers' mess on the first deck, just aft of the waist on the starboard side of the ship. A separate galley contains a refrigerator, stove, oven, microwave, a cook, and his or her assistants. The wardroom itself contains one long table, a television, and a library well stocked with nautical reading. It's lit during the day by three portholes. The wooden paneling and table that graced the wardroom in the German years were removed years ago to comply with fire-prevention standards. *Eagle* has not had the budget to gussy up the ship with synthetic substitutes, so the wardroom has a metal and Formica quality, basic function, with the exception of a linen tablecloth and napkins, brass napkin rings, carpeting, and comfortable couches in the corners.

Paintings and photographs of the ship's past, in black and white, and of her present, in color, hang on the wardroom's four bulkheads. There is an arty framed photograph taken from aloft of German sailors marching around one of the ship's two capstans, long since replaced by electric motors. The sailors are pushing on the wooden capstan bars to weigh anchor, and from above the white uniforms and the spokes of the capstan look like the petals of a flower. There is a photograph of six German sailors in foul-weather gear at the ship's wheels, the tails of their black hat ribbons blowing in the wind; beside it, another photo shows a small group of Germans heaving out of and tricing their hammocks belowdecks. There is one of *Horst Wessel* aground on the banks of the Weser with the bombed and burned buildings of Bremerhaven in the background. It contrasts sharply with a painting of *Eagle* sailing triumphantly past the Statue of Liberty under full sail with flags and pennants flying.

Last evening's meal with the captain was a semiformal affair, as is customary. His officers and guests jumped to their feet when he entered. He bade them sit. The subsistence specialists, who have evolved from the old steward's mate, a petty officer's rate, and the tablemen, who were all Filipinos until the late 1970s, proceeded to serve. The captain has instructed Lieutenant Commander Chris Sinnett, his stocky executive officer, to have two of the officer candidates join the wardroom at the noon and evening meals so he can meet them and observe the cut of their jibs. Last night's candidates sat straight and nervous, knowing that lively and intelligent conversation was expected. The meal began after the captain filled his plate. Fellow officers, expert at reading the captain's moods and, like all career military, practiced in the subtle, nonconfrontational, and often humorous style of disagreeing with points made by superiors, passed the pork roast, potatoes, and green beans. They took great care pouring their iced tea. *Eagle* was still sailing under courses, upper and lower topsails making the windward side of the table higher than the leeward. Early arrivals had claimed the high side, knowing that spilled drinks flow downhill.

The captain quickly put the candidates at ease with questions about their hometowns, schools, interests, and dream assignments. Both candidates were Coast Guard prior-enlisteds and conveyed their dreamsheet priorities in acronym-rich lingo, which pleased the captain in one case but in the other put him in a mock rage at the candidate's decision to become an "Airedale," a flier of the Coast Guard's helicopters and fixed-wing aircraft or to go into marine safety. "Oh, beware the dark force," he advised, referring to the Marine Safety Division, which wages war against pollution. Overseeing the cleanup after the *Exxon Valdez* spilled half of Saudi Arabia into Alaskan waters was the dark force's finest hour. The table joined in the captain's mock disdain for any but afloat assignments, laughing heartily with the candidate on the spot.

"It wasn't *Baywatch*, was it, that inspired you to join the Coast Guard?" asked Tom Dickey, the warrant OCS instructor, smiling. Over apple brown betty à la mode, Captain Papp explained the remark to his guests. Coast Guard recruiters had learned through a survey that a good number of recent recruits had been drawn to the service by *Baywatch*, the TV show featuring perfect butts and breasts in tight-fitting swimsuits and loose plots about southern California lifeguards. Like the cavalry in old cowboy serials, the Coast Guard is a background omnipresence on *Baywatch*, always ready, *Semper Paratus*, to ride to the rescue. "Then the recruiters asked what their other favorite TV shows were, and a lot of them said the World Wrestling Federation," the captain reported with a look of incomprehension. Recruitment ads were thus targeted to the viewers of the weird world of professional wrestling, and by extension, I happened to know because I've watched a few matches, of the likes of Stone Cold Steve Austin, who often drives to the arena in his "bloodmobile," and of the pot-smoking Road Dogg. The Dogg once took on Chyna the girl wrestler in a Dogg Pound match. When Chyna refused to strap on the dreaded dog collar, he floored her with a jab and tried to put the collar on her himself. Mr. Ass attacked him from behind and hung him over the top rope, and the Dogg went without oxygen until X-Pac came to the rescue. Only a few weeks earlier, the wrestler Owen Hart, who had planned a dramatic entry into the ring, fell 200 feet to his death, real death, when his feather boa got caught on the buckle to his safety harness, which opened. His body was carried off, and the show went on.

The captain disapproved of the Coast Guard's advertising on the wrestling programs, and he was not alone: senior female officers had complained of the WWF's misogynistic bent. The captain wondered whether young people addicted to that kinky world were the kind the Coast Guard wished to attract. Certainly a great many recruits had loftier reasons for joining up. Someone very wise in the Guard's old brick headquarters on the Potomac may have decided that advertising with the WWF was a way to throw a life ring to kids drowning in boredom so deep it had them watching Mr. Ass attacking Road Dogg from behind and cutting off his air supply. The sea would be an escape, as it always has been, for those with few prospects on shore who get even a small taste of it. The stakes are high. German youths before World War II were far less idle than the American kids that the Coast Guard and other services seek to rescue from the television swamp — and Germany fell hard.

~

IN REPUBLICAN Germany in 1932, some 10 million young people belonged to the numerous organizations that together were known as the Reich Committee of German Youth Associations. The genius of Hitler's early rise lay in his ability to see and seize opportunities. He put people to work by creating the Labor Front, a mandatory service, but one that came with perks. *Kraft durch Freude* — Strength Through Joy — was a program conceived by Dr. Robert Ley, who said, "It is more important to feed the souls of men than their stomachs." Ships were built and chartered to take workers on inexpensive vacations to places many never dreamed of traveling, including the fjords of Norway and balmy Madeira. The cruises kept the workers close at hand; they spent their hard currency on board and thus within the country. Hitler also recognized the value of uniting the various youth groups under the Nazi banner. In 1931 he named twenty-four-year-old Baldur von Schirach the party's youth leader. His mother was American; her grandfather was a Union officer who lost his leg at the battle of Bull Run. The signatures of two of Schirach's forebears appear on the Declaration of Independence. He supposedly told his American jailers during the Nuremberg trials that he had become an anti-Semite and a believer in Hitler's cause after reading *The Eternal Jew* by Henry Ford, whom Hitler greatly admired.

On the last day of January 1933, Hitler was made chancellor of the Reich with the tentative blessing of the aged President von Hindenburg and the support of the army.

On March 23, the parliament committed suicide, in effect, by passing the Enabling Act, which gave Hitler the power to suspend the democratic process at will. The vote, which made him absolute dictator, was taken in the Kroll Opera House in Berlin, and when the votes were counted, the victorious National Socialist delegates jumped to their feet and erupted in the "Horst Wessel Lied":

> *Raise the banner! Stand rank on rank together.*
> *Storm troopers march with steady, quiet tread . . .*

President Paul von Hindenburg died soon afterward. Hitler was named president and quickly abolished the office. The once lowly corporal in the defeated German army of World War I then named himself führer, chancellor, and commander in chief of the armed forces.

On June 24, 1933, the steel sailing ship *Gorch Fock* slid down the ways at the Blohm & Voss yard in Hamburg. Her purpose was to train naval officers and seamen, replacing *Niobe*, which had gone down in July of 1932. The trainer had been under full sail off the Fehmarn Belt Lightship when a squall struck. The sudden blast pushed her onto her side, and water poured into open hatches and skylights. She sank in four minutes. The watch below had no chance. The captain survived the sinking and the court-martial that followed. The disaster resonated throughout Germany. Everywhere along the Baltic coast, from Königsberg in the east to Kiel in the west, flags were lowered to half staff. The *Niobe* was raised from the bottom; the dead were buried.

"Don't complain, try again," became the rallying cry. A collection was taken up to build a new training ship. The Prussian state mint struck a memorial coin the size of a five-mark piece. Special permission was given to sell it to banks for the benefit of Project 1115 — Replacement *Niobe*. A total of 200,000 reichsmarks was raised, and the *Gorch Fock* was built in one hundred days. She was christened in June of 1933. Then, as if to make the point that the sinking had been an intolerable low point in German naval history, coinciding as it did with the restrictions of the Versailles Treaty, *Niobe* was sunk again in the Baltic, this time with a torpedo in the presence of the new training ship and the entire German navy.

Hitler gained the trust of the previously suspicious military in secret talks in the Baltic aboard the cruiser *Deutschland* in 1934. During the passage from Kiel to Königsberg in East Prussia, General Werner von Blomberg and the commanders in chief of the army and navy, General Werner von Fritsch and Admiral Erich Raeder, accepted Hitler's hollow assurance that the military would maintain its traditional role, unchallenged by the Nazi party's political police. More important, Hitler vowed to rebuild the armed forces from the hobbled status decreed by the Versailles Treaty.

The naval part of the general military buildup, which Hitler had begun secretly even before assuming absolute power, required men as well as ships — far more of both than was permitted by the Versailles Treaty. The solution to the manpower shortage lay in the Marine Hitler Jugend, the part of the Hitler Youth movement that prepared young men who had volunteered to serve in the navy after finishing secondary school. There would be equivalent youth programs for the army and the Luftwaffe. Those who did not volunteer for a specific branch of the armed services were still required to participate in Hitler Youth and, after universal conscription was begun in 1935, were drafted as needed. To make the party's takeover of the youth groups official, Schirach took some muscle over to the offices of the Reich Committee of German Youth Associations and removed its president, Admiral Adolf von Trotha, the retired chief of staff of Germany's High Seas Fleet during World War I. In a speech delivered in November of 1933, Hitler did not equivocate: "When an opponent declares, 'I will not come over to your side,' I calmly say, 'Your child belongs to us already . . . You will pass on. Your descendants, however, now stand in the new camp. In a short time they will know nothing else but this new community." Two years later non-Aryans were banned from military service. In December of 1936, the year *Horst Wessel* was launched, Hitler outlawed all non-Nazi youth organizations.

Johann Kinau, the man whose nom de plume, Gorch Fock, became the name of the first of the great Blohm & Voss training ships, was a national rather than a Nazi hero. This is not surprising. Hitler was Austrian, and while the foundation of his power in Germany had been poured, it had not yet set. He was careful to link himself with German traditions that could be useful. Kinau, who wrote stirring sea stories and poems using old German diction under his pseudonym, was a direct link to Germany's strong seagoing past.

Kinau was born in Hamburg in 1880, and during World War I he served on the cruiser *Wiesbaden*. The Battle of Jutland — the Germans call it the Battle of the Skagerrak — at the end of May 1916 was the defining naval engagement of the war. At great cost, the British succeeded in beating the imperial German fleet back into port, where it was kept bottled up. On June 1, *Wiesbaden* was sunk. Of its crew of 650, only one man survived. Kinau's body was found washed up on the Swedish Island of Stensholmen and was buried there with those of a number of other German and English sailors. It was Gorch Fock who coined the well-known saying *"Seefahrt ist not"* — meaning that seafaring, a life at sea, is a kind of primal necessity. His was the logical name to attach to the ship that rose from the *Niobe* disaster.

⌒

AFTER leaving Hamburg in 1996, *Eagle* rounded Denmark and entered the Skagerrak. She passed the place where the *Wiesbaden* was sunk and Gorch Fock died and the spot off Copenhagen where in 1801 Horatio Nelson famously turned a blind eye to the signal that ordered him to disengage from the enemy. His blind eye resulted in an all-out victory over the Danish navy.

Eagle entered the Baltic proper and was sailing a course of 255 degrees, the wind from the south. We had headsails, lowers, uppers, and the mizzen set. Lightning flashed, and numerous squalls appeared on the radar about eight miles out — and then a big squall came into view. Worse, a large Swedish ferry, barely visible in the dirty weather, was to leeward and not far away. Captain Papp said later that he would like to have fallen off the wind, but the ferry was there and the bridge was unable to make radio contact. Visibility was zero. *Eagle* had 4 knots of headway, but the fore course was backing: the wind was blowing into the front of the sail. We turned 15 degrees, but to no advantage. Then the sails on the mainmast were backing and we started getting stern way. *Eagle* was caught aback. The wind increased to 35 or 40 knots in the squall. The engine was put on line, and the order for left full rudder was given to get the wind coming down the yards. *Eagle*'s bow was then facing where the ferry was last seen, the crew dousing sails as fast as possible to prevent getting caught aback again in the shifting wind.

"The next option would have been sail stations, brace around and sail the other way," the captain told his officers, enlisted mast captains, and first-class cadets later on the mess deck, where he'd gathered them before a chalkboard. His smooth-shaved head shone in the close heat. He praised the crew for the way they'd handled the situation. He said disaster had been averted with quick thinking and good seamanship. But there was something else, and Boatswain Cooper said it: "Thank God for Blohm and Voss." The crew knew he meant, Thank God for the ship's strength. The captain then leaned into them, his eyes meeting and holding each of theirs in turn and reminded them of *Niobe*'s fate and the reason their ship had been built so herky: "It is July, July, July, in the Baltic, Baltic, Baltic."

Just twelve years after the second, deliberate, sinking of *Niobe*, the German navy would scuttle *Gorch Fock* in the Baltic off the coast of Pomerania as the victorious Russian army moved west across Poland and Germany. The Russians raised her two years later. She was refitted and continues to train Russian officers under the name *Tovarisch*.

The end of the nineteenth century was the height of Hamburg's trade, primarily in guano and mineral nitrates, between Chile and European ports. The big "Cape Horners," the steel square-riggers of the house of Laeisz, dominated the trade by sailing the 11,500 miles out and around Cape Horn and, because the winds dictated a longer route on the return trip, 12,000 miles back. They made the round trip in around five months, including loading time, and with no auxiliary power. The Panama Canal, which will deliver *Eagle* into the Pacific Ocean two weeks from now, was completed in 1913, but because of a large area of dead air on the Pacific side it was of no use to the sailing ships, nor could the slow-moving steamships of the day match the Cape Horners' speed, despite the thousands of miles the Canal saved.

The house of Laeisz became known as the "Flying P" line, for its ships' names all began with that letter: *Parsifal, Pirat, Placilla, Pitlochry, Peking*, the five-masted barque *Potosi*, and the mighty *Preussen*, a five-masted, full-rigged ship of 11,000 tons displacement that could carry 8,000 tons of cargo under thirty square sails at a top speed of 17.5 knots. Many of the steel ships were built at Blohm & Voss or at the Tecklenborg yard at Geestemünde during the 1880s. They were specifically built to withstand the stresses of carrying heavy cargoes around the infamous Horn, and not one was lost doing it. In 1903 the *Preussen* sailed from England to Chile in fifty-seven days. The following year she sailed the longer homeward route in sixty-one. "My ships can and WILL make rapid voyages" was the opening sentence in the Laeisz "Instructions for My Captains" manual. The clipper ships of an earlier day enjoy the reputation of being the fastest sailing ships, but they were not. The famous *Cutty Sark* and *Thermopylae*, rivals in the China tea trade of the 1880s, were capable of great bursts of speed with their extra skysails and studdingsails. *Cutty Sark* ran from Sydney, Australia, to England in sixty-seven days, and *Thermopylae*'s record twenty-eight-day run from Newcastle, on the south coast of Australia, to Shanghai was never bettered. But the tea clippers were smaller, just over 200 feet, and carried much lighter freight than the Flying P ships. The size of the Cape Horners allowed them to maintain speeds only slightly slower, and often equal to, those of the clippers, and over much greater distances. Their design owed a debt to the better clippers, however. The sharp cutwater and the strong, rounded stern that allowed the ships to press on even in a big following sea were both American innovations.

The house of Laeisz's Robert Hilgendorf, known as the "devil of Hamburg," drove a number of Flying P ships at an average speed of 7.5 knots, with sails only, over the nearly twenty years he served the company. Born in Schievelhorst on the Gulf of Stettin in 1852, he began working in the Baltic and North Sea trade at the age of seventeen on the small barques and brigs his father was master of. He was drafted into the imperial navy and advanced to the rank of boatswain's mate, a great accomplishment for a merchant sailor in the class-conscious navy of the day. During the years of expansion leading up to World War II, many more merchantmen who had received training under sail on some of the big Cape Horners filled out the navy ranks. Hilgendorf earned his master's certificate within two years of mustering out and joined Laeisz. The company kept scrupulous records of all its ships' passages, and over the years Hilgendorf used these and his own vast experience to anticipate winds with great accuracy. His reputation as a devil, or troll, who could control the wind (a superstition as old as sailing ships and gifted sailors) grew throughout his career and up to his retirement at the age of fifty, sixteen years into the twentieth century. Hilgendorf was considered a natural meteorologist with a genius for finding ocean currents and winds, from the lightest puff to the most violent gale. He obviously had absolute faith in the strength of his Cape Horners and was not one to reduce sail except in the most extreme conditions.

As though mesmerized by the wind and oblivious to the growing roar of fossil-fueled engines and the production of new, synthetic nitrates, Hamburg's ships continued to sail right up until World War I, and some sailed even after that, as the prizes of other countries. The *Pommern* went to Greece, the *Parma* to Great Britain, the *Potosi* to Chile, the *Ponape* to Norway, and the Pola to France. But these countries could not make them profitable, and before long the Hamburg company bought them back. The reassembled fleet included the Blohm & Voss ships *Pamir, Parma, Peking,* and *Priwall.* In 1933 the *Priwall* left from the floating dock at Blohm & Voss, was towed to the mouth of the Elbe, and set out with the Tecklenborg ship *Padua* in ballast to pick up wheat in southern Australia. The round trip was a precursor to "the Last Grain Race," as Eric Newby called it in his firsthand account, by thirteen steel sailing ships in 1938 and '39. It was their last round trip to Australia before the war, the final breath in the slow death of commercial sail.

The race between *Padua* and *Priwall* was nearly a dead heat — the two ships were only hours apart arriving in Australia's Spencer Gulf after sixty-five days of sailing, but the trip didn't pay. And nitrates were no longer an alternative cargo, as they had been during the first war, when they were needed to make gunpowder as well as fertilizer. Laeisz sold *Peking, Passat,* and *Parma* to Gustaf Erikson's Finnish company, and Erikson made a go of it. But then the last grain race proved conclusively that there was less and less need for the old skills. In Germany, however, the Reich recognized the need for trained merchant officers. A trade in commodities, using a number of the remaining sailing ships, was subsidized so that seamen could complete the required twenty months before the mast. In 1938 the *Priwall* was still going, carrying general cargo for Laeisz and the Reich and breaking clipper records. That year, with forty German merchant cadets as part of the crew, she made the fastest-ever westward rounding of Cape Horn.

Once the war began, the system broke down, although sail-trained merchant officers, who were considered naval reserve officers, were at a premium as the needs of the Kriegsmarine, especially the U-boat service, grew. Of necessity, the old class barrier that had hindered former merchantmen from entering the naval officer corps was dropped. It was strange that the barrier existed at all, for both the merchant marine and the navy drew from the same North German, mainly Protestant, populations, especially those of the former Hanseatic cities. Hamburg contributed the greatest number of naval officer candidates. *"Seefahrt ist not"* still exerted its pull, but another important factor was the imperial constitution of 1871, which exempted "the entire seafaring population of the empire" from the army draft, including merchant sailors and fishermen. Still, the imperial navy's exclusionary standards made entering the naval officer corps extremely difficult. Its ranks grew even more elite because of the 1,500-officer limit imposed by the Versailles Treaty. The navy's standards remained high even as war appeared on the horizon, as evidenced by the insistence on sail training, but the expansion that began symbolically with the launching of *Gorch Fock* was done under deadline to produce more officers. Blohm & Voss was awarded the contract to build the trainer because of its enormous experience with sailing ships and because its only real competitor, Tecklenborg, no longer had the capability. The ship was to be ready to train the officer class of 1933, and it was.

An amusing story survives in the Blohm & Voss records about the launching. Admiral Raeder was there, as was the whole Kinau family. The admiral, who was very fond of Gorch Fock's writing, noticed how uneasy the author's mother was amid the pomp, so he decided to pay her a visit the next day. He dressed in mufti to put her at ease. She answered the door, and before the admiral could finish his introduction, she said, 'Yes, yes, I know what you want, all right.' She returned with a penny for the man she took to be a beggar. He tried again to identify himself, and again she interrupted, saying, "It's all the same to me what you are. You're not getting more than a penny from me." The admiral retreated.

The navy and the shipyard were extremely pleased with the barque and at first overly protective. She was smaller than the Cape Horners, of course, but was built with the same sharp cutwater and high round counter. She had their low waist to minimize the surface area that a beam sea could attack, allowing waves to pass over the deck if necessary. Because she would carry more than one hundred cadets, whose backs would be strengthened by bracing yards and hauling halyards, there was no need for the motor-driven donkey winches used by the thirty-man crews of the big steel square-riggers. She did come equipped with an 800-horsepower M.A.N. auxiliary engine.

It wasn't long before Captain Raul Mewis (who had commanded the *Niobe* in the late 1920s) began chafing. He petitioned Berlin to expand the ship's training grounds. "The *Gorch Fock* is a better seagoing ship than any steamer! Real seafaring experience can hardly be gained in the narrow waters of the Baltic Sea. Confined room to maneuver and heavy shipping traffic even pose special dangers. I therefore consider longer journeys to be absolutely essential in order to train a generation of really experienced officers and noncommissioned officers." Admiral Raeder eventually sanctioned trips to Iceland, Norway, Madeira, and the Canary Islands, but warned the commander: "I will tell you one thing, nothing must be allowed to happen."

Three years later, 10,000 spectators, including Admiral Raeder, watched *Horst Wessel* slide down the B&V ways. She was nearly a carbon copy of her predecessor, though a few meters longer, but the crowd that turned out for the birth of the second sister was bigger than the first, and louder.

⟡

May 6, 1999, afternoon

Ten knots of wind, and it's backed a bit. Earlier we braced around three points on our starboard tack to meet it. The sun won't last, according to the mackerel sky off to the southwest. "Cielo empedrado, suelo mojado. A mackerel sky never left the earth dry," says Colonel Charles García, the nephew of the admiral whose ashes we will commit to the deep. García was born in Cuba and looks forward, with some trepidation, to seeing the island again after fifty-odd years away. A Baltimore oriole, a couple hundred miles from home, flies from one yard to the next.

During the noon meal in the wardroom, Margaret Dillmann and Seth Gifford, her friend, told about their pick-your-own high-bush blueberry farm. Last season was their first. They've learned to prune the wood to produce larger, more plentiful fruit. The relative merits of high versus low blueberry bushes were discussed. Gifford and Peg Dillmann are proponents of the former; Dan Reynolds, the engineering officer, who raked them in Maine as a boy, and still does on occasion, of the latter. He allowed that some cultivated blues had become "fat water berries" and agreed that the wild ones have the flavor. The subject of a rise in sea level came up during the noon meal, and the wardroom cook said he had built his house on sand even though the Bible said not to. In the waist after lunch I heard someone ask the bosun, "How'd Karl do?" The test consisted of 150 multiple-choice questions. "I didn't even look," he answered. "I'm sending it in to be graded."

We're under full sail, including the lower mizzen. Several of the crew have brought afternoon fuel — granola mixed with liquid chocolate — topside in paper cups from a supply in the crew lounge. The lounge is one deck down and forward of the crew mess. It's a space rich with the smell of coffee and fatigue. There's a framed, hand-colored photo of the ship under sail, taken before the Coast Guard's orange and thin blue stripes were painted on. It hangs near a TV monitor and a movie-theater-size popcorn maker. A long couch is built into the starboard bulkhead, and a few cushiony chairs are bolted to the deck. The one porthole is kept dogged. The sound of the sea rushing on the other side of the half-inch-thick steel hull is a sweet resonance, like soft brushing on a bell.

The sea produced a deeper, rounder note during the German days and after, until the great open space of the second deck received extra bulkheading athwartships to add structural integrity. Back then the second deck, approximately the same length as the ship's waist, was a berthing area, mess deck, and classroom for cadets. The mess tables, now bolted to the deck, were folded and lashed to the ceiling. The German command was *"backen und banken,"* which meant the meal is cooked, sit down and eat. When the order came, the tables were lowered for a meal. The ceiling also held the hooks from which cadets strung their hammocks. There was no crew lounge per se. The German petty officers' quarters were located forward of the space, as they still are.

Karl holds that fresh air was lost when the great space was sectioned, leaving a smaller mess with adjoining and compartmented berthing areas. The tween decks were once ventilated naturally via air scoops. These have been replaced by air conditioning, which Karl blamed yesterday for his upper respiratory infection and, by claustrophobic extension, for the ill health of many a poor office legionnaire ashore. "You've got the same problem when they take nice public buildings built in the Victorian era and subdivide them into little cubicles so everyone has their own space, and then they bitch because they need an air conditioner because they've cut off the air flow. If you ever look in those vents it's frightening," Karl says.

His is not the only curmudgeonly note I've heard sounded on this issue. Keith Raisch, Stillman's boatswain, underwent a kind of spiritual crisis en route to the Potomac River for the commandant's change of command in '94. He was irritable and would expound on the intrusion of what he called "the Beach," a kind of philosophical shoaling he observed in little breaks with tradition, as well as by the more obvious examples: air conditioning, closed-circuit TV for movies in every lounge and mess, and racks instead of hammocks. During one noon meal he insisted that the cadet wardroom attendant find his linen napkin and brass napkin ring. The table had been set with paper napkins, part of a new austerity that was, he told his fellow officers, an unnecessary break with tradition. Raisch was sailing dangerously close to criticizing an official dictum, and the subject was quickly dropped by his mess mates. The people with the most time aboard seem to view the ship differently, with older eyes, a more fundamental vision wind-stripped of chaff and reinvention. Not that TV monitors and pipe racks have turned *Eagle* into the *Love Boat* — far from it. But Raisch had been to the mountaintop, with eight years on *Eagle*. Enlisted people may choose where to "reup" — have their reenlistment ceremony. Raisch once did so underwater, outside of Los Angeles Harbor, on the bow of the sunken barque *Olympic*. He fought to control his impatience with those who innocently viewed *Eagle* sailing as an exercise and not as a pure form of existence. Europeans had more respect for the tradition. "They have sailing ships on their postage stamps; we have Elvis," was how he put it. He told me he knew he had gotten too involved; he needed a change and thought perhaps he should retire. He would move out west and work as a telephone lineman, because then he could at least climb up the poles and see the world around him. (At this writing, he is serving on an icebreaker in Alaska.)

Karl has climbed aloft on the foremast following an impatient search for the belaying pin on which he hung his rigging belt before entering the wardroom to take the servicewide exam. He's working alone on the fore t'gallant yard to take some slack out of the footrope beneath it.

Bosun Ramos is exhorting a squad of deckies to be vigilant in the eternal battle against rust. He tells them most of it is caused by chlorides — salts — which break down paint. A new paint system is being tried. "If it's rust, convert it. If you need to feather it, feather it. I don't want to see any difference between the old paint system and the new, either through tactile or visible senses. If it's cancerous growth, excise it with power tools." In an aside, he says that when he first came aboard in 1979 the ship was fully engaged in the rust war. Paul Welling was the captain. It was during the period when *Eagle* was going into the yard each winter for her badly needed overhaul. Often the work was not complete by sailing time. Ramos remembers a big hole in the deck "here," under our feet, forward in the waist on the starboard side, where rust had been cut out of the steel deck. There was a corresponding hole on the second deck, so you could see down to the third. The second deck was still undivided at the time, with rows of pipe racks and lockers along the outer bulkheads.

"In my judgment, *Eagle* was on a downhill slope," Admiral Welling said. "My first winter I saw so much doubling. Where the steel deck above was wasting, they had put doubler plates. I kept seeing them on the underside of the main deck. I didn't think that was the way to do things. We'd take a hammer with a pointed nose and beat on the steel, and the hammer would go right through it. That led to the three-year program replacing the main deck, fo'c'sle deck, and poop deck."

By contrast, the steel of the hull has held up surprisingly well. *Eagle* was constructed from the keel up using the transverse framing system, nearly the same method as was used on wooden ships. The keel was laid, and ribs or, in this case, steel frames were placed about 18 inches apart. The external skin was fashioned out of square plates made of half-inch steel (the same lot of Krupp steel used on the battleship *Bismarck*). The plates were welded together top and bottom and riveted at the butts, or horizontally. They were also riveted vertically where they were attached to the frames. In the riveting the plates were placed side by side and overlapping. Holes were made and gauged so that the rivets would be countersunk. The rivets were heated to cherry red in a hot pot, flung up to the riveter, caught in a basket, thrown into the hole and hammered, with someone providing the backing support so that they could be flattened. As the rivets cooled, the plates were pulled together, clinched, to become watertight. Getting the right fit was an art. By 1936, much of the hammering was probably done with pneumatic hammers, although Blohm & Voss was renowned for the skill of its hand riveters. It's certain that at least a portion of the barque's hull was handmade. The transverse framing method allowed steel to be curved and rounded into the barque's classic lines. Her two full-length decks were added, and then the raised fo'c'sle and poop decks. Steel ships are no longer built from the keel up, but rather in longitudinal hull sections, with all decks and spaces completed before being welded together. The method, pioneered by Blohm & Voss and other U-boat manufacturers, is much faster than transverse framing.

Karl is on his way back up the rigging. He must have come down for something, a tool, or hardware. Now he's straddling the yard, a canvas bag with shackles in it slung over his shoulder. He's been up there all afternoon, facing inboard, working what looks like a wrench, which is lanyarded to his belt, as all tools must be.

"We used to call him the Independence Man when he was a boy, like the statue on top of the dome of the capitol in Providence," Peg Dillmann told me earlier. She's reading on the fantail, sitting on the cushioned banquette that backs onto the shaded starboard side of the "captain's coffin," the six-foot-long mahogany box that houses the mechanism for the ship's emergency steering wheel. The wheel is connected directly to the ship's rudder and is used only if the three wheels on the quarterdeck, which can be manned by as many as six helmsmen in severe weather, fail. There's a bench on the port side of the captain's coffin too. *Eagle* is carved into each side of the coffin, the letters emblazoned with gold leaf, just as *Horst Wessel* was before. I have a photograph of the flag-draped body of a sailor named Fritz Neumann lying on the small wooden helmsman's step before the steering wheel. He had fallen from the rigging.

The aft capstan, no longer in use, sits just forward of the wheel, and forward of that is the door leading to the ladder that goes below to the Schlossgarten and the captain's quarters. The door is hung in the after bulkhead of a deckhouse called the C.I.C. (combat information center), where it's always night and the eerie green retinas of *Eagle*'s electronic eyes glow. Here the radar and satellite positioning systems fix the ship's position on the globe to within a few feet and at a place in time somewhere between Captain Cook of the eighteenth century and Captain Kirk of the Starship *Enterprise*. Right outside the port-side door of the deckhouse, latitude is being made by hand with sextants raised to the sun in search of local noon as Chief Warrant Officer Tom Dickey puts a few of his officer candidates through their celestial paces. At sea the ship's day begins when the sun is at its zenith relative to the ship. Both celestial and satellite navigation assume that a ship is at the center, with sun, moon, and stars revolving around it, as Ptolemy saw it. Every day the captain is told of the approach of noon, sometimes informally, other times with: "Good morning, Captain. The officer of the deck sends his regards and announces the approach of noon. The chronometers have been rated, L.A.N. [local apparent noon] has been computed to be 1207. Spaces are cool and dry. The noon meal has been sampled and found to be sufficient in quality and quantity. Request permission to strike eight bells on time and test the ship's alarms and whistles." "Make it so" is the captain's answer. The exchange of words, which tie time and place together and make one person the lord of both, are feudal and reassuring, given the alien world stretching for hundreds of miles beyond our walls.

Mrs. Dillmann is wearing a canvas hat and gardening gloves for protection from the sun. She's participating in a Lyme disease experiment back home and is taking a drug that makes her skin burn more readily. She is small with age and smart in a gray wool sweater. She prefers to keep her eyes, which are gray-blue, downcast when the hands are aloft. "In order to get Karl to go to first grade, we had to get him a sailor suit," she recalls, laughing.

⌒

SUNDAY, MAY 9, 1999, 0830

Three days later. We are motoring, but the wind is now on the water after being absent for two days. We are off Florida and expect to reach the easterly trade winds by tonight. Last night NATO forces bombed the Chinese embassy in Belgrade, according to Armed Forces News. At the end of the Protestant service held on the boat deck this morning, the snipe called "Sparky," David Sparkenbaugh, who led the service, offered a prayer for those who go aloft, for a father about to undergo surgery, for peace at home, adding, "May people who see us not see our riches but our goodness." Karl provided the hymn accompaniment on his accordion. He took lessons in the seventh and eighth grades. "My interest was Alpine music, but all the accordions were Italian — 'O sole mio.' Eventually I was able to trade my Italian accordion for a German one, a Hohner, and found a German instructor. It's a different approach. The Italians want you to draw the notes out. The German teacher tells you to play the keys like they're hot."

The "Teak Beach" part of the fo'c'sle deck is forward of the foremast and its fife rail of belaying pins and coils of line and aft of the headsails, with their dangerous head-high blocks called widow-makers. Sunday, after services, the noon meal, and quarters — and except for watch-standing and sail stations — is a day off. Teak Beach is the place where the crew hangs out: lying on their backs looking up at the lean, hard white bellies of the sails and absorbing the roll of the ship until sleep comes. Playing guitar, a mouth harp, CD's, everything from Jimmy Buffett to Metallica. Wearing bathing suits. This is one of the few times when uniforms aren't required; the women may wear modest two-piece bathing suits. It's a time to write in personal logs, talk dreamsheets and tattoos.

"I'm going to get the silhouette of a hammerhead to cover the Marine Corps dog tags on my back. I'll put a Marine Corps anchor on the inside of my right wrist. The tail of the shark will reach around over my right shoulder." Matt Rawls smiles sheepishly. "I quit the Marines to get married." He quit because his wife-to-be would never know where the Marine Corps might take him. He had to go back to boot camp when he joined the Coast Guard but retained his E-3 rate. He worked in the color guard in Washington and hated it. He loves *Eagle*. The wedding has been called off, but his former fiancée is still his girl back home in west Texas, the high desert by Big Bend. He wants to go to veterinary school to learn to care for large animals. Worked on a couple of big ranches with horses and cattle. "Before I came into the Coast Guard I was making twenty-five dollars a day and lived for free, seven hundred dollars a month. I miss it, but I love this life. I'm a cowboy sailor. Lots of people who pioneered knew how to farm. Kept moving. That's the way I am." A lone flying fish makes a 20-yard flight, leaving a line of droplets upon the ink-blue Gulf Stream water. Now a sea turtle. The bow watch, a young Sea Cadet from Madame Island, off the coast of Cape Breton, spotted it.

A few people are aloft, hanging out, enjoying the view. Others are at work on their diaries. An arm bears a blue and green parrot. Another shows Neptune rising from the waves. There are eagles and a few sailing ships. Karl, Tracy Allen, and Chief Boatswain's Mate Greg Vaught have climbed out on the bowsprit to examine the broken shield in *Eagle*'s talons, tighten the bird, and "tension" the t'gallant stay.

Lynn Hensen is sunning on the starboard side, her bare feet in the scuppers. Earlier she was talking to Wade Smith, the Navy Seabee from Old Ironsides. He was in his B.D.U.s (battle dress uniform) — camouflage pants, a brown T-shirt, dog tags, and boondockers. "Our bowsprit is about twice as long as y'all's," he tells her. They compared their ships' rigging and berthing and tops, which were once called the "fighting tops" because from there Marines could fire small arms onto enemy decks in close combat. The *Constitution*'s tops are wider for that purpose. Old Ironsides shocked all of England when her forty-four guns beat up the frigate HMS *Guerrière* in August of 1812. Four 20-millimeter anti-aircraft guns were mounted on *Eagle* 131 years later, during World War II, one each on the port and starboard bridge wings and two right here on either side of Teak Beach, immediately behind the pin rail.

Hensen had two semesters of college. "Dad paid for it and for a car. I jacked off the whole time." Her dad was with the First Cavalry in Vietnam. When she was a little girl and couldn't sleep, he would tell her about the time he was standing guard and a wild boar charged him. "He shit his pants," she said, smiling at the thought of her old man hightailing it. Finally her dad said he would no longer pay for school, given her performance. "I thought, What am I going to do? So, I joined." She says it's the best thing she ever did, which is impressive when you consider that the "best thing" has included dealing with drowned and rotting bodies. She wants to travel when she leaves the Coast Guard next April. "I've never seen a desert. I have to see the 'Field of Dreams,' in Iowa. I've got to see Tibet, Europe. I'm just going to take a backpack. My best friends hiked the Appalachian Trail together. Then they got married." *Eagle* has no wind. Max, her Caterpillar engine, is grinding away.

"Kwajalein has a Macy's." These words from the other side of Teak Beach start me from a semidoze. My father fought for that island as a Marine; I've seen the pictures of bodies piled high — and now it has a Macy's. More talk of tattoos, of the right-handed tattoo artist who outlined Disney characters on his left arm and let his grandkids sit on his lap and color them in with crayons, of the decorative line designs called "tribals."

"Shit, everybody's got a tribal. I've got a friend who has one that's barbed wire around his bicep with a feather and his dog tags hanging down. His girlfriend is a twenty-four-hour-a-day virgin, a Girl Scout troop leader, keeps apple pie in the freezer and you can see her glow in the dark and walk on water. She brought cookies to a kegger party. She don't know about him. He keeps a skinned squirrel in the freezer with its arms crossed like this. Takes it to parties. Keeps the skin on the top of the toilet."

Charlie Wilkins was on *Polar Star*, an icebreaker, in both the Arctic and the Antarctic, then on *Rush*. Loved Tasmania. *Rush* is a 378-footer based in Honolulu. "We got under way on Superbowl Sunday. The crew was looking forward to a few beers and the game, but we were recalled. At 1600 we were steaming out trying to watch a small TV — a guy on the fantail was holding a small satellite dish. Then we got a migrant call, but it was sketchy at first — a mutiny maybe, a person thrown over the side, a very organized violent group, five or six snakeheads — the Chinese mafia. For $10,000 they'll take you to America. People have no money. Women work it off as prostitutes. The boat was DIW [dead in the water]. The story of the revolt may have been a ruse to get help because their engine quit. The enforcers, the intimidators, were on board, not the big people. It was horrendous — two holds, no heads, men and women sleeping on cardboard. People topside were selling water to those below. We got on scene and boarded. Our helo was overhead. Jumped out of the RHI [rigid-hull inflatable], staked out a piece of the boat. The ship was about 400 feet long, single screw, in Third World shape. If we hadn't arrived when we did, there would have been dead people in the hold. It's a hard job taking care of three hundred people. Our cooks baked bread all night. The boarding teams swapped out six hours on, six off. We went to Kwajalein. Took them off in groups of twenty. They knew they weren't going to the States. Women had signs, 'We want to go.' Sad. It was a lot of hard work. We were gone a month total. We were supplied by C-130s dropping sonotubes packed with food.

"I was three years in Hawaii, and on the *Aquidnick*, a 110 out of Portsmouth, Virginia. The *Eastwood* out of Cape Disappointment. I teach sea ops for the Atlantic Area. Go on different vessels all over the place to see where they're at. We don't have any more money for the program, so I got back under way where I belong. I'm TAD [temporary-assignment detail] on *Eagle*. My grandfather was in the navy — in New London training submariners. My father was a tank driver. He saw Elvis in Germany."

Wilkins grew up on a cotton farm in Virginia. His grandfather on his mother's side was an Italian Catholic, a boxer called Tony the Tiger. His father's family is German. "My dad picked cotton for a penny a pound as a kid," Wilkins says. He joined the Coast Guard "because of a woman, of course." He was working in a paper mill stacking boxes and living with a married woman. At nineteen he took off, joined the Coast Guard, and went to Port Clarence, Alaska, 80 miles north of Nome. "It's the closest thing to the Wild West. Native Americans go hunting, carve ivory, sell it, fly to Nome with a round-trip ticket, and then drink. Went there three or four times in *Rush*. Isolated duty, ALPAT — Alaska fishery patrols. Rescues you wouldn't believe. Boats ready to capsize because they were so iced up. Twenty-foot waves. We have a perfect balance of love and hate with fishermen. The mates and deckhands on those boats come home with $20,000 and blow it. People go there who can't handle society. There's nothing more forbidding, more beautiful."

Quartermaster Second Class Jeff Lukowiak joins the conversation. He was on *Rush* with Wilkins. "In Juneau, there were whales, bald eagles, seals, fishermen making $30,000 in five days halibut fishing. 'We don't stop fishing,' said one guy. The open season is short. There are no women."

"Yeah!" Wilkins agrees. A flock of small flying fish takes to the wind, which has increased. The new wind seems to have improved their glide. "Alaskans are the last of the frontiersmen," Lukowiak says. "We fished every night on ALPAT patrols. An Airedale pulled up a halibut — four or five hundred pounds. The XO pulls out a nickel-plated .45 and kills it. We used to hide from the weather behind Saint Paul, a small island in the Bering Sea. It was a central point to catch Japanese factory ships. We would anchor right next to them. Board three teams at a time checking for legal size. We could seize their whole catch. I've been to thirty-two countries on *Eagle*. Hamburg was my favorite port — the history." Lukowiak's wife worked as a United Airlines flight attendant. "We went to Rome for Easter Sunday. Then we flew to India and ate monkey's brains. They were good," he says, crossing his eyes as though the brains had had a lasting effect.

Kelly Nixon, BM2, soon to be BM1, has joined Seaman Kelly Grothmann on the starboard side of Teak Beach. Grothmann has been working in the galley as the jack-o'-the-dust, the one who brings food to the galley from storage below. Nixon has short blond hair and is wearing pearl earrings and mirrored shades. The shedding of clothes reveals a gold ring in her navel. Bob Marley is on the box — "Buffalo Soldier." The sun feels Caribbean. Nixon grew up in Joshua Tree, California, where her mother is the fire chief. Her uncle was on the *Arizona* at Pearl Harbor, which means he still is on the *Arizona*. "Tracy Allen is following me around without interfering," she says of her breaking in as mainmast captain. "I'm sorry Captain Papp is leaving. I don't know anything about Ivan Luke."

Nixon was not long out of boot camp when she was assigned to the

378-foot cutter *Boutwell.* The cutter had recently returned from a successful weeks-long effort to bring to bay a vessel that had been setting illegal high-seas drift nets off Russia's Pacific coast. The unflagged Taiwanese fishing boat would not permit a boarding. "They cut the net. We got a piece of it for evidence. We kept asking their flag state. Told them we would claim them if they didn't tell us. A week later we were still with them and heading toward super-typhoon Eve. When we threw a weather report on board, they turned." The standoff lasted nearly all the way to Hawaii. *Boutwell* was in the process of getting permission to fire a shot over the fishing boat's bow when the vessel relented. Then *Boutwell* received a mayday. Nixon told of saving a woman who'd been sailing a 65-foot schooner by herself until being overcome by seasickness in 25-foot waves. "I was lowered in an RHI in 25-foot seas with a boarding officer on board in case the woman was purposely trying to sink her boat for insurance. We got her, but getting back onto the cutter we put a hole in the RHI. People on the lower deck were helping, but the RHI tipped over. I was clipped in, and I held on to her. Later it occurred to me: I was a nonrate, and I was the only one responsible. I was in charge."

⌒

TWO BELLS, 1300: Karl, Tracy, and Vaught have returned the fo'c'sle deck after tensioning the stay. The wind has picked up, and Ramos has passed the word that the yards are to be braced onto the port tack in anticipation of sail stations later. He's a bit testy with his mast captains. Could be it's the bosun emotion brought on by two days without wind.

Officer candidate Greg Shouse remains in his trops smoking a cigar outside the galley below Teak Beach. He's older than the other thirty-six candidates. He tells me about his work on Operation Snow Cap from 1989 to 1993 along with the Drug Enforcement Agency and Bolivian police on the Mamore River in the Amazon Basin. The drug laboratories are located on the rivers because they need water to make cocaine. He says the commandant was concerned about the Coast Guard being deep in the jungle until it was explained that the coke makers moved almost everything by river. Shouse describes a ten-day raid during which the labs were blown up along with the cheese presses and microwaves they used to dry the coke. "They would put women and children in front to stop us, so we had to throw tear gas to get them out." Clandestine air strips were destroyed. Shouse talks about Coastie boarding parties on navy ships working the blockade of Iraq. He resmokes the great cigars he's enjoyed while on duty in the Dominican Republic.

Chief Greg Vaught, a tall man, is new to *Eagle* this year. He opens his leather tobacco pouch and stuffs his pipe. In a low voice he tells me about "another example of Karl's magic," which he's just witnessed while tightening the bird and the t'gallant stay. Vaught takes me back a few months to explain. *Eagle* was in dry dock over the winter at the Coast Guard yard in Baltimore. The hull was waterblasted and repainted, but the primary job was to overhaul the foremast. All the yards and the running and standing rigging were taken off so the mast could be worked on. At the same time, two man-sized holes were torched in the hull, port and starboard, and the Nazi pigs — 344 tons of iron ingots placed in the bilge sixty-three years ago — were removed and replaced with heavier lead pigs. This gained some space because it takes fewer lead pigs to counterbalance the ship's spars and the wind upon them. Vaught tells me that when it came time to repaint the waterline, Karl said that the Germans had placed the line higher on the hull, that *Eagle*'s line was too low. He convinced Bosun Ramos to have it painted higher. When *Eagle* first went back into the water, Karl's waterline looked too high even when the yards were put back on and the stores were shipped. "But today, when we climbed onto the sprit to tighten the bird, the line was perfect." He says "perfect" with wonder in his voice. "When there's sail stations, Karl's here, he's there, and you never see him moving from one place to the other."

～

MONDAY, MAY 10, 1999, 0830
Our position is 23 degrees 11 minutes north and 71 degrees 32 minutes west, approaching the Caicos Passage. Fifteen-knot trades from the northeast. Our track will be between the Turks and Caicos and Great Inagua Island. Two small dolphins are leaping in unison with the sun on

their backs. The signal for sail stations, like the *heehaw* of a robotic donkey, sounded five minutes ago.

"Lay aloft. Lay out the headsail downhauls. Ungasket the lowers.
On the fore, on the main, man your course gear!"

Sails are set in order. A scimitar moon sits off the curve of the main
royal leech, making it a Turkish flag. Off the port beam looms one thick
black cloud with gilt edges. The sun's rays and cloud shadows descend
in godly facets in the distance. Captain Papp appears on the fantail and
notes the "silver ribbon" on the horizon. Karl is in high spirits as he
checks the stack of the headsails one above the other, his hands weigh-
ing the balance of them, pointing out to one of his foremast hands how
the balance is attained by sheeting home — adjusting the sheets until
the spaces between the three headsails are equal. Then they will draw
evenly. He feels the whole ship the way a conductor or pianist feels an
entire score with its first notes. *Eagle* is making 11 knots. Smiles all
around and high fives. "Tee-en knots!" Tracy Allen says in Texan. Bama
shouts, "Whoah! Whooee!" The ocean is purple with white horses.
Hot sun, warm wind. Eleven knots feels like Mach 2. Haiti is not far to
the southeast. Tracy explains some finer points to an officer candidate
in the waist:

"We err on the side of tightness, so we don't luff. The belly of the
sail is adjusted with the sheets. The lifts are used to adjust the cockbill
[the cant of the yards]. The braces are set by the quarterdeck according
to the ship's course, our track. The ship talks to us," he says, meaning
that the experienced crew know the language of her blocks, shackles,
and sails. "We hear luff and then commune with the quarterdeck. The
last couple of years the junior officers have listened to us. One time a junior officer wanted to brace sharper 'to see what happens.' We said, No,
you're not going to kill our guys so you can see what happens. If you
want to see, then bear off. We tried his idea, and did pick up a few knots,
and then we braced." Allen goes on to review the outer and inner cardi-
nal points of the compass and tells the candidate that two points equal
22.5 degrees, which is about what the wind has backed — moved counterclockwise relative to the ship — in the past few minutes. "The wind
backs the opposite way, clockwise, in the Southern Hemisphere." Because the wind has backed, *Eagle* is able to keep the same course but is

now sailing two points freer, away from the direction of the wind, a better point of sail. "Oh," says the candidate, looking as though Allen has been speaking Martian.

1010: "Classic puffy cumulus," observes the bosun. "Trades all the way to Panama." A container ship changes course to get a better look at *Eagle*, which is not uncommon. The barque under sail is an uplifting sight to merchant seamen. Karl tells of the time *Eagle* was under way in this kind of wind with a tanker approaching from the opposite direction. The ship radioed for help with a sick crewman. *Eagle* launched a small boat with the doctor and with Karl as coxswain without reducing sail. She later wore around to retrieve the doc.

At quarters in the waist after the noon meal, the captain addresses the entire crew: "Now it gets serious. It's been nice sailing, but now we're down around islands and boats. The ship may have to be worked at night. We will be losing talent soon, and frankly I had hoped their replacements would be farther along. We will wear ship at least twice today." He means that *Eagle* will gain the opposite tack by falling off the wind and putting her stern through it. Wearing a square-rigger is safer than tacking in a strong wind, especially with a green crew. It's the same idea as jibing in a small boat, but with many carefully timed steps involving the bracing of yards and shifting of staysails. It requires teamwork and leadership. The talent we are losing includes Tracy Allen, whose replacement as mainmast captain is Kelly Nixon. The captain is applying some not-so-subtle pressure on the mast captain-to-be, and I think he's applying it to himself, too, perhaps unconsciously, as we approach the latitude of Saint John, where Greg LaFond fell.

I've learned from the old German logs that our ship touched in the Virgin Islands in June of 1938. Saint John is a two-day sail from here and at practically the same latitude. We are only 10 degrees of longitude, though sixty-one years, from Captain August Thiele walking the same quarterdeck, bearing the same grief as Robert Papp does today. A seaman named Fritz Neumann — New Man, of all things — had fallen to his death from the rigging on July 30, 1937, while the ship was en route to Iceland. Even making allowance for the superstitions of salts, I doubt that Captain Thiele would have seen Neumann's fall as foretelling the gruesome plunge of the thousand-year Reich after its short,

pride-bloated climb. A second seaman, named Linde, committed suicide on the same voyage. He was sewn into a sail and buried at sea.

The second wear, smoother than the first, is completed just before
dark, and *Eagle* is back on course to Cuba. "Well done," the captain announces over the PA.

⌒

MAY 11, 1999, 0900
Eagle is flying at more than 10 knots as day breaks between Caicos
and Little Inagua Island in 20-knot trades. From the boat deck, the after part of the fo'c'sle deck, which overlooks the waist, Tracy Allen
shouts the order to set royals, t'gallants, and upper staysails: "On the
fore royal, on the main royal, hand-over-hand the halyards." Greg
Giggi follows up and hails the hands aloft: "On the fore; lay onto the
royal and t'gallant yards and overhaul!" Down on deck Karl tells the
rest of the foremast crew that the Germans tended not to set staysails
when the wind was abaft the beam. "It robs wind from the squares," he
says, pointing out an unwanted ripple in the fore course caused by the
main topmast staysail. The sky holds big cumulus clouds, blue patches,
and squalls on the horizon — wispy, black, dangerous-looking bruises.
One passes aft, and *Eagle* hits 13.6 knots in a hot rain of mist and heels
to 11 degrees. "Captain on the bridge!" shouts the officer of the deck.
The quarterdeck snaps to attention. Good mornings are exchanged all
around. "It doesn't get much better than this," the captain says of *Eagle*'s
squall-powered sprint.

The seas have grown, and with the ship's heel the walk forward to
the fo'c'sle deck is a zigzag affair. Karl has his coffee cup in hand outside the galley and is telling a few people about the battle of Little
Bighorn, saying that the bones of one of Custer's men were found a few
years ago when a grass fire exposed them. The experts could tell how he
died, and it wasn't pretty. He talks about the difference between the
Spanish-American War–vintage 30/40 caliber Craig-Jorgenson ammo
and Springfield ammo and about the advantages of the smokeless gunpowder used by the German-led Spanish soldiers in that war. The former Spanish empire — and perhaps thoughts of Theobolt Dillmann,

who barely missed shipping out with the *Maine* — brings Karl back around to his Marine days in the Philippines. He says he was talking to Wade Smith, the Seabee from Old Ironsides, who was stationed near where Karl was in 1974. Smith mentioned the name of a post, and Karl recognized it. The post had been named after a Lieutenant Jeffries, a Seabee killed in an ambush by communist insurgents on April 14, 1974. "We put his name on the backside of a C-ration box and hung it on a cross," Karl says with an inward look that goes all the way back to the Philippines.

8 PONDER THE IMPONDERABLE

Eleven miles off Cabo Maisi, the eastern tip of Cuba, and heading west toward Guantanamo Bay. The Sierra Maestra mountains are ephemeral outlines. Cuba is a blue shadow with a cumulus headdress. Colonel García is standing on the fantail facing her, crying silently for the homeland he has not seen this close since childhood. It's hot. The black cone, an upside-down witch's hat called the "day shape," points to the fo'c'sle deck, telling the world that we are motoring. Sails are being doused.

"Get it up to the yard," Karl shouts to his people, who are hand-over-handing the heavy mainsail to its yard to be furled.

"Giggi, good job," Karl tells the blond bear as he swings onto the deck from the ratlines. Giggi has shown leadership aloft. "Thank you, boss," he answers, instantly puffed by Karl's endorsement. He has been attached to the foremast since the beginning of the trip in order to qualify as a "BMOW" (pronounced "beemo"), boatswain's mate of the watch. He has already served the requisite time on the mizzen and mainmasts, learned their fife and pin rails so he can find their lines in the dark. Once qualified, a BMOW is the member of the watch who passes orders relating to the setting and trimming of sails from the officer of the deck on the bridge.

Giggi is from Outville, Ohio, "a little town about a hundred yards wide, thirty miles east of Columbus." His love of the sea began as a boy on fishing and skin-diving trips with his dad to Florida, where he visited a Coast Guard station. "It's still my dream station. I want law enforcement. I got on *Eagle* out of boot camp. Couldn't pass it up. I'm glad I'm here. Been here for a year and five months." As Giggi moves along the pin rail, memorizing and following each line with his eyes to its place aloft, he mutters a ditty that has been with the ship since before women joined the crew:

> He lowered her to the sheets
> His face turned clew garnet.
> He lifted up her shirt.
> He saw her leechlines.
> He went in her,
> And out her,
> And up her,
> For a t'gallant, royal time.

The actual lines that correspond to the lines of verse are the lower sheets, clew garnet, fore lift, leechline, inner bunt, outer bunt, upper topsail sheet, fore t'gallant sheets, and fore royal sheets. Giggi says he isn't sure if the females use the same guide. Then he shouts, "The foremast rules!" to his mates, who have finished furling their sails quicker than their counterparts on the mainmast. The mainmast still has the

Foremast hands battle a headsail. (Doug Kuntz)

t'gallant to furl, and "dead men," unsightly lumps in the rolled and gasketed sail, are visible in a few places on the main's lower yards.

The Caribbean reminds Giggi of his friend LaFond: "He was a family boy. He didn't always do good, but he meant well. He came to *Eagle* right out of boot camp, too. His father retired as a chief warrant officer, a gunner. There were too many people at his memorial service for the church to hold. The gym at Raymond High School was bigger, and it was filled when they dedicated a soccer field to Greg; he was a star soccer player. They retired his number. His brother Joe is a Marine. We put on bravos, camouflage field dress, and marched out and raised the flag at his grave. The LaFonds had *Eagle* carved into the marble headstone, with three deckies on the fo'c'sle deck. They are Frank Conka, Dan Burgoyne, and me. Burgoyne is a QM3 on the *Midget* now. The LaFonds adopted me. I call her Mom II. His death was an accident. He stood up, blacked out, you know, the way you get lightheaded sometimes. A freak. I knew him too well." Giggi dismisses the idea of suicide, a possibility that was considered in the investigation. "There were good vibes that day. Swim call. I believe it was one of those things. They did the autopsy right before Christmas. That wasn't right. I think of him out here. He's here. I strongly believe that."

The Falcon jet carrying Captain Ivan Luke to Gitmo is expected to fly over at any time. I'm surprised *Eagle* has cruised so close to the coast, well within Cuba's territorial waters. During last night's evening meal the captain spoke about using *Eagle* to break forty years of ice with our Caribbean foe. Maybe he's hoping for a diplomatic opportunity. Bob Papp's next assignment is as Coast Guard liaison to Congress. He seems born to the job, a natural diplomat who has placed special emphasis on the last of *Eagle*'s three basic missions: to train cadets, to be perceived by Americans as their tall ship, and to represent the United States to the rest of the world. The captain said that *Eagle*'s visit to Leningrad in 1989 served as a rapprochement at the time when the Soviet Union was coming apart at the seams. Her visit was a way for suspicious Cold War enemies to practice cooperation based on a common seagoing heritage.

Eagle's destination after leaving Hamburg in '96 was Rostock, on the Baltic coast of what had been East Germany. Training ships from all

over the world converged there to participate in a race to the newly renamed St. Petersburg on the occasion of the Russian navy's tricenten-
nial celebration. Before the race, *Eagle* was tied next to the Russian
four-masted barque *Sedov*, the former German *Magdalene Vinnen*, a
huge, rusting shadow of her former glory. All the training ships took
turns hosting cocktail parties to encourage the international exchange.
The captain and officers of the *Sedov* were of course invited to *Eagle*'s
reception. But while walking the short distance between ships in his
dress uniform, the Russian captain, having already consumed an abun-
dance of vodka, tripped and bloodied his face. His officers and *Eagle*'s
doctor, who had witnessed the fall, returned him to his quarters, where
he was tucked into bed and reportedly given a fresh supply of the dog
that bit him. It was explained that he had been with his ship for many
years and had fallen into a depression because of his nation's inability to
provide even basic maintenance. Captain Papp observed later, after
Sedov beat the rest of the pack to St. Petersburg by nearly twenty hours,
that a certain justice had been done.

Sailing ships do seem to play a small unifying role these days, as
though they were envoys from a time before the mess of the twentieth
century. They remain bound to the uneven pace of the earth's powerful
nonchalance, a fundamental rhythm now barely felt except at sea. And,
most important, they are able to "make time," in the old definition,
through the combined will of their people. The justice of *Sedov*'s victory
lay in her crew's having heaved and hauled speed from the wind and
their captain's humiliation. It was a human victory. Perhaps the cat was
let out of the bag with the invention of the internal, the infernal, com-
bustion engine. The "cat" in the old expression was the cat-o-nine-tails,
which, once out, was meant to tear the flesh from those who broke shipboard rules. Better, perhaps, to have foregone engines because of how
they have flayed time to hasten it. The wind might have served us
better.

1600: We're anchored in Guantanamo Bay. It's hot and desert-
like. Gitmo is a ghost town with only about forty navy personnel and a
few Marines, a far cry from the emigrant-stuffed camp of the early '90s.
It could fill up again. Bosun Ramos, whose son is in the National Guard
and may be called up for duty in Kosovo, said Gitmo was being con-

sidered as a destination for some of the refugees fleeing that bloody province.

The three navy specialists who oversaw damage-control training en route have donned their trops and brought their bags on deck. They're looking forward to some golf on the Gitmo course. At quarters, the captain bids a formal goodbye to Peter MacDonald, "damage controlman extraordinaire," who's been with *Eagle* for four years. "Mac has touched *Eagle* from stem to stern and made many improvements," says the captain. Mac starts to speak but can't continue and is applauded. The big man tells the deckies, tears in his eyes, that they are the hardest-working deck force in the Coast Guard. The captain hugs him, then presents him with the order of the square-rigger, a prized approbation.

1630: I'm at my escritoire in the flag berth, probably for the last time before Captain Luke climbs aboard to claim his rightful place. I'm recording the morning's events in my log, including a long-overdue nod to the snipes. Departing members of the engine-room crew also may receive the order of the square-rigger. They too are hardworking, but less visible, for they live down deep in "the hole," a hot, windless, noisy place that is alien to the nineteenth century of the weather deck. I'm convinced the snipes love it down there because I believe in natural selection. Grub white, they talk engines and blink in the sunlight — a different species, antipodal from the tanned and calloused deckies. An unspoken competition exists between denizens of the hole and those of *Eagle's* sky works. Each group knows it cannot survive without the other. Deckies prefer the heights and wind, but heat and noise are wind to the snipes. There is less motion in *Eagle's* netherworld, where machinery shines and hisses. And there is oil, with its incomparable smell and feel. There are boilers, gauges, and compressors. Snipes know their own value. Engineers are responsible for the ship's forward movement in the absence of wind so that she can save herself from lee shores and meet her required speed of advancement. They keep the sewage system functioning, along with the refrigeration, air conditioning, and all of the motors on board. Last but not least, they turn seawater sweet.

The desalination equipment now on board is extremely efficient, but in '94, *Eagle* depended on Joboo, the name the snipes gave the temperamental voodoo water-maker. Back then the shrine to Joboo, its spiritual incarnation — a fierce-faced coconut head with dark glasses — was mounted on the bulkhead beside the six-foot-square, brass-tubed evaporator, which was moody and not fuel-efficient. It drank diesel that otherwise was needed to run *Eagle*'s main engine, Max, the big Caterpillar. As a result, water conservation was essential, especially in the absence of wind, when Max required fuel. In the name of keeping time, visits to the rain closet went by the boards, people smelled bad, spaces below decks got close, tempers flared. Only when the wind blew could Joboo be run to refill the water tanks. The Joboo dilemma seemed a perfect metaphor: fuel for speed versus fuel for water, the choice facing all of humankind from now on.

The metaphor topside is that without wind, without moral purpose, the nation that the barque now represents is in danger of becoming becalmed, her crew suffering scurvy of the soul. In '94, word of O. J. Simpson's troubles reached us almost a week late as *Eagle* approached the Bay of Biscay. The news set off a Hobbes-versus-Locke debate that raged on all decks. The younger ones in the fo'c'sle were more interested in the bloody aspects of the crime. Executive Officer Curran, who took Locke's view that man in his original state was good, called the murders a sin. Captain Stillman, who said O.J. had been his favorite running back, saw them as evidence of man's fundamentally selfish, brutish nature.

1 700: A gray navy landing craft approaches the ship. "Stand by to take lines," Karl barks. "Man the vangs." *Eagle* will use its cargo boom, which is stored on the boat deck, to bring a replacement pump on board. Frigate birds circle overhead like black pterodactyls. Captain Luke, small and wiry, climbs the ladder from the barge, stands on *Eagle*'s rail, looks aft, and salutes the flag. He jumps down, salutes the man he is to replace later this summer, and shakes hands. The captain leads him back into the aft cabin and the blond satinwood berth, now prepared for him. Colonel García has been allowed to go ashore to buy provisions for the Cuban meal he has offered to make for the crew tomorrow.

It's difficult to feel surrounded by an enemy on this peaceful Caribbean day, but we are. Only the dry brown foothills of the Sierra

Maestra, where Castro hid out during the revolution, and the black frigates — also called man-o'-war birds — circling, tweak at the sixth sense, the sense of foreboding. *Eagle* is meant to awaken it in her people, and to teach them to carry it lightly. That's the trick. Too much attention to it spawns prophecy of the self-fulfilling kind. A balance must be struck. Sailors call it being forehanded, habituated to always thinking ahead. Captain Stillman used to tell his first-class cadets, "There is no bravado in this business. It's risky because of the Clausewitzian fog. Beware the Clausewitzian fog." The Prussian military strategist Karl von Clausewitz was a favorite of his, an early exponent of chaos theory: that random events are no less influential in war than the most rational calculations. "Nelson understood that, too," said Stillman. "He said that there's nothing in a sea fight more given than the element of chance. He exemplified forehandedness, discipline of mind, willingness to embrace the unthinkable. You should develop a special regime to find responsibility, then have the faith to doubt. If you think there's a better way, share it. It's always the way on a good ship."

Stillman said that in one way it was easier to be forehanded today, at least in the physical sense. The random event that sank *Niobe* — a squall — appeared out of nowhere. Today it would appear on a screen, perhaps in time to make a difference. The crew bore Stillman's philosophizing in a funny way. During his occasional morale-raising speeches at quarters in the waist, crew members would wager under their breaths on whether he would again use the phrase "ponder the imponderable." Morale was thus raised, if not always in the way intended, although by and large they were damn fine speeches.

I once accompanied him to the mainmast crosstrees, and when we arrived he looked out at the horizon. "I don't care who you are; if you don't feel a solid attachment to the good Lord up here, there's something wrong. It's not just the beauty, but the profound connection to the pain of experiment. The sea is unforgiving." At that moment, they seemed the truest words ever spoken. Later on the same glorious day, a cadet spoke with Stillman. Had he been on shore, hanging out and joking cynically with friends, he might have considered one of the captain's short sermons fodder for derision. But here, as he watched white horses gallop over a purple sea and geysers of spray surge up through the hawsehole onto the deck, the captain's words, "You are bearing witness to the purest relationship between our minds and the gifts of nature," had him gulping "yes, sir" and nodding like a proselyte.

Stillman taught political history at the academy before taking command of *Eagle*. He is a short Teddy Roosevelt of a man, a former wrestler, full of bully teeth when he laughs or makes a point, as when he was standing at his favorite perch on the port bridge wing watching *Eagle*'s flight. His master's thesis at Wesleyan, "Leadership During the Great Age of Sail," told tales of Horatio Nelson and his gifted right-hand man, Collingswood. Stillman was at a loss to explain why this subject appealed to him, a kid from Lakewood, Ohio. Later he earned a master's in public administration from George Washington University. After graduating from the academy he commanded the 270-foot cutter *Forward* in deep Caribbean drug operations, and in the Windward Passage collected Haitian boat people. Stillman is now an admiral and assistant commandant in charge of government and public affairs.

I once heard him tell cadets that when they were on watch and felt they must wake the captain, they should "make sure he's awake and understands. As a young man, I thought I needed to understand the total situation before troubling the captain — have my socks in order, suitcased and stenciled, metaphorically speaking."

"Suitcased and stenciled, aye, sir," Keith Curran, his executive officer and unflagging straight man, repeated, chuckling. Their very different statures — Curran is big, a former football tackle — combined to become one authority. "Don't get cozy in the pilot house," Curran added. "Get out there and feel the wind."

Stillman's teeth could clench, too, when he was vexed or concerned about his people. He would sometimes worry aloud that while we, as a society, can see far forward technologically, we do so at the expense of our hindsight, which lives in traditions, which are dying. A moral radar must see equally well fore and aft, and he was afraid that this was not happening. He said that because of the unforgiving nature of the sea, so obvious on *Eagle*, one tended to contemplate life's paradoxes, the imponderables — How could God have allowed the Holocaust? He wanted his cadets to ask such questions. For that matter, how could God have allowed Tyler, Stillman's first child, to be born with Down

Aloft, the air seems sculpted by the sails. (Russell Drumm)

syndrome? "He was born just before I was going to sea. I waited a week. My military experience pulled me through — that and the Book of Job. Then it was all Laurie, my wife. She is a strict Lutheran. Her father founded a church in Nebraska. She said, 'How could God?' A Lutheran friend said, 'God didn't, God simply provided challenges.'" The challenges, Stillman told me, his light blue eyes bright, were opportunities.

I remember being surprised and humbled by the emotion I witnessed on my first day aboard the ship, as *Eagle* was about to leave New London in '94. Stillman, addressing the cadets and crew mustered in the waist, spoke of not compromising where personal integrity was concerned. "Remember this platform and the obligation to duty." He gave the order of the square-rigger to Bob Wiles, his operations officer. Wiles, choking back tears, announced to the crew that he would not be going, that his baby had been diagnosed with cancer. "When it gets tough out there, think about her. I love you all." As *Eagle* pulled away from the dock, the captain's smiling son Tyler stood next to his mother, saluting. The ship's crew, lined up along *Eagle*'s starboard side, saluted back. When Pat Stillman was relieved by Don Grosse in '95, his crew presented him with a gift they had bought in Plymouth, England: a nail and a piece of deck from *Victory*, Lord Nelson's flagship. For once he couldn't speak.

⌒

FROM the main crosstrees, I can see more of Cuba. I can see back toward the Windward Passage, forward toward Panama and the Pacific beyond, and down through the ages. The ship is a conglomerate, displaying faults of many times at every level. *Eagle*'s a bit Jurassic in the hole by virtue of the fossil fuel consumed there. "I cremate old dinosaurs," Bob Volpe, Stillman's engineering officer, liked to say. He read books about fire-breathing dragons and knights, carrying earplugs in a transparent plastic capsule chained to his belt. The next stratum down on the ship is human salt, male and now female berthing areas. Bodies, stacked in bunks, are mended there by dreams woven on the ocean's loom, as always. Last night on the weather deck, Chief Warrant Officer Tom Dickey raised his sextant to a star to compute latitude, while in the CIC the global positioning receiver fixed our position to within a few feet via man-made moons. It's only on the upper yards, on the fighting tops, from which the ghosts of Marines fire onto enemy decks, and even higher, here on the crosstrees, surrounded by canvas and sculpted air, that the past is victorious, unassailable.

9 *The Fall of Neumann*

THE CONSTRUCTION and fitting-out costs of *Horst Wessel* and her sister ship *Albert Leo Schlageter* were included in the Kriegsmarine's overall budget for 1935. In addition to the resources needed for the training of officers to serve in Hitler's new, secretly growing navy, the budget covered several warships. On May 21 of that year Hitler created the Defense Law, which officially authorized Hjalmar Schacht, minister of economics, to direct preparations for war, which Schacht had actually begun the year before. In fact, beginning in 1934, the sole basis of Germany's economic recovery was *Wiederaufrüstung*, rearmament. "The accomplishment of the armament program with speed and in quantity is *the* problem of German politics; everything else therefore would be subordinate to this purpose," Hitler told those close to him, while continuing to talk peace in public. His "purpose" was kept under wraps until March 16, 1935, the day universal conscription was imposed to build an army of thirty-six divisions, about half a million men. The order would effectively break the Versailles Treaty. But until that day, Hitler forbade Grand Admiral Erich Raeder from even discussing the construction of U-boats. Prohibited by the treaty, they were being built secretly in Holland, then the parts were shipped to Kiel and kept in storage. Krupp's plants had already been cranked up, of course. They were turning out the steel that would be fashioned into tanks, guns, and the riveted flanks of *Horst Wessel* once Hitler was certain the world would fail to meet the challenge he had so carefully timed.

As expected, Hitler's gauntlet was not taken up, and the Krupp furnaces continued to roar throughout 1936. The huge I. G. Farben chemical concern was perfecting synthetic rubber and gasoline. The company had saved Germany from early disaster in World War I by inventing synthetic nitrates. The traditional supply, delivered to Germany via square-rigged ships from Chile, was cut off by British blockade.

On August 1, seventeen days after *Horst Wessel* came off the Blohm & Voss ways, the world's top athletes gathered in Berlin for the Olympic Games. The games had never been better organized and were a glittering showcase meant to demonstrate just how well the Third Reich was reinventing Germany. Hitler foresaw Berlin as the permanent home of the games. As it turned out, German athletes did win most of the gold, with the glaring exception of Jesse Owens's five gold medals. His feat changed nothing, of course. Long before the games were held, the concept of Aryan superiority had begun to take shape in the Nuremberg Laws, which stripped German Jews of their citizenship. While the games were going on, the signs that banned "dogs and Jews" from shops and other public places were ordered removed.

Horst Wessel *heads to sea with Captain Thiele's sailboat mounted on the stern.*
(Collection of Herbert Böhm)

The Olympic sailing events took place at Kiel, once the imperial navy's largest port. In 1881 the German navy built a wooden dock outside of Kiel for the torpedo school ship *Blücher*. (General Gebhard Leberecht von Blücher was the gifted Prussian officer who helped defeat Napoleon at Waterloo.) The torpedo ship was later moved, but the name Blücher Brücke — Blücher Bridge — stuck to the wooden dock. The "bridge" was favored by sailing ships because they could approach and leave it under sail alone. No German *Segelschulschiff* had any standing unless her crew could sail to and away from the dock. The *Gorch Fock* showed the world how it was done during the '36 Olympics. There was a sense of navy pride as she paraded.

Kiel Harbor had been the site of the navy's humiliating mutiny in 1918 during the final days of Germany's defeat. Though the war was already lost, the admirals of Germany's High Seas Fleet took it upon themselves to engage the far superior Royal Navy in one last, suicidal battle to regain their honor from the Brits after their defeat in the battle of Jutland two years before. The enlisted sailors balked, however, especially those influenced by communist theory and the successful revolution in Russia the previous year. Thousands of men gathered on the outskirts of Kiel on November 3, 1918, to protest the arrest of 180 sailors from the battleship *Markgraf*. By the end of the demonstration twenty mutineers had been shot to death by a unit of loyal seamen, but the mutiny mirrored the unrest in the war-sick nation. In a hospital near Stralsund, east of Kiel, Corporal Adolf Hitler, still partially blind from poison gas delivered by British artillery, listened to reports of the Red mutiny and to rumors that a general worker's strike was planned for the major cities. Six days later, Kaiser Wilhelm II abdicated. The terms of surrender would be harsh, for the Allies were bent on dismantling Germany's war machine. The British ordered the German fleet to Scapa Flow, the British fleet's base in Scotland, where, as the victors looked on in disbelief, the Germans scuttled their own navy. Hitler did not forget the events of November 1918, and made sure the officers and men of the new Kriegsmarine knew whom to thank for the navy's resurrection. Their feelings of indebtedness lasted too long; unlike the army, the German navy made no overt challenge to Hitler's maniacal course.

What a chilling turn of the wheel it proved to be when *Eagle*, former flagship of the Kriegsmarine's training fleet, sailed back into Kiel in September of 1972, where the Olympic sailing events again were to be held. The main venue was in Munich. Gerry Donohoe was a cadet in his third year at the academy then and remembers it well. September was late in the year for *Eagle* to be heading for Europe. Her schedule had been changed with little notice when President Richard Nixon, otherwise engaged in the Vietnam war, accepted an invitation from West German Chancellor Willie Brandt to take part in a tall ship race from the Isle of Wight to Kiel as a prelude to the Olympic sailing events. *Eagle* was committed. Edward Cassidy, a fine sailor (but called "Crash" Cassidy by his crew because of his penchant for mistreating docks), was the captain. *Eagle*'s crew learned of the challenge en route to New London from Florida. At New London, the Gold Star Bridge, under which *Eagle* must pass every time she leaves or returns to the academy, was being repaired, and the steel safety netting strung beneath it was left hanging too low. Though housed as usual for the return, both of *Eagle*'s topmasts hit the netting and were bent in half at the doublings. Both royal yards came off their tracks and dangled by their chain lifts. To stay on schedule for the transatlantic crossing, *Eagle* went to Electric Boat for repairs. Ship's rumor has it that Nixon personally halted construction on a nuclear submarine so that the yard crew could fix the square-rigger. People from Blohm & Voss were flown in to lend their expertise.

Eagle crossed the starting line off the Isle of Wight 10 seconds after the gun, under full sail, at least an hour ahead of her competition: *Gorch Fock II, Danmark, Winston Churchill,* and *Dar Mlodziezy.* "It was blowing 50 knots and we had no heavy sails, just light Dacron," Nathaniel Wilson recalled. "I remember the moment I was formed as a sailmaker. All through the night *Gorch Fock* was on our weather quarter. The previous evening we had doused t'gallants and royals. *Gorch Fock* stayed under full sail. We reset them at night in 40 knots of wind. The waist was smothered in foam. You couldn't afford to miss stays and get caught aback in those conditions. At dawn we had begun another tack. *Gorch Fock* passed us doing 15 knots. Everything was glistening in the morning light. We were just going through stays. They were more than a half-mile ahead by the time we finished the tack. The duel lasted all day long in 25- to 35-knot winds and a clear blue sky. Then we blew out the lower topsail clews. *Gorch Fock* was on the horizon. They had no problem with their sails. We were spending twenty-four hours a day keeping canvas on *Eagle*. It was a horrendous trip. It punished *Eagle*. Twelve sails blew out. She performed extremely well, but something was wrong."

Donohoe said the tacking toward the north of Denmark and around into the Baltic was supposed to be done within boundaries prescribed by the location of old minefields, but *Eagle's* crew was quite sure *Gorch Fock* and *Dar Mlodziezy* had tacked well inside of the boundaries. The night before *Eagle* entered Kiel Harbor, Palestinian terrorists had attacked the dormitory housing the Israeli weightlifting team and killed eleven of them. "Kiel had been in a great, festive mood," Donohoe said. There were beer stands and bands. It looked beautiful when we first got in. We tied up next to *Gorch Fock*. The *Christian Radich* was there. But the Israelis had been killed. When that happened, everything came down overnight. We got under way as soon as possible. We went to Lübeck and tied up in the heart of the city late in the day. Thousands came to see the ship as we moved up the narrow canal. They shouted 'Welcome, *Horst Wessel*! Welcome, *Horst Wessel*!' The affection for the ship was amazing. The next day, men who had served on her came aboard."

⟳

HORST WESSEL was placed in service under Captain August Thiele on September 17, 1936. Thiele had entered the German naval academy at Flensburg-Mürwik in 1912, in plenty of time for the start of the kaiser's war. He had commanded the *Gorch Fock* the year before taking the new *Horst Wessel*, now considered the flagship of the training fleet, to sea. Thiele first took her from Hamburg to Kiel. Throughout October the crew trained and the ship underwent sea trials. On October 23, Storm Troop Leader von Jagow presented the ship with a portrait of her namesake. The next day the ship left for the Blohm & Voss yard in Hamburg for a few adjustments. En route, as though to receive a blessing, she visited Gotland, off the east coast of Sweden, a region that had supplied the crews of sailing ships for many generations, right up to Gustaf Erikson's fleet of steel grain ships. In November she returned to Kiel, where the crew trained for the rest of the month.

Horst Wessel left the cadet training center and ventured into the Atlantic for the first time on December 1, 1936, bound for Las Palmas in the Canary Islands. Early in the morning on Christmas Eve, the barque was dealing with headwinds 150 miles northwest of the Canary Islands on a port tack. There were thunderstorms on the horizon. The wind nearly died early on — the proverbial calm — and then began to rise throughout the day. By evening it was approaching gale force, over 40 knots. Captain Thiele changed course at 1930 to face the growing seas head-on. By midnight, when Christmas is celebrated in Germany with the singing of "Silent Night," the ship was climbing her way up and over 20-foot seas in a whole gale. The night was anything but silent. By noon on Christmas Day, the wind had shifted, allowing Thiele to keep his southeast course and make time to the islands. They had been able to cover only 76 miles in the previous twenty-four hours; the storm had blown them 16 miles off course.

One month later, the barque, homeward bound, was a few hundred miles north of the area where she had met the December storm when the barometer again began a precipitous drop.

The log tells us that at 1300 on January 19, a dark cloud appeared with rain "on its backside." The wind picked up and suddenly veered to the north. The captain ordered the helm down and the upper sails doused. The barque fell 60 degrees off the wind. The gusts grew stronger, and more sails were doused. Rain fell harder. Strong ocean swells began showing from the northeast. By the end of the day, the wind had swung all the way around to the southwest, opposing and flattening the sea. By early the next morning, all sails were set again, but not for long. As it turned out, the previous twenty-four hours had been only an appetizer. Big swells were now marching from the north-northwest, evidence of something big and mean churning in the distance. What had started as a flat ocean in the morning was a mountain range of 20-foot peaks by afternoon. All through the night and the next day the ship was assaulted by gale-force winds. At five in the afternoon of the twenty-first, while part of the deck watch was aloft dousing upper topsails, those manning the ship's three wheels lost their hold on the rudder, and *Horst Wessel* turned sideways to the huge swells. Water poured into the waist. She recovered her course, but for two hours she took green water over the bow as lightning storms made false daylight in the southwest.

The wind went from west to north and back to west at over 60 knots. At 1800 the ship was pushed sideways again and was in danger of broaching. At some point that day, the flag was lowered to half-staff. Word was received that the ship *Welle* (German for "wave") had sunk in the storm.

As January 22 dawned, *Horst Wessel* was 700 miles off the coast of Spain, having made 400 miles in three days the hard way. There were no weather satellites, of course, no images from outer space showing the speed and direction of the big storm, no way of knowing that things were going from bad to worse except for the barometer, which refused to climb. In fact, between midnight and 0100 on the twenty-third, the glass dropped and the wind blew harder. At 0030, only the lower topsail on the foremast and a storm headsail were set. Because of the increasing seas, the captain ordered the ship turned up into the wind. She was now "lying at orkan," as the log puts it, heaved to in hurricane-force winds with her rudder turned hard to windward, the pressure of the wind on the headsails keeping her bow perpendicular to the marine mountains. The rain fell so hard that it kept the sea down for a time. Lightning lit up the sky to the east. It must have been one of those times when, as in childbirth, you begin to see what brought you to this point, even if it was a splendid idea, as very ill-conceived. At 0345 the wind suddenly veered 40 degrees and increased to 12 on the open Beaufort scale, to something over 70 knots. Beginning at 0900 on the twenty-third, in heavy rain and hail, the crew poured oil into the sea in an attempt to calm it. By 1100, the wind had begun to slow, but the sea was still heaving. *Horst Wessel* rolled, her lee rail at times under water. The wind continued to move around the compass. That evening the ship was still turned into the wind, which was still gusting at hurricane force in a confused sea. Huge swells approached from different directions and collided to form steep peaks. The barque was lifted from the bow, dropped, lifted from the stern, dropped, struck on the starboard beam, the port beam, and on around all the points of the compass. *Horst Wessel* returned to the Blücher Bridge on February 11.

The fierce Christmas and January storms have come down to us by way of the ship's logbooks — thirty volumes, each one and a half feet high by one foot wide, epitaphs of days bound in black leather. The logs must have been left on board, for they came to the United States with the ship and eventually found their way to the National Archives in Washington. Each volume contains ninety days. Each day is given two pages with a total of fifteen vertical columns whose headings account for a comprehensive range of conditions: compass heading, deviation from the heading, magnetic heading, ship's latitude and longitude, nautical observations, depth of water, wind speed and direction, sea size and swell direction, a general description of the weather, barometric pressure, temperature, a wide column to describe the activities of the crew, an even wider column for general remarks, and finally, a column devoted to sails: which ones were set and how. The days are divided horizontally into twenty-four rows representing the hours. Seas can be seen growing on the pages, daylight fading, temperature dropping, sails being set and doused, the ship rising and falling on a swell, and then the captain "making it so" with his signature in the lower right-hand corner of the page. A shorthand key gives seventeen abbreviated ways to describe the atmosphere, including "ugly." The key contains abbreviations for the twelve levels of wind speed according to the Beaufort scale. The various types of cloud formations are keyed, as are the phases of the moon. The comprehensive form of the log was established in another age, at the turn of the last century, when Grand Admiral Alfred von Tirpitz began building an armada in preparation for *der Tag* — the day when Germany would defeat the British navy. Until Tirpitz's time, officers in the German navy considered themselves blood brothers of their English counterparts. The competition between the navies was a root cause of World War I.

As the *Horst Wessel*'s first class of trainees was being hammered in the Atlantic, the second half of the class of '37 was in boot camp in Stralsund. Cadets were required to keep personal logbooks to record their activities and private observations on a daily basis, complete with drawings. Later in life, Franz Jacob of Hamburg used his log to write a memoir for his children. As a boy, he had been a member of the Hamburg Sailing Club and sailed with friends on the Elbe during fall and spring holidays. In the summer months he worked for boat owners who belonged to the club. He volunteered for the Marine Hitler Youth in 1933. He had wanted to study shipbuilding like his father. On the elder Jacob's recommendation, he applied in 1936 to join the navy as a com-

missioned officer and entered the service in April of 1937. He wrote
that he was awed by the sight of *Horst Wessel* "with its three masts and
yards," as he and his fellow "little sailors," fresh from basic training in
Stralsund, approached her for the first time. "After I had learned to
conduct myself as a soldier, knew how to handle a weapon, understood
how to salute my superiors, I approached the ship with mixed feelings."
That was because his father was a builder of sailing ships and had been
the engineer in charge of *Horst Wessel*'s construction at Blohm & Voss.
The son sensed that serving on the barque would be very different from
the sailing he had known. As he wrote in his memoir:

> While we were still in Stralsund [at boot camp], a rumor had made the
> rounds that the infamous bosun from the *Niobe*, a man named Kul, who
> was known as a slave-driver, was now a lieutenant doing duty as officer of
> the watch on the *Horst Wessel*. He had survived the *Niobe* disaster and was
> called the "Lion of the Sea." It was just this man who received us with
> bellowing voice as we stood at attention on the Blücher Bridge in Kiel,
> the perpetual home of the sailor. We stood there after a long train ride,
> our heavy duffle bags on our backs, holding everything we owned. Soon
> thereafter, this man revealed himself to be exceptionally approachable,
> extremely understanding, and quite fond of us, so we named him Papa
> Kul. Incidentally, his awe-inspiring voice was only raised during sailing
> maneuvers so that he could be heard even by those who were working on
> the highest yards. Until July 5, the first day we went to sea, we learned
> the theory of sailing a square-rigged ship, of setting and dousing the
> sails, the handling of lines, and, of course, the name of every line and sail.
> On the first day, everyone had already been assigned to a watch and a di-
> vision. . . . Sailing on a three-master such as *Horst Wessel* was exciting to
> me; it was entirely different from sailing on a yacht, although it is dif-
> ficult, if not impossible, to say which is better. In order to become very
> well acquainted with handling the ship, we first spent a couple of days on
> the western Baltic. On the second day, General Blomberg came aboard.

That was General Werner von Blomberg, formerly minister of defense, who had by this time evolved into the minister of war. By the time
he visited the ship, Blomberg had been named by Hitler commander in
chief of the armed forces, the first such position in German history. On

March 2, 1936, Blomberg, at Hitler's direction, issued formal orders for Germany's first military step: the occupation of the Rhineland. "Germany no longer feels bound by the Locarno Treaty," Hitler stated. "In the interest of the primitive rights of its people to the security of their frontier and the safeguarding of their defense, the German government has reestablished the absolute and unrestricted sovereignty of the Reich in the demilitarized zone." Blomberg would soon fall from his exalted position after it came to light that his new bride, the love of his life, was a former prostitute. When her cover was blown by some working girls who had known her before her marriage, he was dismissed.

Jacob's memoir continued:

> The war minister had hardly left the ship when we set sail for Königsberg, where we stayed for two days. The entire crew traveled through East Prussia, but with a few other volunteers I stayed behind to keep watch on the ship since I already knew quite a bit of the area. We had our fun, too, telling a newspaper reporter a lot of nonsense about the ship, which he then faithfully published the next day in his journal [a disquieting thought]. The important destination during the training cruise was Reykjavik, the capital of Iceland. But before we could leave the Baltic, the Sund, the Kattegat, and the Skagerrak behind us, we had the sad duty of bringing a dead comrade ashore at Swinemünde with military honors. He had fallen from a height of 20 meters out of the rigging.

Fritz Neumann fell at 1019 on July 30. The ship had just passed Copenhagen and was tacking. The wind was out of the northeast and light. He fell while gaining or leaving the main or foremast top (the log doesn't say which it was). Jacob had just finished his watch and had gone below. He was wondering at the beautiful houses along the Danish coast:

> FRIDAY, JULY 30, 1937: While I am belowdecks and the ship is just turning into the wind, I hear above me a heavy thud. One of our comrades has fallen from the crow's nest. The sails are hauled in, and under motor power we return to Swinemünde as quickly as possible. Around noon the captain announces the death of our comrade. He says a few appropriate words and invokes the words of Gorch Fock: "Do not complain, but dare again — seafaring is necessary!" The flag flies at half-

The flag-draped coffin of Fritz Neumann lies on the steps in front of the "captain's coffin." (Collection of Herbert Böhm)

mast. In the afternoon the whole crew stands in formation on deck. Our dead comrade Fritz Neumann, wrapped in a flag, is carried past us to the bridge and put to rest on a bier. We can hardly grasp it that someone who was fresh and healthy among us in the morning, enjoying the wonderful weather with us, should be dead by noon. But we do not want to give up. Our officers tell us to continue to do our duty as soldiers as we did before.

SATURDAY, JULY 31, 1937: We enter Swinemünde at 0100. Dressed in blue, we fall into formation in a square around our dead comrade, who rests on a bier before the mainmast. Deeply touched, we listen to the words of the captain. It is a solemn hour such as I have not seen before. The chief bosun's mate blows the pipe and Fritz Neumann leaves the ship carried by six of his comrades.

Horst Wessel reached the pier at 0107. Funeral services commenced on board at 0130, and Neumann's body was taken off at 0155. The barque was under way again at 0345. The sea was calm. As the sky lightened, the air grew misty. The rigging on all three masts was ordered checked out. At 0700, thunder was noted in the ship's log.

Franz Jacob recorded:

> In the North Sea, after a brief visit on the Faroe Islands, we encountered a storm. Only the storm staysails were set, but nonetheless the ship heeled so much that the railing was constantly in the water. Ropes were spanned in longitudinal and latitudinal directions at railing height so that we could hold on while crossing the deck. The first officer, leaning on one of these ropes, cried "Hold on! Hold on!" louder and louder. To the delight of everyone, including me, who could see it, he lost his grip and fell downward into the water-filled scupper at the foot of the railing. The ship plowed toward its destination with wonderful speed. Iceland greeted us in radiant sunshine, which stayed with us for the five days at anchor there in the harbor. During this time, we visited the city and toured a bit of the country to see the western portion of this particularly interesting, sparsely beautiful island. On the return trip we again headed toward the Faroes. One foggy night during a heavy rainstorm, our ship, which lay at anchor in a fjord, was almost stranded on a shoal. The trip to Kiel continued without problems at up to 14 knots. Just before arriving, I was able to present my watch officer, Lieutenant Petri, with a model of the *Horst Wessel*, which I had built in my free time. He had wanted a model such as this to demonstrate the position of the yards and therefore of the sails in different wind directions.

In appreciation for the model, Jacob was given a bottle of sparkling wine by his division commander. When the barque reached Kiel, Jacob celebrated his twenty-first birthday, "became a legal adult," and was promoted to naval cadet with his comrades at the Blücher Bridge the same day.

He would not have been given a bottle today. Admiral Paul Yost, the Coast Guard commandant from 1986 to 1989, is a Mormon who, according to several of the present *Eagle* crew, attempted to recreate the "Yost Guard" in his Mormon image — teetotaling and coffeeless. The latter privation was unimaginable, of course, but the former went into effect in June of 1986. Gone were the "morale beers," issued, two each, on Saturday nights, although the nonrates were known to lose a beer or two as tithes to their petty officers. Beards went by the board about the same time. The navy had lost its beards two years earlier; it was said that they prevented gas masks from making a proper seal. Karl said the B.T.s — boiler technicians — on the old 327-foot steam-powered cutters, were all bearded. "They wrote their own book," he said, "grotty old bastards." The B.T.s did not have to suffer, weakened from their shearing, for long. They all went the way of steam. Admiral Yost was mailed more than a few shoeboxes containing shorn beards.

Captain Thiele was an enthusiastic sailor. Otto Schlenzka, a cadet who was on board with Franz Jacob and Fritz Neumann, said the captain had a beautiful little sailboat that he raced during the annual Kiel Week regatta. The boat belonged to *Horst Wessel* and was attached to her stern by special davits. She was cadet Schlenzka's "station for cleanups." Schlenzka also crewed with the captain during the races.

⌒

I'M LOOKING down at Guantanamo Bay from the crosstrees and picturing the deceptive tranquility of Kiel Bay, full of sails, before the war. Calms and storms, the alternating currents of the world. Bob LaFond took his son Greg sailing right here in the waters of Guantanamo in a little Laser. It was the boy's first sailing experience. Once the boat capsized in the wind and Greg said he would never go sailing again. His father was stationed here as a gunnery instructor for Coast Guard and navy personnel as well as the gun crews of foreign navies. He struck master instructor in Cuba and made warrant, too. When the navy was recommissioning battleships, he was recommended for the job of resurveying the gun foundations. A navy commander couldn't see a Coastie doing it, so LaFond instructed the squids — as navy personnel are known to the Coast Guard — who were then given the assignment. He was a boarding officer, winging it before the job was given an official designation. LaFond participated in the Mariel boat lift in 1980, picking up Cubans trying to escape from this island and interdicting boats streaming to Cuba to ferry refugees out for a price. Haitians were not recognized as immigrants at the time, although they were fleeing their island too. He remembers one night when a boat overturned, putting one hundred people in the water. Coast Guard aircraft dropped life rafts and all were rescued, then returned to Haiti.

Greg wanted to be a marine biologist. He attended the University of New Hampshire but dropped out. He had some rough times, made some bad choices socially. Bob LaFond said his son confounded him sometimes. "I had always looked over the horizon. He liked to stay home." Dorothy LaFond, Greg's paternal grandmother, was in the Coast Guard Auxiliary. She has written a textbook on celestial navigation entitled *Shoot First, Ask Questions Later,* and she has her 100-ton master's license with a sail endorsement. For a while she skippered the schooner *Harvey Gamage* out of Boston. Bob LaFond told me his son eventually changed his mind about the horizon. "He came to me one day and said he wanted to join the Coast Guard. I knew a nonrate detailer. He recognized the name LaFond and offered help. I told him Greg would probably like something in New England. There was an *Eagle* billet. Greg took to *Eagle.*"

The black frigate birds circle overhead. Most people are not equipped to look beyond the horizon or even at the horizon itself. The line that separates an empty sea from the vast sky triggers an ancient loneliness that makes most of us turn away and become soldiers or farmers or newspaper reporters. But for some, the empty 360-degree horizon generates a primordial joy just because they're the center of it. The view is tattooed deep within such people, on an island in the blood that accompanies them everywhere all the days of their lives, and perhaps beyond.

The other night in the wardroom, Captain Papp told of taking part in a family reunion when the ship touched in Copenhagen in 1997. He, the son of a Connecticut highway patrolman, had never met most of the Jorgensens and Andersens whose blood he shares, but in their homes were models of sailing ships that distant family members had served on and paintings of sailing ships on the walls. "Makes you think," he said. Captain Papp's grandfather was Coast Guard for thirty years. "He got kicked out of the academy for marrying my grandmother, so he enlisted," Papp said. "He was a radioman during World War II, serving on cutters that sank German submarines. His was a vague history. He was a character — married five times. He went around the Pacific creating loran [radio beacon] stations."

That night the wardroom conversation turned toward *Eagle*'s longtime role of training academy-schooled officers and her newly revived role of training nonacademy officer candidates. "We promote *Eagle* as the highlight of the swab summer," the captain said, referring to the cadets' weeklong initiation on the barque the summer before starting their freshman (fourth-class) year at the academy. "I've tried to make it so it's fun." That taste of her gets them through the doldrums of schoolwork, he said, until the third-class summer, when they come aboard for their five-week cruise. "Once on board, it's the bully pulpit. Graduates of the academy must serve two years afloat before going on to anything else. If they fail at sea, we won't recommend. They have to develop The Attitude."

Those in officer candidate school, now based at the academy in New London, have less time to do so. "Seventeen weeks doesn't add up to four years," Papp observed, although some candidates may have achieved The Attitude by virtue of prior-enlisted experience. Half of the Coast Guard's officer corps are academy graduates now and half are from officer candidate school. The latter are assigned staff positions with a reserve commission if they have at least three years of college. Prior-enlisted people get temporary commissions. The captain spoke of cutterman's night at the academy, held each year so that those with experience aboard cutters can inspire the first-class cadets and "talk about boats." The Jarvis Award is presented to a cutterman who has displayed The Attitude in an outstanding performance of duty during the previous year. The award was named for a lieutenant junior grade who drove reindeer across Alaska to save whalers whose ship was frozen in the ice. These days Lieutenant Jarvis would be honored for driving the equivalent of reindeer across Alaska to rescue — and then arrest — the icebound whalers, for protection of marine mammals is now on the Coast Guard's list of responsibilities.

10 THE ATTITUDE

I WAS WITNESS to The Attitude when TWA Flight 800 exploded and rained down into the Atlantic off Moriches, Long Island, on the night of July 17, 1996. A small boat crew from the Montauk Coast Guard Station had been on routine summertime patrol heading back to the station, when their radio began to crackle with word of a disaster 10 miles off the coast near Shinnecock, about 40 miles away. Frank Sabatini, a BM2, was anticipating time off and a flight to see his parents in Atlanta, where he planned to attend the Olympic Games.

By the time the boat reached the Montauk station, its 82-foot cutter, *Point Wells*, was en route to the scene. Boats from the South Shore stations had already responded. Montauk's 41-footer was ordered to stand ready, and Richard Kraynak, machinist's mate third class, paced nervously near the radio room's open window. The Coast Guard was playing musical boats, bringing one from New London to cover for the Montauk boats that went to the disaster. If the 41 got the call, I would go with it.

Kraynak wants to go. Looks up at the clear, starry night. Paces. Wants to go. Has to go. The radio speaks. Then, from the window, comes the order, "Go, go, go!" — and the adrenaline.

Eric Suskevich, "Susky," the coxswain, turns west after rounding the Montauk Lighthouse at full throttle. It will be a two-hour run to the scene. At least the ocean is cooperating: there is a slight swell, glassy, a soft summer night, fertile sea smells. There might be survivors. It is the kind of mission one trains for. The wheelhouse is lit radar-screen green with orange panel lights. Kraynak listens like a doctor to the roar of the twin Cummins engines. Sabatini plots by a small red light to protect

A Coast Guard rescuer reflects on the crash of TWA Flight 800, July 18, 1996. (Russell Drumm)

night vision. Susky is on the horn hailing *Adak*, a 110 out of Sandy Hook, New Jersey, the on-scene command, with his estimated time of arrival. All of it is second nature by drill until we are 10 miles out, where we catch the unmistakable odor of jet fuel — a strong intimation of hell. The boat keeps its speed, but the mind begins to recoil from this different, still-invisible sea we have just entered. Then a small city of lights on the horizon and, above them, more lights, beaming down as if by aliens. And, on the radio, terrible, shocking words.

"*Adak*, this is Coast Guard 41394. Do you have more gloves?" — meaning bioprotective latex gloves.

Air is replaced by a mixture of jet fuel and the acrid exhaust of the searching boats. The sea is on fire in places, and where it isn't burning it is silky with fuel. No wind. The hanging mist makes it feel as though we've entered the set of a B-movie rendering of hell. Then I, who have asked to come along as a reporter, realize that, yes, of course, hell would be clichéd and this is indeed hell, and it is not one big city, but villages of lighted boats with blackness in between except for the fires and the "sun" in the form of white phosphorus flares descending from planes high above. The suns set when they burn out. Short days, unnatural.

Our searchlight sweeps as we approach a small private boat waving us over. We move slowly on the River Styx; with quick looks at one another, we know why they want us.

A man floats in a standing position in a kind of dance. His hair, waving on the surface, is filled with thousands of multicolored sequins, a cargo of Paris-bound party glitter. We take him aboard and cover him with a blanket. The condition of the body tells us there is no possibility of survivors. God is not present, so there is no ceremony. The crew makes an attempt at black humor, but it's awful.

The boat turns and moves across an unlit stretch of silky sea, lifeless, dotted with thousands of things that had been part of a whole — a happy journey to France, with a new language to learn, romance, fine wine.

Pieces of insulation, the plane's aluminum skin, small personal belongings, pocketbooks, backpacks, shoes. If the crash was caused purposely, who would do such a thing? the crew ask one another. We look deeply at each other when our eyes meet accidentally.

It's 1 A.M. A small white jacket floats past, empty, in an upright position. The radio never stops talking, its voice friendly, reassuring in tone, if not in content. A helicopter, announcing yet another debris field, squats over it in the distance, staring with its beam.

A trawler named *Night Moves* beckons us, deck lights on, three forms covered with blankets beneath the net reel.

"Do you want to take them? One's a stewardess."

"Can you hold on to them, unless you're planning to go home?"

"We'll hold them."

Then, as we depart, a hellish banter about quotas between the fishermen and the Coast Guard crew, which, in the real world, might board the boat to enforce fishing laws. In other words, we are all fishing, and he's asking, What are the rules in this fishery? There are none.

Because time would be lost organizing it, the *Adak* is not attempting a formal sweep. Instead, helicopters have dropped lighted buoys around the outer extremes of debris, and boats search at random. The

Adak advises all boats that it has learned the jet had eight liters of HIV-positive blood on board in a Styrofoam box. Be on the lookout. Hell has levels, and we're descending, it seems.

We approach a lone man in a skiff looking up at us beseechingly. A form is draped over the gunwale of the boat.

"Can you take her?" he says, "I've had her a long time."

There is a reluctance. Sabatini calls *Adak*, asks if we are to take victims from civilian boats and, again, "Do you have more gloves and body bags?" Yes and no. No body bags. More are being brought. Come and get gloves first, then go back and collect the victim. *Adak* orders all Coast Guard small boats to begin collecting victims from private boats and from the larger cutters. Word has come from shore that we must start bringing them in.

We return to the lone man in the skiff and the woman who fell from the sky and are made desperate by what we see. Kraynak grasps her hands and pulls her on board. She is young, pretty, naked. The young crewmen, appalled by the immodesty of death, cover her quickly. As we pull away, the man in the boat has the saddest look I've ever seen. He has been protective of her. Now we've taken her, and he seems to realize how ridiculous his feeling was. The same illogical weed has taken root on our boat. Sabatini nips it in the bud, ordering the crew to "think about it tomorrow."

The cutter *Bainbridge Island* calls, advising that she has victims for us to deliver ashore and giving us her position. We move slowly in that direction, our searchlight sweeping. What looks like light snow is ash falling from the phosphorus above. The festive sequins are on our clothes, covering everything. There are so many things in the water, so many parts to what had been a whole. Could someone possibly have done this in the name of God?

We arrive at the *Bainbridge Island*. It's wonderful to see her officers and crew, hear their voices. Everyone is friendly, helpful, speaking the shared language of rote seamanship. No confusion. She is a refuge of order, and we tie up alongside like a child to a mother, who says, "We have four for you — three female, one male. They are in bags. Thank you." We lift them aboard and separate. It's 4 A.M.

We turn toward Moriches and move slowly until we reach what we believe is the perimeter of wreckage, then throttle up. I lie down on the deck not far from the dead and sleep for an hour. When I wake, the sun has made a soft, gauzy light to the east, and the boat is about to enter the long, winding inlet to the Moriches station. We eat at last, sliced watermelon from a plastic bag someone gave us back in Montauk. A beautiful dawn: misty heat, no wind, egrets stalking along the banks, the high-pitched cries of terns. Behind us, a cortege of small boats creeps along single file past people casting for bluefish beneath feeding birds. A fishing boat approaches, and a man points toward the sea and asks if he can go fishing. The crew doesn't understand the question.

Helicopters land and take off somewhere nearby. We wait our turn at a low floating dock crawling with men in white, bioprotective jumpsuits. A city has been created overnight, its purpose streamlined. A bearded rabbi prays and prays and prays.

THURSDAY, MAY 13, 1999

Still anchored in Guantanamo Bay, but not for long. Caribbean smells and birds — vulture, pelican, frigate bird. Breakfast in the wardroom with captains Papp and Luke. The talk is of Jamaica beef patties brought to the cutter in the old days by bumboats — "roach coaches."

"It don't Gitmo better'n 'is," says Captain Luke, his words recalling his past here, their honey flow revealing his southern roots. He and the captain are telling war stories about the near invasion of Haiti in '94. There were fifty Coast Guard cutters on scene. Airborne troops had been inserted at Great Inagua, as well as Marines. "I was SAR [Search and Rescue] for the airborne force," Captain Papp recalls, "a commander at the time, chopped to a navy CTU [command task unit]." The two captains agreed, over cereal, that Able Vigil, the damming of the migrant flood, which lasted from January of 1993 to November of '95, was the Coast Guard's finest hour. There were twelve 110-foot cutters, two or three 270s, and two 378s, *Chase* and *Midgett*. The *Midgett* had been en route to fish ops in Alaska when she got orders to head for the Panama Canal. It was a time of great professionalism in the service, they concur. After the Coast Guard stood down from Vietnam, it was put back together, and there was stability in the service. There were first-class petty officers with fourteen and fifteen years' experience.

Captain Luke was on the command ship *Mount Whitney*. He says he talked to Cuban migrants in '94. "They were like my neighbors. They wanted jobs. It was not an ideological thing. I did a paper while at the Navy War College on why we should do away with the Cuban embargo. I said lifting the embargo would be the downfall of the Castro regime."

Eagle is getting under way.

"Bosun, the anchor is up and down."

"Bosun, there's two shots [90-foot lengths of chain] on deck. Anchor is at six o'clock, light strain." The anchor detail hoses Guantanamo mud off the chain as the electric capstan pulls it through the hawsehole.

"Engineman, engine ahead one-third."

"Aye, my engine answers ahead one-third." A leisurely school of dolphins grazes beside the ship.

"Shift colors." The union jack, which flies when we're at anchor, is lowered. *Eagle* moves out of the bay, her engine chugging in six/eight time. Small waves break on the low coral cliffs. The sun catches a pink hangar in the distance, a watchtower. A cloud shadow moves across the green, sparsely vegetated foothills of the Sierra Maestra. A big billfish chases prey into the air. A Caribbean day laughs at the smallness of people. Captain Luke is on deck sniffing the breeze, glad to be under way. "Land is a navigational hazard," he declares. The PA system announces the test of the ship's alarms and whistles: fire, chemical, collision, sail stations, ship's whistles. "Report all discrepancies to the bridge." Then "Sweepers, sweepers, man your brooms. Make a clean sweep of the ship fore and aft." Our course is southwest toward Jamaica. Once out of the lee of Haiti, we will find 15- to 18-knot trade winds. Bosun Ramos says he is Cuban on both sides of his family. "I could live real good in Cuba when I retire. We were upper crust in Cuba. My great-grandfather was Ignacio Díaz, a nationalist during the Spanish-American War. There was a statue of him."

The heat has softened the Stockholm tar that coats the shrouds. It gives off the smell of old medicine or the first whiff of a long-unopened attic. Karl wants to shorten a crane line, a steel-cable footrope strung athwartships between the port and starboard shrouds. These particular tightropes allow one to reach the main royal staysail where it's furled, close to the mast, about 50 feet off the deck. The handhold along the way is another crane line above the climber's head. Because shorter people have trouble if there's too much slack in the footrope, Karl has decided to shorten it. Bosun Ramos told me that the only rigging change made to accommodate females has been to rig the ratlines closer together to allow smaller steps while climbing. Less slack in the crane lines serves the same purpose. Karl removed the offending cable ropes before the noon meal, and now he and Kelly Nixon, who needs to learn the procedure, carry them below to the bosun's hole. Karl is alternately whistling and reciting. I hear the words "with nothing but a star overhead" in Cockney as he disappears down the narrow ladder to the first deck. The verse is from what sounds like a Rudyard Kipling poem, in which a soldier in the field is thinking that if he were home he'd be mowing the squire's lawn. "I make him sing it when we're aloft," Nixon says. Karl drifts in and out of Cockney and German as he makes theater out of showing her how to peel the old parceling — covering — from the cable rope and to cut — *abschneiden* — a foot-long piece off it with a hydraulic snip. The end of the cable must now be reparceled and reserved. "Worm and parcel with the lay, turn and serve the other way," he chants. The worm is the "small stuff" — marline that's laid between the strands of a rope to make a smooth surface and keep water out. Kelly fetches a roll of parceling, one-inch-wide number-10 canvas and tries her hand at making a tight wrap with it over the wormed rope. Next Karl shows her how to rig the serving mallet, a hand tool with a spool on it that "turns" or tightly wraps another layer of small stuff over the parceling.

Once again Karl's world seems a cat's cradle made of thread, small stuff, and rope. Last night on deck he told me about "the forgotten soldier" in a book he'd read. He recreated the scene, as though he had been there, in which a German grunt digs his way through the snow toward Stalingrad, learns that the city has fallen, and then digs his way back, weak and frozen. Like Kipling's limey, the German soldier is left to try to survive a mess not of his own making. It was not right, Karl said, that the German tank troops were shot because their black uniforms with death's-head emblems were mistaken for those of the SS.

The tank cavalry had descended from the death's-head hussars, an honorable military regiment, unlike the SS.

Karl's appreciation of German history and culture halts abruptly with the rise of the Nazi party. He told me the story behind the song "Wacht am Rhein," written well before World War I. "It's talking about the national duty, an almost spiritual duty to defend the Rhine. Between the 1600s and 1813, France invaded Germany no less than thirteen or fourteen times, Sweden wiped out thousands of German villages, France probably eliminated 30 percent of the German population during the Thirty Years' War. Germany is right at the crossroads of Europe. Everybody in their quest for glory has overrun it. I find that most cultures that are pissed off at somebody — the way the French are pissed off at the Germans, and the Irish are pissed off at the English — if you go back far enough, you will find that they opened up a can of whip-ass, paid for it, and then thought they were oppressed. There wouldn't be any such country as England if the Scots hadn't stayed on the north side of Hadrian's Wall where the Romans pushed them.

"Germans do things well because they're German. Watch a German sailor get ready to paint something. He is neat. He cleans the area, puts down the drop cloth. Just the preparation and thought. He could go out in his dress uniform and not get paint on it. The Nazis didn't do anything particularly well. They were a bunch of idiots, but once the system was in place, it got done. The Nazi party kept all its promises, but unfortunately, not everyone realized what all their promises were. There was no television, so you could tell each group what it wanted to hear. Hitler could tell the industrialists, We will get you back on your feet, and tell the military, We will rearm you, and tell the anti-Semites, We'll get even with the Jews. Hitler was *Time* magazine's man of the year in 1937.

"My father never spoke German. I don't know if it was because of the war. He was pretty proud to be an American. He was a Marine in World War II. He didn't go on much about the Germans. When he was growing up he was immersed in it because his father took him down to New Jersey to visit relatives, and everything was very German. My dad's father came from Union, New Jersey. Even though his father — my great-grandfather — was born in England, his first language was German because Union City was all German back then. The Dillmanns came to America about 1840. The family came from Koblenz originally. I have my great-great-grandfather's obituary and a picture of him in 1860. His name was Karl, too. I'm his namesake. He was the sexton of a church in Koblenz. He moved to England and married an English girl whose mother was possibly an American Indian, but back then nobody talked about that. The old aunties used to tell these stories. The part that made sense was that she had married an English sailor, and she was free to sail to England where she was probably treated pretty well, like Pocahontas."

Karl's stories travel through time the way he travels through the rigging. His knowledge of the old intricacies of the ship verifies his time travel, substantiates his visiting of other times and places, as though the journey were only a matter of applying the correct blocks and fairleads and then hand-over-handing his way there with the help of a strong and loyal crew.

I was here in the bosun's hole on a previous occasion with Karl and Tracy Allen when they were repairing a block. The subject of Vietnam came up. As Tracy and I talked about the terrible Ia Drang Valley battles, I looked over and saw tears rolling down Karl's face. "Human bait," was all he said through tight lips before leaving. Tracy followed him out.

Kelly has the serving mallet in hand, but before she begins wrapping, Karl saturates the parceling with Stockholm tar, a mix of pine tar, asphalt varnish, and spar varnish in equal parts. "This is what sailing ships have always smelled like," he says, offering his "slush"-covered hands to our noses. He says the "pregreasing" of the parceling is done more effectively with bare hands. "In the days of wooden skis, you'd put Stockholm tar on the bottom and hit it with a blowtorch" to waterproof the wood. Karl is no stranger to the ski slopes of New England. He shows Kelly how to "bury the marline" so there are no loose ends. He asks if she understands, and she nods. He tells her, "Go forth and worm, parcel, and serve."

11 SEPTEMBER 1, 1939

IN THE fall of 1937, having twice tasted the fury of the North Atlantic and the shock of the death of her fallen crewmen, *Horst Wessel* sailed up the Elbe to attend the launching of *Albert Leo Schlageter* at Blohm & Voss. When that barque was put into service in February of '38, the navy had three square-riggers on which to train its officers. *Schlageter* was named after an army lieutenant who received the Iron Cross First Class for his service in the 1918 war. After the armistice, Schlageter joined the Freikorps, a paramilitary group that sprang up in the postwar chaos to fight for German-claimed land in the east and against the spread of communism. In 1923, when France occupied the Rhineland to enforce the German payment of reparations, Schlageter was among those who sabotaged trains carrying coal from the disputed territory to France. He attained martyr status when he was arrested, found guilty by a French military tribunal, and executed by firing squad on March 26, 1923, at Golzheim near Düsseldorf.

In November of 1937, the same month that *Schlageter* slid down the ways, Hitler announced to General Blomberg and Admiral Raeder "the aim of German policy — to make secure and to preserve the racial community and to enlarge it." It was therefore a question of living space, *Lebensraum*. He was by then speaking of Austria and Czechoslovakia, which the Reich would absorb by using bullying diplomacy under the pretense of uniting ethnic Germans. The Rhineland, of course, was already back in German hands. Blomberg, who was skeptical of Hitler's plans for acquiring *Lebensraum*, or at least of the timing, nevertheless conveyed Hitler's wishes to his generals in June: prepare for war as early as 1938 to "make possible the military exploitation of politically favor-

Captain August Thiele looks aloft. (Collection of Herbert Böhm)

able opportunities." But by January of '38, the man who had walked these very decks as minister of war the previous July had been dismissed. Hitler used the sixty-year-old general's disgrace to weaken the old-guard military caste, which was largely suspicious of the führer. On February 4, 1938, he announced that he had taken over the High Command of the armed forces, having subsumed Blomberg's office of commander in chief. He abolished the Ministry of War at the same time.

On March 19, one week after the nation of Austria became a province of the German Reich, *Horst Wessel* set out on the longest voyage of her German years, to the West Indies, with calls at the Canary Islands, St. Thomas, and Bermuda. On board were nearly two hundred trainees and sixty permanent crew. After two and a half months at sea, she returned to the Blücher Bridge, put in at Kiel's Deutsche Werke shipyard for a week, trained in the Kiel Bay for another two weeks, and then left on a trip to Scotland and Norway.

During this time, Hitler was plotting the Reich's absorption of

Czechoslovakia. Nazi party operatives had agitated the Sudeten Germans into demanding unification, as France and England watched, incredulous. It's possible that *Horst Wessel's* visit to Britain was part of Germany's mask of innocuousness at the time. According to the log, Hitler came aboard on July 22, the afternoon the barque left for England, and visited for an hour. The tops were flagged for the occasion. Behind the scenes, General Ludwig Beck, the army's chief of staff, and others were plotting a coup. Beck, an early believer, saw that the führer was now leading Germany toward a war it could not win. By late August the conspirators had a plan. When the führer ordered X-Day, the invasion of Czechoslovakia, he would be seized and brought before one of his own people's courts and charged with endangering the existence of the nation. According to Hitler's urgent schedule, X-Day would fall at the end of September.

From August 19 to 28, naval exercises were held in Kiel Bay. The *Horst Wessel* log entry for August 19 shows that the ship participated in a great flag decoration for the admiral of the fleet. The next day, flags were at half-mast for the burial of a machinist from the *Scheer.* On Sunday, August 21, *Horst Wessel* was cleaned and polished from stem to stern.

The log entry for Monday records that a "great flag decoration" began at 0800 to mark the launch of the armored cruiser *Prinz Eugen.* Hitler and Admiral Miklós Horthy, the Hungarian regent, were present, along with other dignitaries. The new cruiser's name was a not-so-subtle reminder of a past alliance. In the days of the Austro-Hungarian empire, Prince Eugene was the Austrian hero who saved the city of Belgrade from the Turks. Hitler entertained his guests aboard the ocean liner *Patria* and encouraged the Hungarians to ally themselves with Germany and share in the spoils that would result from the takeover of Czechoslovakia. "He who wants to sit at the table must at least help in the kitchen," Hitler was reported as telling his guests.

At 0905 on the twenty-second, *Horst Wessel* took her position in a parade of ships. The log does not say if Hitler sailed on *Horst Wessel* during the parade, but he was aboard at one point that day. There is a shot of Stroppi, one of the ship's dogs, greeting the visitors and another of Hitler, accompanied by Admiral Raeder and Captain Thiele, in-

Adolf Hitler reviews the barque's crew with Grand Admiral Erich Raeder and Captain Thiele. (Collection of Herbert Böhm)

specting the hands lined up on the starboard side of the waist. The pictures were later added to a photographic diary that Thiele must have compiled after the war, documenting his time on board from the autumn of 1937 to the spring of 1939. Thiele, a gifted amateur photographer, took most of the photos and supplied captions for his diary. The shot of Hitler on board, taken by a crew member, is accompanied by a caption that reads: "The führer's visit made a lasting and disquieting impression on me. His eyes were not clear, and they darted this way and that." The caption accompanying a photo of the ship's eagle figurehead clutching a swastika reads: "We wished our figurehead were a mermaid." The comments, and the fact that the ship's log barely mentions Hitler's visit, make one wonder what Thiele thought of his commander in chief, the upstart former army corporal, and of his using the beautiful barque as a public relations strumpet.

Tolerating the visits and spectacles of politicians has remained this ship's cross to bear. It's safe to say there's been a great improvement in their quality since 1938, although time has a way of dulling perspective. When President Bill Clinton came aboard after speaking to the academy's graduating class of '96, there were Secret Servicemen on the fighting tops, divers under the ship, and not a whole lot of respect for the president beneath the crew's hospitality. He had recently blocked an investigation into his alleged dalliance with Paula Corbin Jones while he was governor of Arkansas by invoking his rights as an active serviceman — commander in chief — under the Soldiers and Sailors Relief Act. Messing with a female subordinate and lying about it while never having served in the military did not sit well with many Coasties, although *Eagle*'s officers were careful to keep their opinions to themselves. The enlisted crew were not so reticent.

Most U.S. presidents since Harry Truman have climbed aboard *Eagle* for the requisite photo op. One boatswain's mate recalled the humiliation of having the Coast Guard's own photographers ask that sails be set even though there was not a whisper of wind, then requesting that *Eagle*'s engine drive her backward to fill the sails for a public relations photograph.

Prinz Eugen was with the *Bismarck* during the battle in which the British battleship *Hood* was sunk. *Prinz Eugen* returned to Brest while *Bismarck* proceeded to her doom. The cruiser survived the war and was taken by the United States as reparation. She was sailed into the Pacific by way of Philadelphia, where, as we shall see, she was involved in an episode that had repercussions for the German members of the crew that brought *Eagle* to America. Once in the Pacific, *Prinz Eugen* was placed in harm's way during an atomic bomb test off Bikini Island to see how a ship would do in a thermonuclear attack. She was badly damaged but refused to sink. Eventually she was scuttled there, a victim of the nuclear age, and a long way from her christening in Kiel Bay.

Thiele had a gift for narrative in addition to his talent as a photographer. Midway through his diary are several photos of a large shark caught by the crew during *Horst Wessel*'s visit to Bermuda and hoisted into the waist. Thiele saved one photo of the shark for the last page of his diary, I think to put his departure from the barque and the beginning of World War II in its true light. The picture is a close-up look into the toothy maw of the giant man-eater.

Throughout September, as X-Day approached, and France and England offered more and more generous terms to Germany in the disastrous policy of appeasement, *Horst Wessel*'s crew trained at Kiel and made ready for a cruise to Portugal and the Canary Islands. The conspirators' plan to overthrow Hitler soon evaporated when, with the support of France and England, Germany was allowed to carve the Sudetenland out of Czechoslovakia without the use of force. What became known as the Munich Agreement was signed on October 1, 1938.

On November 22, Admiral Raeder and Hitler, triumphant after his visit to Prague, boarded the *Deutschland,* a pocket battleship, and sailed east to take back Memel. The city had once been East Prussian territory, with its port city of Stettin, but after Versailles it was annexed to Lithuania. A seasick führer kept the pressure on Lithuanian diplomats throughout the night until they caved in. At the time, the German navy consisted of two large battleships, seventeen destroyers, two heavy cruisers, and only forty-seven U-boats. Stettin would later become the eastern Baltic home to the *Horst Wessel* and her sister ships. As the navy commander and Hitler were sharing in their minor naval victory, *Horst Wessel* was already a week into her second trip to the Canary Islands.

Among the trainees was Ludwig Brenner, who remembers:

> There was little or no free time. Everyone was constantly needed to man the sails, sometimes setting and dousing them every ten minutes. We only sang songs in harbor, at the pier, or when there were visitors on board. There were often storms, but we had no accidents except for one death, a man [named Linde] who took his own life. He was sewn into a sail and buried at sea. My colleagues and I found the training bearable. We were, at that point, already seaworthy since we had spent several years on other warships. I was twenty-four years old. On the outbound trip, we primarily encountered headwinds, but on the return trip to Germany we set a speed record which lasted for years. Our tour in late 1938 was the last training mission aboard *Horst Wessel* and her sister ships before the war. None of the ships left the Baltic after that. One noticed little of the coming war. It surprised us, came out of the clear blue sky.

From out of the sky is exactly where the war came, of course, seven months later when the warplanes of the Luftwaffe dived on their

The barque and one of her sister ships in Stettin, 1940. (Jürgen Gumprich)

prechosen targets. The blitzkrieg began at first light on September 1, 1939. All through the spring and summer Hitler had played the stunned nations of the world as though they were pieces in a game of solitaire chess, one in which he already knew when and how checkmate would occur.

With the outbreak of the war, *Horst Wessel* lost her freedom. Neither the Atlantic nor the path to it were safe for a German sailing ship. Germany would not take "control" (a relative term) of Denmark and Norway, and thus the vital Skagerrak, until spring. Tens of thousands of mines were seeded throughout the area during the war. The dangerous defusing and removal of them was undertaken by the Allies after the war with the help of a great many German navy volunteers.

It would have been ironic indeed if this barque, under American flag, had been lost to a mine eight years after the war's end. Captain William Earle, her ninth American captain, was an officer serving under Captain Carl Bowman at the time (1953). Earle recalled, "We had been sailing full and by in a moderate gale for the Skagerrak when we encountered a heavy squall and wind shift that left us driving for old minefields under full sail. All hands scrambled aloft at midnight in driving rain to get the sails in, including available officers. I found myself

The masthead of a Hamburg newspaper, 1940.

fisting canvas in torrential rain on the main royal yardarm. The cadet on the footropes beside me was also wildly fisting canvas and passing gaskets — lumps or no. 'Great!' he said when we got the order to 'lay in and down.' Elmer [the original engine] coughed and came on line. We slowly and painfully clawed off that lee shore against 35-knot headwinds and rain."

The Germans occupied Denmark without a fight and Norway with not much of one, although Germany's surface navy was crippled in the process. Already the battleship *Graf Spee* had been scuttled in Montevideo, Uruguay, after a fight with three British cruisers. Soon the high hopes attached to the 41,000-ton battleship *Bismarck*, which had been constructed at Blohm & Voss four years earlier, were dashed when she sank — some say she was scuttled — during a battle following her victorious but punishing encounter with Britain's *Hood* in 1941. *Horst Wessel*'s former steward went down with the *Bismarck*. Karl told me that when the *Bismarck* was sunk, an English sailor saw a wounded, armless survivor in the water. The sailor jumped over the side and put a bowline around the man to lift him aboard. He was later disciplined for abandoning ship, such was the anger over the loss of the *Hood*.

Hitler blamed Admiral Raeder for the ineffectiveness of Germany's surface force. He exploded in January of 1943 upon learning of the losses the navy had suffered in the unsuccessful campaign to stop the Allies' Russia-bound convoys in the Arctic Ocean. He demanded that the High Seas Fleet be broken up as scrap. Raeder, who had commanded the navy since 1928, was replaced by former U-boat commander Karl Dönitz. The war at sea would be conducted by submarines. The decision clinched the fate of many of those who trained on *Horst Wessel* during the last three years of the war.

12 $\mathcal{S}$AILING $\mathcal{U}$NDER

It's a hundred degrees or close to it up on deck. I'm in my stateroom aft
and one deck down, out of the heat. The smell of sweat adds spice to the
Stockholm tar. Lieutenant Mike Summer, the *Constitution*'s XO, has the
bunk below me. He is off making a selection from the movie locker for
viewing after the evening meal in the wardroom. Old Ironside's first
crew in 1812 could not have imagined such a thing. According to the
Armed Forces News summary I've borrowed from the wardroom, the
Chinese have broken off diplomatic relations with the United States
because of the bombing of their Belgrade embassy. Last night Captain
Papp joked about making a side trip to Cartegena because the crew had

*Eagle's second captain, Miles Imlay, was a
hero on D-day.* (Courtesy of U.S. Coast
Guard)

a good port call there last winter. It might be off-limits now because of U.S. involvement in Colombia's war against cocaine guerrillas. I'm hot from climbing aloft to watch Karl Dillmann and Dave Valentine, a red-haired seaman's apprentice, make the shortened crane lines fast to the topmast shrouds. As Karl secured them with wire and marline, he became a Cockney again and sang us back to World War I, to the tune of "Men of Harlech":

> What's the use of wearing braces,
> Hats, or spats, or shoes with laces,
> Vests and pants you buy in places,
> Down on Broughampton Road?
>
> What's the use of shirts of cotton,
> Studs that always get forgotten,
> These affairs are simply rotten!
> Better far is woad.
>
> Woad's the stuff to show men.
> Woad to scare your foemen.
> Boil it to a brilliant blue
> And rub it on your legs and your abdomen.
>
> Ancient Britons never hit on
> Anything as good as woad to fit on
> Necks or knees or where you sit on,
> Tailors, you'd be blowed!
>
> Romans came across the Channel
> All dressed up in tin and flannel.
> Half a pint of woad per man-o
> Clothed us more than these!
>
> Romans, keep your armors,
> Saxons your pajamas!
> Hairy coats were made for goats,
> Gorillas, yaks, retriever dogs, and llamas!
>
> March on, Snowdon, with your woad on,
> Never mind if you get rained or snowed on.

Never needs a button sewed on.
Good for us today.

◦～

KARL TOLD US that woad was a blue dye made from the leaves of a plant in the mustard family. The ancient Celts covered their naked bodies with it before going into battle.

"Secure all ports, doors, and scuttles due to oncoming weather." The pipe is broadcast throughout the ship and wakes me from a short sleep brought on by "Men of Harlech" and the resonant brushing of Caribbean upon Krupp.

Topside again, looking for a squall to quell the heat. The t'gallants are being doused as a precaution. Matt Welch, the mizzenmast captain who's been hanging with Karl's crew on the foremast to finish his qualification for BMOW, sees a problem with an upper topsail leechline and sings out: "It's pinched in the cheeks of the halyard block!" And from aloft, the answering call, "Pinched in the cheeks, aye!" Laughter all around. "Are all the lines made up? Are they made up clockwise? Are they neat? Are there any questions?" Karl growls in mock-drill-sergeant voice, the gang enjoying the grilling. *Eagle* heels into her port tack as she passes the island of Navassa, off the west coast of Haiti, where guano was once mined. We will no doubt hold the same course for the next week. The trade winds blow unobstructed. We're running down the trades, doing almost 10 knots toward the southeast coast of Jamaica in a four-foot swell. The wind in the rigging sounds like owls and doves. As the sun sets, the sails turn from orange to black. The upper topsails keep the orange longest, proving that the earth is round after all.

It spins back to 1939.

After *Horst Wessel*'s last training voyage, to Portugal and the Canary Islands, before the blitzkrieg, she was stationed at Kiel and assigned to the number-one training section for both commissioned and noncommissioned officers under the command of Captain Kurt Weyher. On May 20, 1940, the ship was moved east to the naval base at Stralsund, where she was used to train members of the Marine Hitler Youth. Lieutenant Commander Martin Kretchmar was in command.

The barque was reassigned in January of 1941 to stationary duty.

In fact, she was reduced to serving as an auxiliary to the fleet tender that served as Admiral Leopold Siemens's headquarters in Stralsund. On May 25, 1941, she was moved once again to the number-one ship's staff division in Kiel, but as a stationary training ship, first under Corvette Captain Ernst Eiffe and then Lieutenant Commander Bertold Schnibbe. Eiffe, a U-boat commander in World War I, distrusted the Nazi party and so was out of favor among its higher-ups. He was best known for a book of humorous and instructive short stories called *Spleissen und Knoten* (Splices and Knots), which he wrote for navy recruits in 1926. A sample vignette:

> Emperor William II was visiting a submarine in 1914. He asked for a shave. The barber/sailor put a white towel around his neck. In one hand he held a piece of soap, a brush in the other. The sailor spit on the soap and began making foam. When he finished the shave, the emperor asked him whether he did the same for his fellow crewmen. The sailor answered, No sir — crew members, I spit directly into their faces.

Such humor aside, the underlying message was that the navy could better one's life. The book attempted to dispel any notions that would-be seamen, or their mothers, might have about sailors being a bunch of rowdy drunks.

It's not clear why the barque finally set sail again, first in 1942 under Eiffe and then, for her last German deployment in March of '43, under Schnibbe, except that the war was not going well for Germany. The ports were no longer safe from air attack. In addition, the U-boat war in the Atlantic, which had taken such a great toll on Allied shipping early on, was now a disaster for the Reich. Trained officers and crew were badly needed to replace the thousands already lost. One-third of the 245 U-boats built by Blohm & Voss during the war had been sunk by the end of 1943.

By then, *Bibb*, the 327-foot cutter that years later would become Karl Dillmann's first Coast Guard assignment, had been escorting Allied supply convoys for over a year. She dropped her first depth charges on April 3, 1942, off the coast of Maine. Throughout that summer, *Bibb* escorted Iceland-bound convoys. On September 21, she rescued sixty-one survivors of torpedoed convoy vessels near Reykjavik.

The effort in the Atlantic became more and more effective. More than thirteen thousand U-boaters died or were captured between August 1942 and April of 1943, primarily because of advanced Allied radar. The situation was so bad that Dönitz ordered the withdrawal of all U-boats from the Atlantic in May of '43. But not for long.

"There can be no talk of a letup in submarine warfare . . . the Atlantic is my first line of defense in the west," Hitler reportedly railed at his new commander in chief upon hearing of the withdrawal order. U-boat production was cranked up from thirty to forty new boats per month. Hitler agreed with Dönitz's basic premise, that the underwater war against Allied convoys had been lost, but he insisted that the battle not be abandoned. It was keeping the enemy busy and away from the Continent. U-boats and their men, therefore were to be sacrificed. The training of candidates, younger and younger, was abbreviated. The caution promised after the sinking of the *Niobe* and the christening of *Gorch Fock*, like so many other promises, was abandoned. Training under sail, despite its dangerous exposure, would deliver more men to U-boat service faster. For protection, four 20-millimeter antiaircraft guns were placed on *Horst Wessel* sometime during this period, two on the foredeck, port and starboard, and one on either bridge wing on the poop deck.

Detlev Zimmermann joined *Horst Wessel* in March of 1943 for the hands-on part of the basic schooling for noncoms, which he had begun at Lindau on Lake Constance. He remembers it being terribly cold on board. "We had to bathe on the foredeck, and the boatswain's mate held a fire hose for rinsing. We had to pack our hammocks and stand on deck for the hammock inspection. It was miserable cold." And he remembers a man falling to his death. After leaving *Horst Wessel*, Zimmermann received training on 20- and 37-millimeter antiaircraft guns aboard the old battleship *Schlesien*. Submarine training followed in Gotenhafen, where he was billeted aboard the *Wilhelm Gustloff*, a ship built in 1938 at Blohm & Voss for the German Labor Front for its "Strength Through Joy" cruises. In the final days of the war she was part of the motley armada attempting to rescue the tens of thousands of soldiers and civilians fleeing East Prussia and the Baltic states before a vengeful Russian army. *Gustloff* and her charges would come to a tragic end. Zimmermann was sent to Bordeaux, arriving one month before the Normandy invasion. Soon after, his first U-boat was sunk out from under him, along with most of the crew.

Sailing ships occasionally "sail under," burying their bows in big seas, the wind in their sails driving them down and down. Zimmermann's wife, Ruth, once told me, over fresh-baked *Apfelkuchen*, that her nephew was a crewman on the *Pamir* after the war, when the old Flying P ship was in service as a merchant trainer. He was drowned when *Pamir* sailed under off the west coast of Africa with the loss of almost all her crew. I think of the rest of Detlev's first crew, and all the other lost U-boaters, as having sailed under. They started out high on these same crosstrees above me, lifted into the wind with dreams of glory. But in 1943 this same wind bore the charnel pall from the awful ovens, and the weight of it forced them down and down to die in pressure-crushed boats. Theirs was more than a military defeat.

Tido Holtkamp, who today lives in Connecticut, trained on *Horst Wessel* in 1944, and he visits his old ship in New London on occasion. He told me he had learned the truth of things even before joining the navy, and that was how he came to be on *Horst Wessel* in the spring of 1944.

When the war began, a new trade school in my hometown of Wittmund was taken over by the Luftwaffe. I was fourteen. New recruits began to show up in town. Within a few months the local Hitler Youth organization, of which I was a member, arranged to have the Luftwaffe instructors give night classes to teach Morse code. I decided I would join the Luftwaffe when I was old enough. All this happened with the approval of my dad and under the eagle eyes of Aunt Irma, who had appointed herself my guardian after the death of my mother a few years before. Aunt Irma, unmarried and a teacher at a high school in Wilhelmshafen, 20 kilometers away, smoked cigarettes incessantly and wore her hair short, almost like a man. She was tough, believed in school and discipline, and as long as I maintained my grades, she tolerated my interest in "that military nonsense," as she called it.

By the fall of 1942, Germany was winning on all fronts. In Africa Rommel was marching into Egypt. In the Atlantic the U-boats were sinking Allied ships in record numbers, and in Russia our army had occupied the oil fields on the Caucasus and was pushing into Stalin-

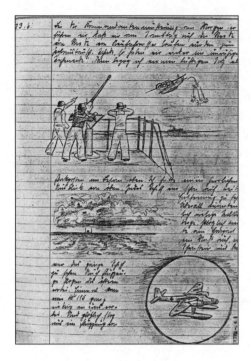

A page of Tido Holtkamp's logbook shows the barque's crew firing on a plane. (Courtesy of Tido Holtkamp)

grad. While the Luftwaffe still played a major role, we boys — I had just turned seventeen — became increasingly enthusiastic about our soldiers, who were singing and marching their way into Russia.

Then one day during our Saturday Hitler Youth service, we had an unexpected interruption. Two officers from the Waffen-SS, the fighting divisions of the SS, appeared and gave us an enthusiastic and lively presentation. They made it clear that they had little to do with the black-shirted SS, but rather fought alongside the army. With their medals and their well-tailored uniforms, they looked sharp. Their arguments sounded convincing and so, together with several others, I signed up for the Waffen-SS. All I needed was my father's permission.

When I presented the news to him that evening, he turned very serious and immediately called Aunt Irma, who told him to do nothing until she came. She arrived promptly on the next train. Aunt Irma and my dad then had a conference, and when they emerged they announced that I was to go with Aunt Irma to Wilhelmshafen, where she would discuss in more detail my decision to join the Waffen-SS. On the train she told me: "George S., whom you know, is home on furlough. He is an officer in a

Waffen-SS division. I think you should talk to him!" From the station she took me straight to him. He was big and rugged. He met me in civilian clothes, and that surprised me. But I saw his uniform jacket on a hanger, and it showed the Iron Cross First Class and the close-combat and tank-destroyer medals. I was impressed. After some chitchat I asked George about his furlough. His face became very serious and he looked at me.

"I have the rank of lieutenant and lead a platoon. My division fights in the middle sector of the eastern front, and my company had served in the line for weeks. So, finally, fourteen days ago, the division sent us to the rear for a rest. It was great. Then one morning we get drummed out of bed and told to get ready for action. We march to the neighboring village. Here we halt. We are told that a German soldier has been killed. We are to assemble one hundred hostages, Jews if possible. We go into the houses and drive out the people, mostly women and children. After we have lined them up at the edge of the village, we are told to get ready to shoot them. Shoot them? I look at the woman in front of me with her baby, crying and begging for mercy. Shoot them? I cannot do that, and I will not do that. I joined the SS to fight, not shoot women and children. I walk back to the company commander: 'I have fought on many fronts and always done my duty. But this is something I cannot do.' The men stand and listen to us. The commander tells me to go back to my quarters and wait there. As I walk back, I hear the guns, and I shudder. Is this what we have fought for? I think of the woman and her baby. The company commander later tells me that he has decided to give me fourteen days' furlough so I can recover from my 'nervous breakdown.' So here I am. I don't know what I will do if I have to go back. Maybe they will send me to a hospital. So now you know what you have signed up for, Tido: to shoot women and children. Think about it!" I was shaken and speechless.

Later, in her apartment, Aunt Irma lights into me: "Now you know what is really going on, and that's just a little of it. Our men are doing this all over the place, and everybody hates us. When this war is over, and it will be over in two years or less, the victors are going to take these men and hang them — the SS first. This regime is a bunch of criminals, the worst thing that could happen to Germany. We will have to pay for this for years to come." Stunned, I replied: "The war is lost? We are winning on all fronts." She laughed. "The war is lost, we cannot win, the others have too much men and materiel. We are losing our best people. You will soon see." I told her that maybe I should go back and join the air force, but she had that covered too. "There will not be much air force left a year from now. No pilots and no gasoline. Then you would be shipped off to the infantry, or, God forbid, even to this terrible SS. No, you should volunteer for the navy. There will be months and months of training, mostly for submarines, and when your training is completed, there will be no submarines to go to, and soon this whole thing will be over. It's the best thing for you. You will be wearing a nice blue uniform, have a warm place to sleep, get fed, and stay in one piece for months to come."

Beginning in the summer of 1943, Hamburg and its factories, including Blohm & Voss, were bombed. In August, British bombers fixed their sights on the factories making the V-rockets at Peenemünde, a small island near Cape Arkona east of Kiel. *Horst Wessel* was just outside the harbor there when the bombs began to fall. Walter Grübel, a carpenter and member of the foremast crew at the time, recalled that crew members ran to the ship's 20-millimeter guns and the captain shouted to them to stand down lest the sailing ship become a target. A section of the engine-room log found among other ship's papers also records the barque being caught in a raid on December 13, 1943, with damage to the radio antenna.

The captain's log of 1943 is missing, and the logs don't begin again until June of 1944, but after the war, when a young *Eagle* seaman named Gene Trainor was removing lockers as part of his "practical seamanship training" he found a logbook written by cadet Hans-Heinrich Frickhoffer. The log, which begins in May of '44, reveals that Frickhoffer was living in a barracks at Stralsund and training on land in anticipation of joining *Horst Wessel* later in the summer. Even before joining the ship, his class would go aboard for training and day work while she was tied up.

FRICKHOFFER'S LOG

24 APRIL 1944: We had an alarm from 2330 on 23 April to 0045 this morning. I mended my socks during that time. We were barely in bed

when we got another practice alarm. This alarm was called as our punishment for being too slow at the previous alarm. We cursed a lot as we hauled our equipment up and down the ladders. We finally got to bed at 0210 with a promise for a day of fun. The promise was not kept. The day started with marching eleven times around the drill ground carrying full packs. Then we had signaling practice, which seemed like recreation by comparison. This was followed by a lecture on sea duty and then the only nonswimmer fell in the water. Next we had rifle instruction. And finally we were able to do some recreational exercise.

25 APRIL 1944: Another day with strenuous exercises on the drill ground. Received a letter from father.

26 APRIL 1944: We were assigned to transport beds and material for mattresses from the town of Steinhagen. Spent the whole day in a truck.

27 APRIL 1944: Class in weapons and knowledge of duties. I have to work on a paper, "Behavior Toward Your Superiors." Had a lecture on "The Navy in War and Peace" followed by four hours of drill. Then we had a lecture on gas masks and had to sleep while wearing gas masks from 2130 to 0015. I had no difficulties, but most of my comrades moaned and groaned a lot.

28 APRIL 1944: Class in Rifle 98. This was a good exercise. During field exercises we had a fast march for one and a quarter hours wearing gas masks.

. . .

5 MAY 1944: Class in ballistics . . . boring. Lecture on weaponry. Two hours of enjoyable physical sport. In the afternoon had an extremely strenuous drill with complete field gear and rifle. Had to run around while wearing our gas masks and with complete field gear. I felt nauseated. Afterward we had written examinations. In the evening the whole company had to again march with complete field gear while singing, as punishment for our poor performance.

6 MAY 1944: Gas duty. Cleaned ship fore and aft. Armory duty.

7 MAY 1944: Attended Mass at the church in Stralsund. It was wonderful. The time for swearing of the oath was changed due to an air raid warning, but it ended up as a very festive occasion. Our division commander, Captain Steffen, gave a very good speech.

MAY 8 1944: Had one hour of drill duty followed by practice in

Morse code. Seamanship training was interrupted by air raid warnings. Had classes in etiquette, weaponry, and ballistics.

9 MAY 1944: Had five hours of drill duty and one hour singing. Watched the movie *The Virgin from Bischofsberg*. Received letters from friends and 50 marks from father.

16 MAY 1944: Five hours of drill. Knöpfchen is in a bad mood and we have to endure a lot. Shortly after finishing we had two air raid alarms. Just finished cleaning our weapons when we heard the noise. Through the window we saw two planes flying low over the nearby airport. One flew toward the ocean while the other made a loop over Rügen and shot an innocent biplane from the rear. Right before our eyes! The beast swung around and dropped all of his bombs at our DO 18 anchorage. Then the enemy plane disappeared. From windows on the other side of the barracks some of our mates watched an innocent Fieseler Storch being shot down. Another plane was downed over Stralsund. During the action something caught fire at the airport, but the smoke rapidly cleared. It was an interesting, horrible, and sad experience. We watched at close range, and at times the enemy flew at a lower level than where we were standing. The biplane had dropped like a rock 100 meters into the sound right in front of our window. I'm going to the movie tonight.

17 MAY 1944: Air raid warnings at night. I belong to the "immediate readiness commandos." Classes in signaling and knot tying. Also had firing practice and I'm doing good. Letters from "Cu" and "Ka."

18 MAY 1944: Classes in seamanship and duty knowledge. Four hours' drill duty. Had an argument with Petty Officer Knog. He made a mistake and I argued with him about it. Hope he won't break my neck. We are very dependent on his moods. Letters from Au and father.

19 MAY 1944: Field training was canceled because of air raid warnings. We stayed at home and had an easy time.

28 MAY 1944: Woke up to music. It is a beautiful Whitsunday. I'm going to church and in the afternoon to the theater. They're showing an operetta, *Drei Alte Schachteln*.

29 MAY 1944: Whitmonday. Free day. Letters to Feh and father.

30 MAY 1944: Weather is gorgeous. We exercised outdoors in shorts. Then we saw a very thrilling movie, *The Weird Change of Alex Roscher*.

5 JUNE 1944: Had five hours of intense drill duty, double-time. Reiman seems to have the drill-duty disease. We had to do eleven rounds. I changed my shoes. Big cleanup at the ship and gear. All this for tomorrow's visitors.

6 JUNE 1944: Cleaned ship fore and aft. Senior officers visited for six hours. There were a large number of admirals, generals, and SS leaders. Everything went satisfactorily. Got news about the beginning of the invasion at Le Havre. Hopefully the enemy will be beaten to the ground and won't move again. But I hope I get an enemy commando so I can demonstrate my fighting ability.

One of those whom young Frickhoffer hoped would be beaten to the ground on that D-day was the man who was to become the barque's second American captain. On June 6, Miles H. Imlay was in charge of all landing craft on the southern half of Omaha Beach. That afternoon he assumed command of the assault group in that area. After the initial assault, Imlay acted as port director for the artificial harbor that was constructed there. For service under fire, he received the Silver Star, the Croix de Guerre with silver star from France, the Legion of Merit with combat V, and the Gold Star.

Time weaves invisible threads that appear only when backlit: throughout 1944, U.S. Coast Guard officers Karl O. A. Zittel, William B. Ellis, and Chester Steele, the men who would become *Eagle's* fifth, sixth, and seventh captains, fought U-boats on convoy duty in the Atlantic: Zittel in command of the Secretary Class cutters *Spencer* and *Ingham*, Ellis on the USS *Pettit*, and Steele aboard the frigate *Abilene*. Prior to the war, Steele had commanded the three-masted schooner *Vema*, a trainer for the maritime service. Carl B. Olsen, *Eagle's* third skipper, and Carl Bowman, her fourth CO, were both involved in search and rescue operations in the Pacific Theater.

FRICKHOFFER'S LOG

8 JUNE 1944: Four hours of drill duty. Had two classes in company leadership and a class in duty knowledge. I have intimate knowledge of my entire certificate of conduct. I know the content word for word: ". . . honest, respectable soldier with good character and disposition and

moral strength . . . personality is a little reserved and must be harder on himself and more lively." The invasion is moving slowly ahead with the enemy taking heavy casualties.

14 JUNE 1944: Sea duty. We practiced signaling all morning. We all had a great time swimming in the Baltic Sea.

15 JUNE 1944: Relaxed drill duty. Enjoyed a wonderful evening with classical music played by the Yonte Trio. I personally enjoyed a piece from Brahms played with violin, cello, and piano.

16 JUNE 1944: Platoon and group leadership practice. In sports we did gymnastics. We used the retaliatory weapon (V-rocket) for the first time. Apparently it can reach London and southern England with artillery.

17 JUNE 1944: Had a coastal alarm shortly after reveille. Our platoon was very slow and the chief petty officer was angry. I relaxed during ship cleaning. Wonderful feeling.

25 JUNE 1944: Quiet day and wonderful weather. Heavy terror bombing of Bremen yesterday. Letter to father.

29 JUNE 1944: Four hours' drill in very hot weather. Swimming. Postcard from father. Movie.

30 JUNE 1944: Platoon and group leader classes. In sports I did great in jumping: 5.7 meters broad jump, 1.5 meters in high jump. I ran 100 meters in 14.2 seconds. A lot of confusion in field training.

8 JULY 1944: Company chief class on *Die Hanse* [a ship]. Gas duty — had presentation on the detoxification of a street. Company restructured . . . Why now? We sailed [small boat] in the afternoon with Staff Sergeant Reiman. Enjoyable. Had a relaxing swim.

9 JULY 1944: Woke up at 0530. Sailed with Knöpfchen. In the afternoon I courageously sailed alone. It was wonderful! Got tan while sailing. Went for a swim.

11 JULY 1944: One and a half hours' drill duty getting ready and marching in the funeral parade. We shot a three-salvo salute for an army first lance corporal.

20 JULY 1944: We heard about the attempted assassination of our führer. Thank God we will not lose him.

21 JULY 1944: We heard the texts of speeches by the führer and Admiral Dönitz. We received a secret order at the same time. All guards

from every group in the Reich must be reinforced. It was immediately implemented. We got reinforcements at every location. Ours included machine guns, 20-mm heavy guns, increased supplies of ammunition, and doubling of guards at every post. We have as many additional men as normal guards. The entire company is under alarm readiness. We continued our normal duties after finishing guard duty. Classes in Mg-34, gas varieties, and sport. We got all the news regarding the attempted military coup. Hopefully all will go well and we can continue to fight under our führer.

29 JULY 1944: Cleaned the ship fore and aft. Alarm during the night. Sat around all day waiting for our transportation, which never showed up.

At this point *Horst Wessel* was moved east to Zoppot, near Gotenhafen. Frickhoffer's company made the trip by train, perhaps because another class of cadets was manning the ship. His turn was about to come.

30 JULY 1944: Went to the railway station loaded down with our heavy sea bags in the morning. We climbed aboard a closed freight train in the afternoon. I'm in compartment 4114. Left the station around 1700. We were in good spirits even though we traveled through a thunderstorm. The train went from Greifswald to Pasewalk, where we were fed at 0030.

31 JULY 1944. We continued our journey around 0300. We lay on the straw-covered floor, crowded like sardines. I had to sleep on top of the very uncomfortable sea bags. Could not really sleep as the freight car was very uncomfortable. We traveled through Stettin, Neustettin, and Schneidemühl until Stargard. It was a very boring trip, as we traveled very slowly and stopped for a long time at a very little town. Finally we went faster through the beautiful lake district of Pommern, surrounded by pine forests. I stood at the open door most of the time.

1 AUGUST 1944: We rattled through the night without stopping. It is so uncomfortable. We arrived at Dirschau in the morning, where we stopped for four hours. During the stop our group got caught breaking into a sealed container and opening a package that contained our health and leadership records. I didn't participate in it. Hope we won't be punished or get a bad performance record. After our stop we continued on to

Danzig, Zoppot, to Gotenhafen. You can immediately see the difference in landscapes between Germany and Poland. Oh, how desolate and deserted Poland looks. Even in Gotenhafen the row houses look awful. We returned from Gotenhafen to Zoppot, where the *Horst Wessel* was anchored. We were met at the gate by a midshipman. We marched in formation to the seashore carrying our heavy bags.

4 AUGUST 1944: As I left my hammock this morning I never thought this would be the worst day of my military career. The morning was spent cleaning the ship for inspection during the planned visit of the fleet admiral. We are anchored in the roadstead, where our sleek ship rolls and pitches in the Baltic Sea. This, of course, does not bother the old instructors, but my companions and I are having a terrible time with seasickness. I threw up three times in the morning. First Lieutenant Knopf put me on report for sitting a moment during ship-cleaning duty. We listened to a short speech by the fleet admiral. Trip to Danzig.

5 AUGUST 1944: Cleaned ship and ammunition magazine duty. Had a great swim in the Baltic. On board I feel like I'm at Saint Peter's.

6 AUGUST 1944: Quiet day. I wrote in my logbook and a letter to father.

7 AUGUST 1944: Alarm. Our platoon had guard duty and our schedule was changed slightly. We were ordered to load food and provisions. We got fresh bread and beer. In the afternoon I was excused from normal duty but ordered to war-guard duty. Can't leave the ship. Around midnight we were awakened by a shrill-sounding whistle, which means "Guards to your stations." I think this is rotten, but since there was no choice I quickly got dressed and ran to my gun. Although it is only a small cannon, it is effective against low-level attacks. Here we are, three of us manning our guns while the others sleep. We cursed everything that flies and after an hour and a half returned to our hammocks.

While Frickhoffer was training ashore, waiting to join *Horst Wessel* in early August, Tido Holtkamp was already on board. "The invasion has begun," his log entry of June 6 begins. "The Anglo-Americans have landed airborne paratroopers, and troops landed from the sea into the battle along the Seine Bay. Our ship left Zoppot this morning."

Holtkamp's entry of July 20, made at sea, speaks of the failed attempt to assassinate Hitler, the last of ten plots by army generals to stop his madness. "During the evening, the radio program is interrupted by the news that an attempt was made on the führer. Thank God he remained unhurt. We breathe easier. During the night we hear that it was traitorous officers who wanted to eliminate the führer at the height of his life. With satisfaction we hear that the responsible ones have been brought to justice."

On July 24, he writes: "At 0900 the captain tells us that according to the wishes of our High Command, from now on the official salute will be the Hitler salute instead of the traditional raising of the hand to the hat, in order to demonstrate our bond with the führer. This moment I will not forget for a long time. We all find it difficult to part with the dear old military salute."

It should be remembered, Holtkamp told me in New London, "that we had to turn the logbooks in every couple of weeks to the watch officer for his review. They reflect our caution. As we used to say, 'Precaution is the mother of the porcelain box,' that is, 'Precaution protects the china cabinet.'"

Holtkamp recalled that the directive to change salutes came when the ship was at sea. "Captain Schnibbe told us, 'I've grown up with the old salute. You are used to it. Many heroes died with that salute. If you do not remember the new salute, and make the old one by instinct, I will not mind.' The only problem we had was back in port, when we ran into some SS guys who gave us a hard time." Holtkamp described Schnibbe as handsome, always with a rakish angle to his hat — a ladies' man. "He was interested in the next port of call. He loved Zoppot, near Danzig, which was a spa. Even in 1944, Hungarian royalty, rich Swiss would go. There was a casino, a long pier. When the *Horst Wessel* was tied, he was the first off. The war was over as far as he was concerned."

It was far from over, of course. Holtkamp was on the ship, anchored outside Kiel Harbor, as the shore facilities and parts of the city were destroyed in a bombing raid. On another occasion, three of the ship's four antiaircraft guns opened fire on a plane that appeared to have an unhealthy interest in the ship. The pilot had failed to respond when warned in code, but as soon as the firing began, he banked his plane to reveal the iron crosses on its wings: *Horst Wessel* had fired on a German reconnaissance seaplane. The furious pilot set his plane down and came to the ship in an inflatable boat. He demanded to see Captain Schnibbe and the ship's logs. As it turned out, the code used in the attempt to contact the plane was twenty-four hours old.

There are stories that seem to cling permanently to the ship. One, that *Horst Wessel* fired on and even shot down one or two Russian planes, has never been confirmed.

13 THE MIRACLE

FRIDAY, MAY 14, 1999, 0800
Eagle is making 6 knots without her top hamper or spanker, which have just been ordered set. "On the fore, on the main t'gallants — let fall! Sheet home. Lay to the halyards. Hand-over-hand the halyards!" The upper two yards on the fore and mainmasts climb into position with a groan, matching that of those doing the hauling. Large squadrons of flying fish take wing, flushed by the bow wake. They land and disappear as though each were the soul of someone sailing under. Mrs. Dillmann said that several people had approached her as she sat on the bench beside the captain's coffin and asked if she'd seen all the flying fish. She said no, just birds, and then laughed when it was pointed out that her birds were in fact the fish. Karl, upon hearing of his mother's "birds," said it reminded him of the lost colony of Norsemen in Greenland that disappeared in the 1400s. When their old dwellings were eventually found, they were inhabited by Eskimos. Then, Karl said, someone noticed that the Eskimos had blue eyes.

LATER THE SAME DAY: Life on the diagonal again. We're heeled to 12 degrees with all sails set. At the noon meal, officers on the lee side of the wardroom table pour only a swallow or two of water in their glasses at a time. The wardroom quickly warms to Captain Luke, who says he grew up in Georgia but discovered his attraction to the sea while fishing with his grandfather in Beaufort, North Carolina. "He used to throw a net for shrimp, but usually threw his teeth into the water, so I had to decide, Did I want to learn how to throw the net or keep going into the water to retrieve his teeth? Ha ha." Luke first served on *Eagle* as an officer in 1984 and '85, and he returned each summer for five years while teaching nautical science at the academy. He was aboard when Captain Ernst Cummings took *Eagle* on her eight-month voyage to Australia and back in 1988. He also commanded the 327-foot *Taney* — another testament to the Coast Guard's skill at keeping old ships afloat. *Taney* was the last U.S. ship on active duty that had helped defend Pearl Harbor on December 7, 1941. In August of 1945, Carl Bowman commanded *Taney* as part of the Osaka area relief force during the initial occupation of Japan. The ship was named for Roger Brooke Taney, who had been a secretary of the Treasury, the Coast Guard's mother agency. Later in life, however, Chief Justice Taney was the man who ruled against the former slave Dred Scott in that infamous case in 1856. Like *Horst Wessel, Taney* was able to transcend the burden of being named for an ignominious figure.

"Are you a Kantian or a utilitarian?" Captain Luke asks the officer candidate who has just presented his curriculum vitae. A philosophy major and former navy medic to the Marines at Camp Pendleton, the man has been in the Seals and served at Subic Bay in the Philippines.

Accordion music lightens the work at the capstan. One of the barque's four antiaircraft guns can be seen in the background. (Courtesy of Tido Holtkamp)

He wants to be an Airedale, go to flight school. "I'm an empiricist," he tells the captain.

"Flying's like making love," Ivan Luke quips. "If you do it for money, it's not the same. I do it for a hobby [he's a pilot and has built his own aircraft]. My favorite philosophers are Jimmy Buffett and Dr. Seuss." Asked to explain, he quotes Buffett: "If we couldn't laugh, we'd all go insane," and Seuss: 'From there to here, from here to there, funny things are everywhere. Not one of them is like another, don't ask me why, go ask your mother.'"

Chuckling all around. Chris Sinnett, the XO, moves the conversation along, talks about being on *Eagle* and seeing suspicious freighters in the Windward Passage just begging to be boarded. "Someone once had the bright idea of *Eagle* carrying listening devices to collect intel." He then spoke of the impossibility of keeping this secret. "The ship would never be invited anywhere again."

At quarters after lunch, in the waist, Captain Papp announces his intention to tack ship for practice. *Eagle* is ahead of schedule. The bosun and his mast captains break off and discuss the tacking strategy. Kelly Nixon asks Ramos if the order to douse staysails comes after "tacks and sheets." He tells her, "Don't worry about that right now." At that moment, one of the crew says under his breath — not in response to Nixon's question, but with unfortunate timing — "This is going to take a while." Bosun Ramos continues his instructions. Nixon, who believes the complaint was aimed in her direction, takes a step backward and closer to the ear of the critic. Keeping her eyes straight ahead on the bosun, she says softly but with feeling, "Fuck you."

On the fo'c'sle deck, Karl again explains the tacking process to his mostly green crew and tells them the Germans on the *Gorch Fock II* can do it with a twenty-man watch in six and a half minutes. "They will douse headsails and let the mizzen push the ship around. The U.S. Navy's 1903 *Houlihan's Deckwatch Manual* called this windjamming and outlawed it." Karl sees no reason to reinvent what has already been perfected, procedures that live on in centuries-old traditions, some more closely followed on German trainers, that can be studied and put into practice. This is what he stands for on *Eagle*. His insistence on the old ways sometimes grates on the bosun, I think. There is a tension between them — creative, perhaps, and it will be kept bottled up by two veteran sailors who know how small a ship can get — but a tension nonetheless.

Eagle "makes stays," completes her tack, slowly but without a hitch. *"On the main, on the fore, on the mizzen: well done!"* the captain shouts. The crew is beaming, sweating over the chaos of lines they have begun to make up between high-fives. "You never missed a beat," Karl tells his smiling foremast hands.

For the rest of the day the painting, cleaning, and war on rust continue. The seas are larger now, and *Eagle* lifts off their tops. Seaman Casen, on bow watch with a quid of snuff in his lip and the flying jib taut above his head, spits over the side into a perfect slice of sea peeled by our cutwater from beneath the golden figurehead. He's on temporary assignment from a buoy tender in Michigan. "It's like the missing piece of a puzzle," he says, letting the ship's powerful roll explain the non sequitur.

At the afternoon weather briefing, Motisola Howard presents a satellite view on her laptop of a high descending to below Jamaica. We're between this high and another that's retreating to the south. The "pinch" will cause winds to veer from the current east-northeast to southeast during the night. The captain tells the bosun that he wants to bring the ship about sometime this afternoon in order to make distance to the east in anticipation of the forecasted wind change. The bosun pipes sail stations and prepares to wear but belays the order after the captain tells him not to rush, to set the watch and let the rest of the crew have the afternoon off.

A dozen or so are teak-beaching on the fo'c'sle deck. *Eagle* is climbing up and dropping down six-foot waves. Spray occasionally makes it up over the windward bow, cooling the sunbathers. The relative grace with which people navigate the deck is directly proportional to their time on board. Newer members seem drunk. Like *Eagle* herself, veterans anticipate each rise, roll, and fall without thinking. The smells of Colonel García's Cuban meal of black beans, rice, and pork roast visit every corner of the weather deck as they pour from the galley vents and join the up, down, and sideways drafts coming off the sails. Some of the foremast hands ask Karl why the order to wear was belayed. Affecting the king's English of Mr. Bush, Horatio Hornblower's first officer, he tells the hands that the French were closing in. "We faked a wear. They turned, and we kept going." *Eagle* finally wears at sunset, back onto her port tack off South Point, Jamaica, according to the quartermaster's chart in the pilot house. A mackerel sky is lit orange. Royals are doused as the old saw advises: "Mackerel skies and mare's tails make tall ships carry lower sails."

⌒

BY OCTOBER of 1944, Germany was being squeezed in a vise of its own making. The Russian armies were poised to enter East Prussia, the Americans were at the Rhine. By this time, Detlev Zimmermann had made it back from France and was in Norway, assigned to the U-boat *Schwartze Hand*, which had received orders to destroy shipping in Murmansk. He realized later that it was meant to be a suicide mission: each crewman was issued a pistol with which to go down fighting if the battle ended on the surface. They first cut through the steel submarine netting that stretched across the mouth of Kola Fjord, the entrance to Murmansk Harbor. Once inside and confronted with a formidable number of enemy ships, the young captain realized he could not escape a counterattack. He decided that discretion was indeed the better part of valor, and *Schwarze Hand* slipped back out. The decision cost him his command. Today Zimmermann and the surviving members of the crew refer sarcastically to the Murmansk mission as their "Strength through Joy" cruise.

Around noon on November 14, 1944, *Horst Wessel* sailed into a bay south of Arkona, a cape known for its high chalk cliffs, on the island of Rügen. Hans Frickhoffer's log continues:

> Our sister ship, *Albert Leo Schlageter*, was ordered to pick up a film crew at Sassnitz to make a movie of both of our ships for the weekly newsreel. We were supposed to meet her at green fireboat number three at Arkona around 2000. Because of this we were free to sail around all afternoon and hauled in the sails around 1700. I had aft flag duty from 1800 to 2200. We saw the *Schlageter* also under sail about 1700. We signaled back and forth for a while and then followed her for 20 kilometers. She didn't have the film crew with her, as they failed to show up.
>
> We were told that the commander would like to set sails around 2200.

We took care to be ready and laid out our clothes. I felt something in the air. No reason for it — just a feeling. I got into my hammock and fell into a deep sleep. I didn't hear the explosion but was awakened by my comrades shouting, "The *Schlageter* ran into a mine. Get dressed immediately and put your life preserver on." Meanwhile, an alarm sounded to secure all bulkheads and for everyone to report up on deck with life jackets. Since we were moving toward the *Schlageter*, we could run into a mine at any time. We got ready to rescue their crew. All cutters were lowered into the water. We maneuvered our ship close to the *Schlageter* to rig for towing. We slowly backed our stern toward her stern and threw them a line. It was difficult due to the heavy seas and high wind. The first line broke immediately because of the stormy sea. The second line was heavy manila and held. We realized the *Schlageter* had lost her buoyancy as two bow sections were flooded. Our cutters returned loaded with rescued crewmen.

Werner Fistler, who was on *Horst Wessel* as an instructor at the time, told more of the story. He wrote to me that it was difficult to see *Schlageter* because of the storm. Sails were doused, and *Horst Wessel* proceeded under power.

It was around three in the morning when we heard a dull thump. I knew the sound from my time on destroyers. *Schlageter* had hit a mine. I heard the captain shouting, "The *Schlageter* is sinking! Volunteers in the rescue boats! We have to save the crew." Visibility was bad and disembarking the ship was difficult. It was done from the lee side. In that sea, without light, rowing was a matter of sheer luck. We only got to the ship because the *Schlageter* constantly sounded her emergency horn. Her bow already lay deep in the water and she could no longer maneuver. Her crew could only board the rescue boats using the ropes from the listing mizzenmast. It became clear that *Schlageter* was not sinking any further.

In the morning we began to tow her backward across the Achtersteven against the wind using a 100-meter hawser. Later, the destroyer *Lutzow* took over. With three happy hurrahs we said goodbye to the *Lutzow* and our comrades on the *Schlageter*, whose bow was almost entirely under water. We returned to Danzig-Neufahrwasser. We wanted to dock on the starboard side, but all the lines were thrown too short and landed in the water. A heavy gust of wind pushed the ship back, so that it threat-ened to crash into the opposite pier. When the next set of lines also landed in the water, we were in grave danger. Then one of the sailors from the radio deck tore the cap from his head, dove into the icy water, and grabbed one of the lines and swam it to the pier. By the time the lines were cleated in place, the ship was at most three meters away from the opposite pier and had picked up speed. Our captain had observed the dif-ficult situation from the bridge and called out, "The bold diver, report to me." The two disappeared arm in arm into the captain's quarters. A dashing man.

Fear can be read between the lines of young Frickhoffer's log, while Fistler, who was older, was less surprised by impending defeat, better able to put it out of his mind. Memory is careful to walk upon stepping stones, and in a letter to me, Fistler chose to remember the happier times, the isolated and confined life on board, where mundane events were magnified to become the world. Life is Shakespearean at sea after a time: *A Midsummer Night's Dream* on nice days, *Hamlet*, *Macbeth*, and *Lear* rolled into one when, for example, the officers' ward-room has been unhappily existing on "green" decaffeinated coffee be-cause of an alleged screwup in supply and then learns that the fo'c'sle has been drinking the real stuff for days. This unreal quality must be even more pronounced when the world offstage is going to hell, as it was by December of '44. Hitler was only a few months away from declar-ing his scorched-earth policy. As the High Seas Fleet did in 1919, Ger-many was ordered to self-destruct in the face of the victorious enemy. Railroads, factories, bridges, communications, gasworks, waterworks, stores, were to be blown up, ships scuttled. *Horst Wessel* and all other navy ships carried an explosive device belowdecks that was to be deto-nated when the scuttling order was given. I think it must be the bitter, never-forgotten taste of approaching disaster that brought the humor-ous and playful to the surface of Fistler's recollections:

> For several weeks we had a famous professor as marine illustrator on board. He was always carrying a sketchbook. One cadet could draw and paint beautifully, and so a scheme was hatched. At the earliest opportu-nity, the professor's sketchbook was snatched for a short time, and Ca-

det Lambert Johrmann drew the old gentleman with a beautiful naked woman on his lap, and surrounded by many other naked girls. The next day, the captain steered the topic of conversation in the officer's mess to the professor's painting. In response, the professor took out his sketchbook (he had not noticed it missing) and opened the first page. It hit him like a bomb. The old gentleman turned pale, then red, and finally laughed out loud. The captain asked the professor for the drawing, but was refused. The professor would not part with the picture for anything in the world.

Reality entered the world aboard *Horst Wessel* in the eerie tales told by Herbert Kruse, who had been on the crew that had served the then-longest U-boat mission, eighteen months; he was radio mate under an ace named Luth. Fistler wrote, "We were simultaneously inspired and shocked. It was incredible to us how Luth had introduced variety into the monotonous, sad, and irritating sardine life in his underwater ship."

Fistler wrote that a dog named Whiskey, brought aboard the barque by one of the cadets, "stole our deck shoes. We were constantly running somewhere or other with a mop because of the dog. Whiskey had to leave the ship." Fistler was chosen by the captain to lead calisthenics. An athlete, he recalled ice skating around the ship when it was frozen into the harbor. The captain, finding that Fistler had learned how to wrestle at school, asked him to demonstrate his prowess. "I selected a strong cadet and practiced with him on the mat." On the day of the match, "the captain sat on the quarterdeck in his big leather armchair, the officers perched on stools, and the rest of the crew stood in a semicircle around the mat in the waist. My opponent was taller and weighed 80 kilos to my 64. The crowd cheered when those 80 kilos flew through the air and the opponent kissed the mat pretending to cry out in pain. Everything was acted out, and the crowd loved it."

Fistler remembered that Günther Wessel (apparently no relation to Horst) was the ship's political officer, but by this time not a very inspired one: "In December while wintering in the Greiswald shoals, our cadet chorus often went on land to sing in restaurants and taverns. Note! Only sailor songs. I would like to state firmly that during my six-month training period, no national or political songs were sung. We were conscious of the fact that we served in the 'imperial' navy."

Tido Holtkamp sounded the same note:

We would never have sung the "Horst Wessel Song" on the ship. We were unhappy about the name of the ship. I did not think a Nazi name was right for a navy ship, and I was not alone. It was the only ship in the navy that had one. The rest had traditional navy names, like *Tirpitz.* The only time we sang the song was in basic training on New Year's Eve. They wouldn't let us go to town, but they served tea and rum. At midnight, we had a big parade on the third floor of our barracks. We imitated all the leaders. One of us played the führer. He had Hitler's mustache and shouted about "unconditional war." No two wore the same uniform. One guy wore boots and nothing else. It was spontaneous. Not one of us said it was not right to do. A petty officer came up, saw what we were doing, and just told us to go to bed.

Obviously, however smitten the barque's crew might once have been with the Third Reich, they had by this time retreated to the illusory redoubt of the Imperial German Navy, something that no longer existed except in song and shipboard tradition. Tradition was all that remained afloat amid the wreckage as the war raged on. They bridled at the sanctimonious first officer, a pastor by profession. Nor did they like the arrogant Lieutenant Streiss. Tido Holtkamp remembered Streiss:

He disciplined us excessively. We would come back from shore leave at 0100, and he would call for a sock inspection, check to see if you had holes in your socks. Who didn't? It was snowing out on the pier. He had a searchlight. We had to run up a hill. If he whistled once, we had to hit the dirt. We did this from one to three in the morning. A bunch of us looked for him after the war. When I was with IBM, I traveled to Heidelberg. One night in a bar, I see him walk in with a couple of people. I waited for him, wanted to throw beer in his face. I drank beer, more beer, nearly passed out. Never confronted him. Then another time I saw him in a shop looking at cuckoo clocks. I said, "Herr Streiss, do you remember me?" He said, "No."
"I served on *Horst Wessel.*"
"Oh, how sweet."
It all fell into place. He was homosexual. All the anger went out of me. He would have gone to the camps if he had been found out.

Werner Fistler mentioned a curious thing in a letter to me, and the image has stuck. He was stationed on the foremast when a "miracle" occurred:

> We were in the process of hauling in the sails when a cadet on the lower topsail yard slipped off the footropes. He couldn't hold on any longer and dropped 20 meters [over 60 feet] onto the taut forestay. He bounced off and landed on his feet on the deck. No one noticed the incident. The young man was 4 meters away from me. He grinned at me and went back to work. It was a small wonder, although for him certainly a miracle.
>
> The winter passed. We returned to sailing. There was suddenly uneasiness. I had been asked by my crew senior to organize the entertainment for the last evening aboard. We had the use of a tavern on land with a large meeting room. Several of our comrades sang songs with humorous verses. The next day, the captain told me, "You are to report immediately to the weapons crew aboard the battleship *Emden*. Really, Fistler, I would have been happy to see you as a sailing officer."

In his letter, Fistler added, "Unfortunately, I cannot give you the exact dates of these events since my logbook, with many other things, was destroyed by a bomb."

⁓

MAY 15, 1999

We've passed between Morant Cays to the east and South Point, Jamaica, with a warm wind increasing in strength and nothing between us and Panama but the Caribbean Sea. A four-foot swell will likely grow from the far fetch: a thousand miles of unobstructed trade winds between us and the Windward Islands. Today is the anniversary of *Eagle's* commissioning as a U.S. Coast Guard vessel in Bremerhaven in 1946. Karl says the galley usually bakes a cake. *Eagle* is making 12.6 knots and flushing thousands of flying fish as she goes. The sea is purple under a hot sun. A few snuff dippers are standing around on the fo'c'sle deck spitting into paper cups, swaying unconsciously to adjust to the ship's heel and roll. The sails are drawing perfectly with the t'gallant leech on the verge of luff. Peace and power. Pretty Lynn Hensen is at the helm with one other seaman, steering full and by. Line shadows and sail shadows move geometrically around the deck as though someone above were designing something beautiful. Tomorrow the ashes of Richard Oaks Patterson and his wife will be committed to the deep.

Fistler's story of the naked-girl drawing reminds me of Marlene Dietrich and the besotted old professor who fell in love with the "Blue Angel." It also brings to mind a Polaroid picture of a battery-powered accessory owned by one of the female crew who served on *Eagle* during the transatlantic passage in 1994. The vibrator had been kidnapped. The photo, showing a knife held to its slender plastic neck, was left in the woman's mailbox, along with a ransom note: it would cost her $10,000 to get the vibrator back. The kidnapping and ultimatum became known throughout the fo'c'sle, which gleefully awaited her answer. In two days it came: she agreed to pay the $10,000, and she wrote the check, but the kidnappers would have to wait until payday. Payday — $10,000. Oh, what mirth. The drama took place without the knowledge of the officers living in the after section of the ship, of course. They would not have approved, because it would send the wrong message to the cadets — most of whom knew about the kidnapping anyway.

Many of the permanent crew are the same age or only slightly older than their future officers. And while the two groups have much in common, fraternization beyond work and training is discouraged. The old Lucky Bag tradition draws a good-natured line between them. Enlisted crewmen have permission to collect clothing and other items not properly squared away by cadets. The items are later auctioned off in the waist amid jokes and jibes, their owners forced to pay for their return.

In the overall interests of the ship, one-on-one friendships between cadets and crew, even of the same sex, are forbidden. The same is true for relationships between cadets and between members of the enlisted crew. Of course, the prohibition on male-female bonding is especially enforced. The ship's officers assume the worst when two people are observed spending too much time together. Counseling follows, and if, after questioning, love is confessed, then the couple will be given separate Coast Guard assignments ASAP.

The Coast Guard is proud of its relatively smooth transition to something approximating the ideal genderless society of the modern military. Coast Guard women worked the blockade during the 1990–91 war with Iraq and thus were among the first American women ever to be placed in combat situations. Women, Captain Stillman once told me, were the key to the Coast Guard's modern mission. Because there is no restriction on opportunities for them, they are assimilated quickly. "From my perspective," Stillman said, "there is a positive balance from a mixed crew. Freud was full of shit. Jung had it right: the authoritarian versus the communitarian voice. The female voice is the glue that holds the whole thing together. Ironically, look at Nelson — more female than authoritarian. His people loved him because he loved them. Here people give up their human urges, which would ordinarily be unbridled, for the good of the ship."

Easier said than done, or as Dan Reynolds, the engineering officer, said, quoting his grandmother in Maine on the subject: "Love will fly into a pile of shit." But in the Coast Guard it is agreed, in theory, that the sanctity of the first marriage, that between human and ship, must be protected. The directive against fraternization is based on the concept that when trouble comes in the form of an iceberg, hurricane, or other emergency, the fundamental, one-hand-for-yourself, one-hand-for-the-ship rule would be broken. Lovers are likely to fend for each other. It is better for one half of the couple to be left ashore, to act as a gravitational pull, an incentive for a safe return, as was the case in the past. I've noticed the furtive glances between two of the crew and the seemingly accidental bumps and brushes. It's none of my business. I'm not the love Gestapo. Romance on board today is far more heretical than was anti-Nazi sentiment on the same ship in 1944. Both have occurred, however, which is a good thing, considering the far greater dangers of dogma. When Captain Papp spoke to the cadets who joined *Eagle* in Hamburg, he said: "People have loved this ship, and so she has loved them back. These are the enduring values: caring for each other and for that which sustains you."

Fistler's story of the crewman's falling almost 70 feet and bouncing off the forestay onto his feet — "for him certainly a miracle" — has caused me to conclude that the fallen man's life was a gift of the ship. Having taken Horst Wessel's name in a forced marriage witnessed by the devil nearly ten years earlier, by late 1944 the barque was ready for a divorce. I like to think that this was the moment — following as it did the rescue of the *Schlageter* — when the ship developed a taste for saving lives simply because salvation, of one kind or another, was foremost on the minds of her crew. Tido Holtkamp said that all were greatly relieved when ordered to remove the *Horst Wessel* ribbons from their hats "for security reasons."

The barque's last voyage under a German flag, when many of her children had been drowned in underwater boats, and with suicide in her guts, was her first voyage in a new role. Heinz-Joachim Meinke, who was witness to the transformation, wrote to me of it:

I was nine years old and living with my mother and my younger sister in Putbus, on the island of Rügen. My father died in the war in 1939. Putbus has a small harbor called Lauterbach. Outside the harbor near the island of Vilm the water is deep. Beginning in 1943, the sailing ships *Gorch Fock* and *Horst Wessel* lay there at anchor and trained cadets. Sometimes the *Albert Leo Schlageter* and *Sote Deern* were there too. My uncle, Willi Lewien, served as a medic on board *Horst Wessel*, so it was natural that my mother and we two children were often visitors aboard on Sundays and holidays. In January of 1945, I visited the *Horst Wessel* on ice skates, as the water was frozen solid. In April we were notified that the island was destined to become a battle area. During a heavy air attack on the port city of Sassnitz on Rügen, many ships filled with refugees were destroyed in and outside the harbor. At night too we could hear the thunder of guns from the approaching front in the east. We all feared for our lives.

Then the order came to move the *Horst Wessel* westward to an unnamed destination. All members of the crew received permission to have family members from Rügen join them for the trip. And so it was that on the morning of April 28, *Horst Wessel*'s pinnace picked up my mother, sister, and me from Lauterbach Harbor and brought us on board the ship. On the dam we could see the first signs of the collapsing order: the small hut on the southwest side of the dam was empty, the door open. Gone was the sign above the door that said "Edelweiss Laundry." It was there the sailors had washed their clothes during the many months at anchor.

Now the wash basins were gone. When the pinnace left the harbor, many women were aboard with their children. On the boat deck stood a sailor in white uniform, legs apart, holding a boat hook with both hands. The weather was of springlike beauty, the sea calm. The mothers had tears in their eyes and waved back toward Lauterbach. No one stood at the shore. We children did not share this sadness. We looked forward to the sea voyage with expectation and joy. Our baggage consisted of two midsized suitcases and a rucksack, which my mother carried. We children each carried a small rucksack and a school folder.

After we had climbed from the pinnace up the gangway, helped by sailors, we were greeted by a bosun. There were only women and children from Putbus on board, no men. In addition to the regular crew of about forty, there were also ten sailors on board from Croatia. They wore German uniforms, but the Croatian emblem appeared on their hats. Cadets and Hitler Youth students from Rügen who had been trained for two years on board *Horst Wessel* and her cutters were no longer on board. Immediately after we arrived, the anchor was raised and the ship started to motor out. The pinnace was brought on deck and placed next to the motor launch and lashed down. We watched this before a sailor took us below to our berths. We reached them from a walkway in the aft third of the ship via a down ladder. It was a fairly large room with two rows of double berths, ten in each row. It lay on the starboard side above the water level, and the bull's-eyes [portholes] were about 1.5 meters above the water.

After our baggage was stowed away, we were asked to the officers' mess. During lunch — we got rice with baked plums — an officer gave us a presentation of the ship's size, sails, machines, armor, characteristics, and conduct on board. The guests on board — we were called guests, never refugees — were taken to the meals in three turns. We belonged to the third turn. I can still hear it in my ears today when the boatswain with an especially long whistle on his pipe would sing out: "The third turn to the O-mess!" After our first meal we went out on deck. We were shown the armament. Two quad antiaircraft guns were mounted solidly midships. They could be turned 360 degrees. There were solo guns mounted on the foredeck and on the afterdeck. Then we received instructions on our life jackets and on the function of the four lifeboats which were hanging from davits. When the instructions were finished, the commandant, Lieutenant Commander Schnibbe, gave us descriptions of the white chalk coast of Rügen, which was slowly sliding past us. Many of the mothers cried because they sensed that for most of us this would be a farewell forever. Joining us from Sassnitz was a minesweeper, which assumed the lead.

Next morning in a calm sea a tugboat brought a barge alongside. That must have been to the northwest of Cape Arkona. Many German soldiers came aboard. They looked ragged and carried nothing except their weapons. Talk among the sailors was of one hundred bug-ridden infantry men from Pillau. Because they were starved, they were fed right on deck. They washed on deck and were afterward deloused by a medic and several helpers. Their hair was cut short, too. As many were sick or wounded, the ship's doctor, Dr. Schwanecke, and my uncle Willi had a lot to do. My mother and Mrs. Eitel also helped in the cleaning of wounds and in applying bandages. Many of the soldiers had abscesses and infected feet. You could tell they were happy to be on the ship. I often heard the sentence: "Now the war is over for us!" And when they said that, they smiled just like my grandfather when he used to tell stories.

Much of what happened and was said around a nine-year-old I did not understand. Only years later did I fully comprehend the events that are firmly impressed in my mind. In spite of the strains and the crowdedness, one sensed a certain hopeful joy on the ship. We children were forbidden nothing except what might endanger our safety. And so we often rambled through the ship, admired the hammocks of the sailors, tried to climb into them and would not stop swinging back and forth in them. I especially liked the walkway to the O-mess and the captain's room. Here one could view many ship models in glass cases. Later it occurred to me that they may have been used to teach the cadets vessel recognition. I would have loved to take one into my hands or even abscond with it to my cabin. My favorite spot was the bow on the port side. Here I could sit, just see over the side, and the wind would play in my hair. Every day was warm spring weather, with sunshine and hardly a breeze. I would imagine how 750 horses were pulling this big ship, for Uncle Willi had explained to me that the machine that was pushing the ship forward had the power of 750 horses. We were altogether eight children on board, among us three teenagers who had been trained to be soldiers. We were the darlings of the crew and of the soldiers. Everybody had a friendly word for us. The captain was especially nice. He gave every child a blue hatband with the golden inscription *Segelschulschiff Horst Wessel*. He also gave each child a mouth organ with the inscription "When We March." That turned out to be the wrong gift, because at once a gruesome noise made by eight children swept across the decks, and even the soldiers called them mouth rasps. Our mothers, however, solved the problem when they simply confiscated the instruments.

We liked the captain's dog. It was a white great poodle, cut in the classical fashion, and answered to the name Peeda. It knew a lot of tricks and spread a lot of laughter. We boys were especially attracted to the midship guns. Under the supervision of a sailor, we were allowed to climb into the seats. When we turned a hand wheel on the right, we could make the gun rotate like a carousel. We liked that, and the girls did too. In this way the days at sea passed quickly.

During the night of May 1, the loudspeakers blared into our sleep with a special bulletin from the German High Command. It was announced that our führer, Adolf Hitler, had fallen in the heroic battle of Berlin. Our mothers got dressed and went on deck. The next morning found many empty bottles in the garbage. Officially the First of May was celebrated as Labor Day, but I heard from a sailor: "We have drunk away Adolf's skin!"

The saying has its roots deep in Germany's drinking traditions. During the Middle Ages, hunters and trappers would sometimes pawn the skins of their quarry for a drink, with the promise to return with cash to retrieve the skins. Given the context of the night's drinking aboard *Horst Wessel*, the sailor was recognizing one truth — the skin of the animal Adolf Hitler had been spent — and the far darker truth that so had the millions of skins he had pawned for his orgy.

When we woke the next morning, we heard no motor noise, only the humming of the electric generators, as my uncle Willi explained later. We had dropped anchor in Glücksburg, near the city of Flensburg. Originally rumor had Kiel as our destination, but the ship's officers had decided to change course. The change saved the ship and our lives. Kiel was destroyed by bombs that day, I found out forty years later. At first we could remain on board. Life and duty on board continued as ever. But on May 3, a British prize crew came aboard and the ship was disarmed. The gun barrels were taken off and brought on land. The soldiers from Pillau had already left. The cook, sailor first class Gerd Stiebel, prepared the children's favorite meal, rice with baked plums, one last time. Toward evening we said our goodbyes and thanked the captain. To my friend Berthold Eitel, the captain said that his first name was also Berthold and that he could call him Uncle Berthold henceforth. But we never saw him again. After a short stay of only two days in a Catholic home in Glücksburg — where we were treated badly — we lived for several weeks in the naval academy in Mürwik. Here I experienced the last days of Admiral Dönitz as head of Germany and his arrest close by.

Horst Wessel was only one of an armada of merchant marine and navy rescue vessels that began evacuating East Prussia beginning in the second half of January. What was left of the German army was engaged in a slow, bloody retreat along the Lithuanian coast and into East Prussia. The Russians, after four years of fighting and the mass murder of civilians, were bent on revenge. The desperate retreat and evacuation by sea was organized by Admiral August Thiele, *Horst Wessel*'s first captain, whom Dönitz had put in charge of operations in the eastern Baltic. Refugees were taken to Kiel at first, and later, when Allied bombing raids closed the harbor, to the few German ports available and to Denmark. On May 1, *Gorch Fock* was scuttled by her crew in the waters off Stralsund.

On Friday, May 4, 1945, *Horst Wessel*'s log at Flensburg records: "1400 hours refugees put ashore."

Saturday, May 5, 0800: "Armistice announced." (Schnibbe drew a black rectangular box in heavy lines around this entry.)

Monday, May 7: "Flag and pennant hauled down."

Friday, May 11: "Arms and ammunition turned in."

Across the Atlantic, in the hours between "Armistice announced" and the final hauling down of *Horst Wessel*'s flag and pennants, U-853, Moby Dick, died with all hands off the coast of Rhode Island. Detlev Zimmermann was back in Trondheim, Norway, after a marathon mission aboard *Schwartze Hand* in the cold North Atlantic hunting convoys. The U-boat was equipped with a snorkel and had stayed at sea for three months straight, most of the time underwater. Zimmermann would soon be taken prisoner and begin his long journey to a POW camp in Avignon, France. There prisoners slept on the ground and stayed low, out of range of the periodic machine-gun fire. There was not much food. Every other day a recruiting table was set up and the same announcement made: those who would like three meals a day need only come up and sign. Detlev's friend, another prisoner from Norway, signed the enlistment papers and, like many Germans, entered the French Foreign Legion. He later died in Vietnam.

Zimmermann's future wife, Ruth, survived the war by a twist of fate four months earlier. "I was with a group of twelve or thirteen girls working in a munitions factory. We could hardly believe what was happening. We could hear the battles in the distance. We were offered a ride to the *Wilhelm Gustloff,* but we went back to Danzig and took a train west because our leader was an older girl who knew her way around." On the night of January 30, the *Gustloff* was sunk at Stolpe Bank, northwest of Danzig, by three torpedoes from a Russian submarine. Only a few of the 6,000 to 8,000 refugees on board survived.

The promise of Tido Holtkamp's Aunt Irma, that in the navy he'd have a nice blue uniform and a warm place to sleep for the duration of the war, fell short. By the fall of '44 Holtkamp had finished his training at Schleswig, but the U-boat service he'd been destined for was no longer an option.

"There was a huge army presence in Schleswig," Holtkamp said.

We were ensigns by that time, so enlisted soldiers and sailors had to salute us. It was sad to see people who had lost an eye, a hand. They were supposed to snap to and salute us, but we walked on one side of the street and looked away on purpose. I was sent into the country to help harvest crops. Then, at the end of the war we were put on a train for Berlin in our gray uniforms. We were a battalion. We were stopped north of Berlin because the Russians had interrupted the trains. We marched west. Our battalion commander would not let us go into combat until we were properly armed and trained. The SS stopped him and were going to shoot him for delaying, but his officers stood around him with guns. I had been in a farmhouse and heard on the radio that the Russians had control of Berlin and that "a mouse could not get in or out."

We fought for two weeks. Then we ran like thousands of others. My goal number one was not the survival of the Fatherland. I ended up on the Elbe River. The only reliable source of information was the latrine, where the troops talked. I learned there was one bridge left, but it was lying in the water. The Americans had taken it. Before we got very far, some SS troops wanted us to fight to the last man. Some old soldiers took care of them. On the other side of the river we saw beautiful U.S. tanks with stars. The Americans were eating breakfast, and their clothes were so good. There were thousands of them. I asked in my best high-school English if we could cross. They said yes, if we threw our helmets, rifles, and hand grenades into the Elbe. Before that, we could not be without them — German field police would shoot you if you were not armed. I hate to think of how many were shot in Berlin.

I was happy to be a prisoner; I was a prisoner for three months. The first month was under the Americans, then the British. I went home and back to high school. One day someone said that *Horst Wessel* was in Wilhelmshaven, and I went to see her. The captain and some of the non-commissioned officers were there. The captain said he had no idea what was going to happen. He told me he thought the Russians would get her. He asked did I want to come back and help sail her to a Russian port. I said, No thanks.

Holtkamp came to the States in 1949 and was drafted into the U.S. Army the following year. He was sent to Germany as part of the occupation force for eighteen months. After his army hitch, he went to the University of Connecticut and then began a long career with IBM as a systems engineer. "I never knew what happened to the ship until I saw her in New London."

14 E~AGLE~ B~ORN~

S~UNDAY~, M~AY~ 16, 1999

A gray day. Big seas at breakfast. Subsistence Specialist Eric Spurlock is trying to reset the wardroom table as Captain Luke holds forth on the subject of OCS versus academy training — "I don't make the distinction. It's all mind expansion. I'm proud of the academy, but many OCS graduates are hungrier, more eager for their first assignment because they've worked for it. I take it as the highest praise when people think I'm a mustang." He said there was a small battle being waged within the Coast Guard about the value of using *Eagle* for OCS training, given that relatively few graduates go to sea after getting their commission. Then, noticing that Spurlock is having trouble working around his audience, Captain Luke urges that "all supernumeraries, non-load-bearing members, and supercargo get the hell out of the way of people who actually have a job to do."

Church is rigged: Catholics on the fantail, Jews by the mainmast in the waist, and Protestants on the boat deck. Arlington Williams, a large officer candidate from the Bahamian coast guard, testifies, in strong Caribbean English, on the boat deck: "We may look all right on the outside, but there is a battle within. I was drunk. I made up evil things and tried to perfect them. I never thought I'd be speaking like this, and on *Eagle*. I'd seen pictures of the ship. Now I'm here and crazy for the love of Jesus. I pray that you will prick your consciences. Now is the day of salvation. Father God, know their ups and downs," he prays.

Eagle has reduced sail. Karl joins his mother on the fantail. We speak about the burial scheduled to take place at quarters after the noon meal. Karl points out how square the yards are, perpendicular to the masts. He says it used to be the tradition to purposely cant the yards in port, make them "acockbill," to announce that a crewman had died. And speaking of the departed, he reminds his mother that John Knowles Hull, a relative, who is buried in a local cemetery at home in Rhode Island, was killed during the Civil War by a rebel sniper. Karl says the ball was meant for the man next to him. "It hit his neighbor's breastplate, ricocheted, and went through him. A soldier crawled in under fire and got him. It's a nice cemetery that buries people the proper way, in the right direction, laid east to west. That's the way it should be — the sun rises in the east and sets in the west. He pauses. "I have a picture of my mother's great-grandfather Martin Van Buren Knowles in his frock coat before the Civil War and another of him in his blue sack coat after the war. In the first picture he's standing erect, his cap is on straight, his mustache and hair are trimmed. In the second picture he's leaning on his rifle, his hair is hanging, his mustache is over his lip. His face is old and horrified, but what's shocking is his eyes — you don't even need a magnifying glass to see his eyes."

Karl looks away for a moment, then says he hopes the ceremony goes well. The wind has been known to take the ashes, and the crew are embarrassed when they have to wash them off the deck. We talk about boats. Karl is a boat builder. He says he's made a lapstrake Viking boat for rowing. "I had a cedar tree; milled it, tarred it, made thole pins out of the branches. I keep it in a pond at Matunuck."

At quarters we commit Richard Oaks Patterson and his wife to the deep. Captain Papp speaks of the fragility of life as *Eagle* rolls and flying fish soar and then sail under. Mike Summers, from Old Ironsides, reads a prayer. Colonel García ascends the steps set up to reach *Eagle*'s leeward, starboard gunwale. The ceramic urn is broken with one of *Eagle*'s brass belaying pins. A small white cloud is given a cyclonic twist by the wind coming off the sails, then disappears. The admiral and his wife descend into the Caribbean, where they wished to be. They are given a twenty-one-gun farewell from the fantail by Karl, Tracy Allen, and Matt Rawls, firing M-16s seven times each in unison.

Being one of the non-load-bearing members of the ship's company leaves me time to ponder the imponderable, and this afternoon I laugh out loud when I'm brought back to earth by the pipe: *"Now! the sewage system has been secured"* — which means that the heads will be closed until further notice. The ship's toilets work via a vacuum system, and the pipes can get clogged easily, by a wad of toilet paper or a tampon. These are never to be placed in the system, but force of habit causes an occasional shutdown, usually at the beginning of a cadet cruise. I've been far away in a deep daydream, the kind summoned by the rolling sea, until the thought intrudes of a headless ship with more than two hundred people on board.

Yesterday I was in the ship's business office, where a yeoman was goofing off, playing a video game on one of the computers. He was flying a fighter jet, hot on the tail of an enemy plane trying to outmaneuver him, but when *Eagle's* rolling fell into synch with that of his virtual jet on the screen, he freaked out. "It's too real," he muttered, and left the room.

I had been thinking that the sea has made it easy for Karl to slip into the skins of soldiers or sailors from many places and times and usually of similar rank, a channeling of sergeants and boatswain's mates from the brotherhood of enlisted men, all of them pinned down by circumstances beyond their control, all doing their duty. He's been reading a book about von Tirpitz's decision to begin the buildup of the German navy, which made World War I and a showdown with the Royal Navy a certainty. He told me that German naval officers used to train on English ships. They shared traditions and were friends; it was making him physically sick, as he read, to see the hostility between them grow toward the inevitable cataclysm. He was upset, as though the old arms race were being repeated somewhere within his English/German genes. I pondered briefly the possibility that the emotion Karl brings to his stories, to his rescue and resuscitation of men long gone, of whole cultures sometimes, might be an expression of present-tense worries such as the servicewide exam, his minor beef with the bosun, or a concern back on shore. But the imponderable thought is that the voices in his stories call out from the larger, even less forgiving world that Karl also inhabits, where honor, even more than survival, is perpetually at stake. He seems to see it as his duty to save from dishonor or oblivion the souls purgatoried there, just as it's his responsibility to teach the rigging of blocks, the lowering of boats should a man go overboard, and the way to ascend the futtock shrouds so as not to fall. His friends understand this. Doug Cooper, the former bosun, told me how Karl had reacted to Greg LaFond's fall. "Karl tried to act like nothing had happened," he said, "but we know about that." I believe that for Karl, LaFond was still falling — in a sense, might still be saved.

Because he spends the better part of his life at sea, Karl hasn't needed a house of his own. When *Eagle* is in New London, he stays with his mother and Seth or with his girlfriend. Behind the Dillmann house are six kettleholes and numerous ponds. Mrs. Dillmann is from an old Rhode Island family that was granted its land in Point Judith when the property they owned in Jamestown, Virginia, was taken by the British. Most of the Point Judith land was condemned by the U.S. government during World War II to build the navy base where Karl's father did security duty.

One of Mrs. Dillman's great-grandfathers was Martin Van Buren Knowles, the one with the thousand-yard stare in the old photo, who fought with the twelfth Rhode Island at the first battle of Fredericksburg in 1862. By strange happenstance, Karl's great-grandfather on his father's side fought in the second battle of Fredericksburg the following year, in which there were three bayonet charges. Karl was not absolutely certain, but he thought his great-grandfather Dillmann was in the third charge, which made it through the rebel lines. "He was wounded at Settler's Church and spent a year and a half in the hospital."

Mrs. Dillman's mother was orphaned when she was three. Her grandparents, John and Mercy Congdon Brown, raised her. They had owned two big farms in Point Judith for generations. One Thomas Brown was in the Rhode Island militia during the Revolutionary War, as was his father, Peleg Brown. John and Mercy Brown eventually sold the farmland because there were no sons to carry on the work. At one point, John dug up the relatives who were buried in Point Judith and moved them all into a small cemetery in Wakefield, where they rest today under a big oak tree, with one stone for the whole family.

There are four farms between the Dillmann house and Block Island Sound. Along the shore is a federal wildlife refuge, which Karl helped clean up after an oil spill in 1996, when he was on the *Bittersweet*. The Narrow River separates Narragansett from South Kingstown. On the marsh island near its mouth, Peg Dillmann's father built her child-hood home, and it's from there that she set out to tend her lobster traps and sail her dory. Karl lives now in a house built in the 1930s that his mother and father moved into in the 1950s. It had been rented by an Egyptian during World War II. When they were kids, Karl and his brother, David, found a radio transmitter hidden under the floorboards in the attic.

"I've learned a lot about Karl on this trip," his mother said ear-lier on the fantail. "He told me that he liked to row his boat in the pond, in the clear water where he could see the darning needles and the bottom."

I wondered: Did she know that he's terrified of the bottom, any bottom, and grows more so all the time? He'd told me this two weeks earlier over the clatter of the Adler in the sail locker while repairing the jib. "I was a diver in the Marine Corps. I can't do it now because it's like stepping into a grave. Whenever I even jump into the water I'm afraid. Even in six feet of water, I'm afraid I'm going to kick my foot on the bow of that U-boat. I have nightmares about it. Sometimes I see it be-ing sunk, and I float out of it and I see everybody lying dead. Sometimes I can just be driving along and I'll think of that boat and I'll just start to cry, and I can't stop."

I asked him if he'd had those dreams in the Marine Corps. "No, I did all right in the Marines. You know, part of the uniform. I could tough it out, muddle through. The diving had to be done, but after I got out I remember there was something wrong with the plumbing in the house, and when I crawled under to check, I got claustrophobic, and I actually saw 853 lying on the bottom. I panicked and scurried out from under the house, and that night I dreamt of it sinking. I dreamt there were holes blown in the side of it, and I could see guys just lying there floating. In the dream I kind of floated up and looked down on it."

I asked Karl if he thought he had been drawn to the *Eagle* by some-thing or someone from that time? What if one of those men on U-853 had trained on the ship?

"Once in 1980, before I was even considering joining the Coast Guard, I was in Germany for the summer. I went to visit my high school girlfriend, who was from Germany. I worked on a farm that grew barley for a brewery. It had been a Roman fortification, then a monastery that was bought by a family after the Reich confiscated the land. One day I fell asleep and dreamt I was up in the rigging and was standing on the ratlines. I looked down at my foot, but I wasn't wearing American shoes or trousers. They were German shoes. I remember seeing them in the dream. They were German shoes and trousers."

Later, below in the petty officers' lounge, where Karl had invited me for coffee, he opened his wallet and pulled out a folded piece of paper. On it were the names of U-853's crewmen. Rhode Island wreck explorers have researched the submarine thoroughly. Comprehensive magazine and newspaper stories have been written about it, and I assumed that this was where Karl had gotten the manifest. He said no one seemed to know what had happened to the crewman identified as Hoffman. The other man who floated to the surface was buried in a military cemetery in Newport. The stone reads "Here lies an unknown German sailor." He said he visits it every few months when he's home. Someone, from the German embassy, he thinks, keeps holly and flowers on it.

How, I wonder, did the spirit of a drowned U-boater invade the soul of a young man from Rhode Island, and how did he wind up on this particular training ship? Grand Admiral Dönitz once described a submarine crew as a *Schicksalsgemeinschaft*, a community bound by fate. What if Captain Helmut Frömsdorf was not a diehard Nazi, as his suicidal venture into the shallows of Block Island Sound would seem to indicate? Perhaps instead he took it upon himself to save his crew from eternal dishonor. There was no place to return to, no honor left on the surface. Honor would have to survive another way. What if some essence escaped on a radio wave, a desperate message from the U-boat to an empty house on the coast from which a spy had already fled? Could it have hung in the air of the attic until it was finally received? Or did honor survive on a more primitive level: a seaman trapped in a submarine, pinched and fed upon by a lobster or crab caught in a young woman's trap and eaten for dinner — and so to a boy even before he was born? Illogical, I know, ridiculous science fiction, but both scenarios floated into my head before the pipe interrupted my thoughts. I had put it all together — that's what a gently rolling deck will do.

The final piece of the puzzle was a recollection from Rostock in

'96. I was on the deck of the yacht *Lili Marlene,* named for the lovely girl in the German song who forever waits outside the barracks gate for her lover. The yacht was tied to *Eagle's* starboard side with a gangplank between the vessels. Karl and I sat on the yacht's deck facing the morning sun, with coffee provided by a white-jacketed steward. He told me about the eternal rebirth of sins and virtues. I thought of Herbert Werner, the decorated U-boat commander who had trained on *Horst Wessel.* After the war he wrote the book *Iron Coffins,* a chilling account of the battle for the Atlantic. In it he told how his crew had adapted a verse of the popular "Lili Marlene" during one of their anesthetizing booze-and-song fests ashore between increasingly dangerous missions:

> Should we sink to the ocean floor,
> We still shall walk to the nearest shore.
> To you, Lili Marlene — to you.

Somehow, in some form — call it a vivid imagination (but what is a vivid imagination and where does it come from?) — perhaps one of the dead on Karl's list made it ashore. And so the honor of sailors doomed by an evil cause struggles to be reborn each time Karl passes his knowledge and confidence to another, who then goes on to save a life — and so on and on. At least that's what a rolling deck might tell you. Karl never would, even if he believed it.

In any case, the heads were working again half an hour later.

⌒

THE "commandos" that young Heinz-Joachim Meinke witnessed coming aboard *Horst Wessel* to dismantle her guns were a contingent of Royal Marines under the command of twenty-one-year-old Major Norman Ricketts. The young officer had fought in the Normandy invasion and was later attached to the U.S. Navy. After the war he became involved in divvying up what was left of the German fleet among the U.S., British, and Russian navies. He was put in charge of deciding what pieces of the German military infrastructure should be demolished and what saved. Among the German vessels were the barques *Horst Wessel* and *Schlageter* and the cruiser *Prinz Eugen.* "I was ordered to take command of the ships in order to hand them over," Ricketts told

me. "Schnibbe had *Horst Wessel,* and Hans Brauers, who had sailed
with the Hamburg-America line, had *Schlageter.* They went in company
through the Kiel Canal to Wilhelmshaven. When we first seized the
ships, a young lieutenant aboard the *Schlageter* signaled frantically that
the German crew was going to blow her up. The ticking he heard
turned out to be her radio." The *Schlageter*'s carpenter made Ricketts a
hand-tooled box that was signed by the remnants of her German crew.
During his inspection of the ships, the young major found some ladies'
black silk stockings in a drawer in the captain's quarters. Apparently the
captain's wife had been on board, but the stockings remained after she
left. It was explained that the captain had worn them under his uniform
to keep warm.

Representatives of the three Allied navies gathered in Berlin just
before Christmas 1945 to haggle over the ships, which, except for those
U-boats that hadn't been scuttled in Flensburg Fjord, no one really
wanted, according to Ricketts. Neither the U.S. nor the Royal Navy
had much interest in the sailing ships because they did not fit into their
training regimes. Apparently no firm decision was made about the two
square-rigged vessels. The Coast Guard had its eye on *Horst Wessel,* but
it was left to the American inspection team to decide which of the
barques would be claimed. *Schlageter* eventually went to England, then
was sold to Brazil. The Brits had already taken the hull of the *Herbert
Norkus, Horst Wessel*'s and *Schlageter*'s unfinished sister. They filled her
with ammunition and scuttled her in the North Sea, an action that was
later regretted. A coin was tossed, literally, for the *Prinz Eugen.* The
United States won the toss, and the cruiser headed off for her fatal encounter with the atomic bomb. *Horst Wessel* and *Schlageter* were towed
to Bremerhaven to await their fates.

On January 1, 1946, the navy returned command of the Coast
Guard to the Treasury Department. Not long after, Gordon Mc-
Gowan, who had risen from apprentice seaman to commander during
his thirty-five years in the Coast Guard and whose first afloat assign-
ment had been to chase rumrunners during Prohibition, was ordered
to the U.S. Navy base on the Weser River in occupied Bremerhaven.
After the attack on Pearl Harbor, McGowan commanded the cutter
Tallapoosa in action against the Japanese. He was teaching seamanship at

the academy when he received the orders to lead a ten-man advance team to Germany to prepare a stripped and weathered sailing ship for her passage across the Atlantic to New London and to do it on the cheap. As for crew, that would have to be figured out later. The Coast Guard's budget, like those of the other services, shrank after the war. Academy cadets might or might not be available.

"I was due for sea duty. For that, I was fully prepared, but not for this turn of events," McGowan wrote at the beginning of *The Skipper and the* Eagle, his book chronicling the rebirth of *Eagle*, published in 1960. McGowan had risen fast in the undermanned Coast Guard of the late '20s. He had served on destroyers, on patrol in the Arctic and the Bering Sea, and had even had a go at international ice patrol. For the three summers during the war that *Danmark* had served as the academy's training ship — mostly sailing out of torpedo range in Long Island Sound — McGowan rode along as seamanship instructor, but he admitted he had been content to let the Danes work the ship and hadn't paid close attention. In his book he wonders why he was chosen for the assignment, given his limited sailing experience. He clearly understates his abilities, concluding that the choice was an example of the one-eyed man being king in the village of the blind. McGowan also playfully admits to having been at least in part responsible for the price of Cuban rum going from $6 to $14 a gallon in Key West because of the antismuggling actions he was involved in before receiving his commission.

"Chesty in the knowledge that I had been selected as first skipper of the *Eagle*, my efforts at becoming modesty were almost without humility in the excitement of seeing my name in the orders. It took a few days for ugly doubts to arise." What McGowan might have lacked in square-rigger experience he made up for in leadership smarts, according to his crew. And he possessed that most valuable of gifts in the chronically underbudgeted world of the Coast Guard — the knack for attracting "cumshaw," that is, hardware procured without payment, and for finding the right people in the hour of need.

The journey to postwar Germany aboard tired transports flown by tired pilots was a halting affair via Labrador and Iceland and, after seven fogbound days in London, to Bremen. Ed Lowe, the chief electrician's mate on the advance team, recalled the plane landing on a narrow strip of runway bordered by bomb craters. "We were taken by bus to our quarters at the naval base in Bremerhaven. It was still daylight. We were told we might get a bite to eat at a Red Cross club near the river. That's when we first saw her. From a distance she looked good."

Up close, however, *Horst Wessel* resembled the gutted and broken buildings around her in defeat. In the fall of 1936, this barque had been a symbol of the Third Reich's glorious future, her taut t'gallants heeling her as she charged the sea. But on the day the Americans found her, grounded, stripped, and stained, with the scuttling charge only recently removed, she was a symbol of Germany's fall. She had come full circle, tied to a dock owned by Rickmers-Werft, a venerable shipyard from the age of sail, whose owner represented the fifth generation of Rickmerses to rig, load, and send ships forth from that bank of the Weser. *Horst Wessel* needn't even have been tied, for she barely floated at high water. At low tide she rested on her keel with a small list to port. Captain McGowan and his team took a closer look. "This could be our ship," he said, "but let's check out the other." After the team examined the nearby *Schlageter,* Lowe, a meticulous man, said, "There was something more damaged on *Schlageter* than what we surmised might be wrong with *Horst Wessel,* so we went back and concentrated on her."

After a short stay in the navy barracks, the ten Americans were billeted in buildings spared in the single bombing raid at the end of the war, which had reduced Bremerhaven to ruins. Lowe heard the story of the bombing from a local resident. "The man was a watchmaker, not a repairer; he could make the parts. I had some watches to get fixed for the boys, so I figured if I can get baking powder, flour, and sugar, this is the way we pay for it. So we put together bags of goodies. He lived in a residential area outside the city that hadn't been too badly hit. They didn't speak much English, but they had a beautiful garden in the back. It had berries and they made berry wine. We brought the goodies in. They made coffee for themselves, and we drank the wine. They had a little red-headed girl and she ate the candy we'd brought. The man told us that during the war it was verboten to listen to the British radio, but he listened anyway. He said, 'They kept warning us to leave our homes. If you're in the city, get out. My wife used to watch by the window, I would listen in the other room behind the door. We hid the radio. Finally, they said it was our last warning and we left. The airplanes came

The barque as she was found by the Coast Guard team in Bremerhaven, February 1946. (Courtesy of U.S. Coast Guard)

Captain Bertold Schnibbe sits with his dog, Peeda, 1945. (Courtesy of Tido Holtkamp)

over and in twenty minutes there was no Bremerhaven. Twenty minutes
— that was it.'"

Slowly the Americans got to know the German sailors who, with
no place else to go, were living on their ship. "It was like a tent city,"
Lowe recalled. "The berthing area below was divided up with canvas and blankets — just drops. The captain and two officers lived aft,
but the crew was divided forward according to groups — engineering,
deckhands — and by rank. They were like living skeletons, most of
them. They didn't have much food. They barely existed. It was dis-
heartening. We were cautious. It was a mixed group, like it would be in
any service. Probably some were believers in the old system, some
weren't, some real old-timers and some youngsters. I don't think you
could call any of them cadets, though the younger ones might have
been. When circumstances got to the point that the war was hopeless,
there wasn't going to be any further training. We looked at them and
they looked at us. Little by little, they dropped their defenses, and we
dropped ours."

Being shot at did not help the rapprochement, however. "We'd
found this hatch up on top of a hill, up the river," Lowe said. "There
were all these underground tanks. The word was that the Germans had
built these oil tanks underground all the way up the river to Bremen but
never got the fuel, so they were never filled. They put spare parts in
them and shut them up. Gene Bagwell, or it might have been Mike
Pasko, and I were knocking the cap off the hatch to get a look. I opened
the hatch. You needed a light. Somebody behind us somewhere had a
rifle, and it came *peeooooooow!* right by. Boy, you talk about eatin' dirt. I
never got to the ground so fast in my life. We looked around and
couldn't find the guy, but down in the valley there was a shack. I said,
Maybe there's a guard. We shut the hatch. I said, 'We'll come back
when we get help.' I went back to report to Captain McGowan. He
said, 'From now on you take a .45. You go armed.' We went back with
some of the German crew and a truck. We didn't know what we'd find
down at the bottom of these bunkers. There had to be an entrance —
we couldn't carry stuff up that ladder — so we went down in the valley
and found this German sentry. He had the shack. The bunker had a
great big door with a lock. It looked like there was a tunnel that went

down to these tanks. I asked the German did he have a key. 'Do you understand key?' I asked one of the guys the word for key — *Schlüssel.* He said, *'Nichts.'* Well, somebody had to tell him he'd better open up the door. So he talked to one of our Germans, who said, 'He's saying you can't go in there and he doesn't have a key.' 'Well,' I said, 'if he doesn't have a key and can't open the door, we'll open it.' The radioman with me had a rifle, and I had my own armed guard, and I said, 'Just keep him from giving us any trouble.' I'd seen John Wayne do this in the movies. I said, 'If we have to, we'll break down the damn door.' He found the key and opened it up. The tunnel went down, down. It was something. You stood at the bottom and looked uphill, and all you could see was a pinpoint of light. The tunnel connected to rooms every so often, and somewhere about the third or fourth one is where I found a lot of the electrical stuff I was looking for. We loaded up."

It would take nearly four months of schmoozing, barter, and the special understanding among chiefs of all navies to put the ship back into shape, a difficult job, but one especially suited to those assigned to it.

Lowe said, "McGowan called us together. He told us: 'We don't have any money, and we're not going to have any when we get home, so find anything you think you can use now, and in the future.' He broke us into three departments; the third was to scrounge for all the equipment for which there were no American counterparts. A shining example was the Anchance gyrocompass, an amazing piece of engineering, a fascinating thing. Most of us in the Coast Guard in those days existed on the idea that scrounging was a way of life. You never had money to buy supplies, so you always looked for another way to accomplish the job, whether it was repair or whatever. You lived this way. You thought this way. You ran your ships this way, kept them running with bailing wire."

McGowan was staggered by the barque's design and workmanship. He admitted he was intimidated at first, like a poor man who must prepare for an evening with a beautiful woman beyond his station.

I had never even seen a barque rig before. The more I explored this vessel, the more fascinated I became with her complex arrangement. Going from bow to stern, one encountered seven distinct areas that can be isolated as a damage-control measure. Her watertight doors are battle-ship caliber of the rack-and-pinion sliding type, with steel-wedge seal-ing. In four of the bulkheads, watertight integrity is complete, with no penetration, making it necessary to go up and over in order to get into the adjoining compartment. She had a barber shop and a tailor shop, a generous sail locker, a soft drink manufacturing plant equipped with car-bonating and bottling machine and an ice cream maker. Plenty of space was set aside for wine lockers against the rigors of long cruises and visits of state in foreign ports.

McGowan marveled at the unfamiliar grandeur in officers' coun-try. "Lush" was the word he used for the captain's cabin. It had

an entrance passageway, a large cloakroom complete with mirror and dressing bench, a pantry, cabin office lined in mahogany, a bedroom of rippling golden satinwood, a tiled bathroom with a large old-fashioned tub on legs, and a dining saloon paneled in mahogany. The wardroom resembled an intimate night club. Dining niches were done in natural oak and red leather. The overhead lighting was indirect and rheostat-controlled. A dial phone system was wired throughout the ship. There were no warrant officers in the Germany navy, but the chief petty of-ficers occupied a position slightly higher in the service scale than do sim-ilar ratings in our service. The CPOs had their own wardroom and indi-vidual staterooms together with pantry and messboys. Their wardroom was handsomely decorated with oil paintings.

McGowan pointed out that by contrast the German seaman who lived in the cavernous tween decks, with a hammock hook to call home, led a Spartan existence. "He had constantly before him concrete evidence of the material rewards which accompanied promotion."

Bertold Schnibbe had stayed with his ship, and now, with no clear idea of his position on board, he dedicated himself to helping McGowan with the refitting. McGowan took the measure of his coun-terpart:

The German captain was thirty-five years of age. He bore the rank of Kapitän-Leutnant. He loved his ship and his crew. When he discussed problems with his officers or directed the crew members, he bore the stamp of leadership without harshness. At all times he upheld the dignity of his subordinates. As a mark of affection, German enlisted men use a diminutive when addressing an officer. When the captain gave an order, the acknowledgment was always: "Ja-wohl, Herr Ka-Leut." He was tall and thin and had a musical baritone voice of remarkable range and color. He was blond and handsome in a hawklike way. His aquiline features gave him a distinguished appearance. Add a monocle and the typecasting would be perfect . . . He never varied from his meticulous politeness, but a warmth bordering upon firm friendship crept into the atmosphere. Little by little, I began to see World War Two and its effects through his eyes . . . He pointed out the spot where the demolition charge had been built into the ship, and explained that under Hitler, all German navy vessels had been ordered destroyed if faced with possibility of capture. Admiral Dönitz had countermanded the order. Upon receipt of the message, Schnibbe had gathered about him those of his crew known to have stable personalities and unquestioned loyalty, and directed them to stand guard while he personally rendered the charge harmless.

Schnibbe was there to greet McGowan as he came on board each morning. One morning, about a month after arriving, McGowan found Schnibbe waiting,

. . . stiff and formally correct. When we got into the cabin, instead of sitting down, he stood by the desk and announced in a colorless voice that he had received word of his mother's death in Bremen, and formally requested permission to go to her funeral . . . The next morning he was back on board. He was subdued and uncommunicative until we had finished our coffee. Without preliminaries, he unwrapped a package. Discarding the paper, he handed me a slender crystal decanter. With a slight smile he said: "Take this home to your wife. No one I care for is now alive." Late in the war his brother had been captured in East Germany. His father had died some years before. His wife had deserted him before Germany fell, and had disappeared into East Germany. He had heard that she was a popular figure in the Soviet officers' clubs.

The bürgermeister had seized his mother's apartment, and he was told he could not take any of her belongings, but he had smuggled the decanter out.

Ed Lowe said the Americans were aware of the German captain's deep sense of pride. "I think Schnibbe's pride and feelings of duty led him to care for his crew, and he did not want to give up what had been the pride and joy of the Reich. I wondered, Was he putting on a false face, or did he know in his heart that the ship wasn't his anymore? And was he going to have a chance to stay with the ship? It was a sad thing in some ways. The Germans liked their captain. The attitude of the crew was astounding, really. The war was over, but nothing was slipshod. It was like it wasn't over. Even toward us, they were sharp. It was part of their training."

Lowe knew his technical stuff as well as the feel of a sailing ship under way, for he had served on the *Danmark* and on the schooner *Atlantic* under the chain-smoking Miles Imlay. He marveled at *Horst Wessel*'s compass. "Picture a small, round bathtub and a large bowling ball. Most gyros have motors placed at different angles. They turn at 30,000 rpms. Once aligned, they don't want to move, no matter what happens to the ship. In the Anchance, the motors were placed within a ball. Wire connections were spaced around the outside, but the ball floated in a bath of distilled water, benzoic acid [the electrolyte], and glycerin, which enhanced buoyancy. It was balanced to float exactly midway in the hermetically sealed bath. Once energized, the ball would stabilize while the ship rotated around it. Because it was frictionless, it had the advantage of more freedom of movement. Our gyros were not as good. The Anchance was more sensitive to changes in the ship's heading."

Captain McGowan would have good reason to thank the Anchance before *Eagle* made it to New London. To hear Lowe tell it, the gyrocompass seemed to be from another, more advanced world, as though what at first appeared to be an old-fashioned sailing ship was, like Captain Nemo's *Nautilus*, something out of the future. The excellence of the compass begged questions of technological superiority, of great innovation. Lowe also observed the "overboard" meticulousness of fuses built with jewelers' screws, evidence of a baroque search for perfection and Old World hand craftsmanship. "Whenever we scrounged things, I would take them apart just to look. Beautiful precise craftsmanship, but when you ran out of something, you had a problem."

McGowan and his men were faced with finding miles and miles of cordage and at least 3,000 yards of cloth for a new suit of sails. *Horst Wessel* had been without new sailcloth for well over a year. What there was in the sail locker had been patched and patched again. Electrical supplies of all kinds were needed. The two big German generators were ten years old and produced direct current. Eventually, the ship would have to be rewired, but in the meantime, where to find the stuff needed for repairs?

"You had to lay out a plan," said Lowe. "You couldn't just walk out into the countryside. You went out and tried to make contact, talk to people, befriend them. The navy had control of vast areas, ordnance, and equipment, so you went out and had a few beers with the old chiefs, and eventually you got what you were looking for." Eugene Bagwell, the motorman machinist's mate, headed the search for engine-room supplies. The search became easier when they realized that after the Allied bombing had begun in earnest, much of the prefabrication of U-boat parts and munitions was moved to small towns well inland and done piecemeal.

The team's greatest asset was Lieutenant Commander R. S. "Gary" von Burske, the supply officer. A mustang, he was known to fellow coasties as "Von" but was respectfully addressed as *"Graf,"* or Count, by the Germans, who recognized his aristocratic lineage. He had immigrated to the United States from Germany at age twelve and still spoke his native tongue. He was able to make some good strikes on line, twine, and paint, items the ship could use abovedecks. The team traveled to warehouses that reportedly contained large stores of the needed supplies, only to find piles of scorched bricks. They finally found sailcloth, 9,000 meters of it, far inland and brought it to Hamburg, where members of a sailmakers' guild set to work cutting and sewing the new suit. Before the bombing, the guild had made sails for five separate companies. It was resurrected for the *Eagle's* sails but faced oblivion as soon as the work was completed. When one of the team dropped by to check on the sailmakers' progress a few weeks into the job, he reported to McGowan that "the sail lofts were unheated and the sailmakers, blue with cold and weak from lack of food, were getting nothing done." Von Burske took a truckload of food to Hamburg and arranged for "a mysterious windfall" of fuel for their stove heaters.

Members of the guild attempted to put the squeeze on for the balance of von Burske's stash of flax. Their attempt failed because the Russians would be needing a supply for the *Schlageter*. And McGowan learned that the guild was to be paid by the city of Hamburg as part of the reparations agreement. He didn't fault the sailmakers for trying to profit, however. People were living hand to mouth, many without shelter except in the basements of gutted buildings. Ed Lowe remembered that the only shops were "Goodwill kinds of things here and there. The Germans took whatever possessions they had and brought them into these thrift shops. They were looking to barter anything to eat. It was pitiful."

Two weeks after McGowan and the ten original *Eagle* plank owners arrived, they were joined by forty-five other Coast Guardsmen. Except for Lieutenant Commander R. M. Hutchins, the new XO, and an electrical engineer, the group consisted mostly of what the skipper called "downy-cheeked apprentice seamen, many of whom had never been to sea before." McGowan assembled them in the chapel of the navy base. I am reminded of the scene in *Moby Dick* in which Father Mapple climbs the ladder to his ship-shaped pulpit and pulls the ladder up behind him before addressing his congregation. "Yes, the world's a ship on its passage out, and not a voyage complete; and the pulpit is the prow," Melville wrote. McGowan warned his young seamen that the price for tasting the wares of the "candy bar circuit" — the droves of girls selling themselves cheaply to get by — was venereal disease. He also told them, "You're going to find out what handpower means. You've got an opportunity here to get to know more seamanship in a short time than any of the petty officers who taught you in boot camp. When you get back, you're going to be sought after as qualified able-bodied seamen. In my opinion, you should make the best petty officers the service has seen in many years."

One of the jobs below decks was to remove *Horst Wessel*'s ballast, the iron pigs, from the bottom of the tanks that held recycled wash water. Their placement there was a rare example of poor design, for the pigs trapped material and fouled the water. The Rickmers crew were given the job of removing them from the tank deep in the ship and carrying them about twenty feet down a narrow passageway to where they could be hoisted out and placed elsewhere below. Days later, very few had been moved. McGowan asked Captain Schnibbe about the delay. "Yes, sir. I must tell the truth. These yard workmen are very weak. They are not strong enough to lift the ballast pigs. They have very little food." McGowan noted that the official government ration in Hamburg of 1,100 calories per day was

> not-so-slow starvation. I did not know precisely how scarce food was in Bremerhaven, but it did occur to me that the workmen were a gaunt-looking lot. The hang of their clothes suggested that scarecrows were repairing *Horst Wessel.* My boys were impressed with the Germans' willingness to work. They became sympathetic to the plight of these men who were trying hard and accomplishing so little. Spontaneously, food began to disappear in small bits here and there from the American mess hall. I looked the other way.

Strange how, after I had been witness for weeks to the barque's graceful lines, to the synergy of muscle and sail, to the blond satinwood cabinetry, and to the wind's unyielding imperative, what took root in my mind was being in the presence of *Eagle's* trove of corroded iron pigs. Karl took me to see them as part of a tour of the ship's netherworld — climbing down tight scuttles, through narrow passages, until I was kneeling on *Eagle's* keelson, the floor of a damp sweating valley of steel. It resounded with the ring and roar of the sea's passing. I could feel the flare of the hull to port and starboard with arms outstretched athwartships. And there before me, stacked on either bank of the steel valley, like old black gold, were the pigs, all 344 tons. They are the barque's gravity, that which keeps her upright, the deep dark soul of her poetry.

Lowe said that the Americans had more money than they knew what to do with in Bremerhaven. "You got cigarettes, and if you didn't use them, you sold them and ended up with cash, military currency that was worthless once you left. I got shoes, pants, dungarees for my German engineers. The stuff they had was ratty and worn. When they got new shoes, that was really something. They didn't even want to wear them." Lowe felt disgusted after investigating a bonfire that had been lighted the night before some army troops were due to be shipped back to the States. The fire was fueled by military currency the soldiers no longer needed but that the people of Bremerhaven certainly could have used.

One of the individuals whose trust McGowan was able to win was Mr. Rickmers, at whose family shipyard the barque was being transformed. McGowan described him as

a dark, wiry, intense man. He stood five feet seven in a pair of shabby sea boots, which were constantly caked with mud and grime. His shiny, faded blue serge suit stood out in immaculate contrast to his foot gear. How he slogged around the muddy yard and climbed through the tangled wreckage without soiling his clothes was a mystery. His faultless courtesy and perfectly enunciated Oxford English erected an invisible barrier between Rickmers the man and Rickmers the ship builder, hellbent upon getting a difficult job done against terrible odds. The level stare of his deep brown eyes and the stainless steel polish of his speech transmitted only facts and figures.

Like the sailmakers' guild, Herr Rickmers looked upon the *Horst Wessel*'s rerigging as a godsend. His formality melted and his fears came to the surface one night after a three-man wine tasting to which he'd invited McGowan and Captain Schnibbe. "Captain, I was fortunate enough to salvage some rather special wines after the bombing of Hamburg. I inherited most of them from my father and had them buried in the ground. Would you be good enough to join me in my office tonight at seven?" McGowan arrived to find a "painfully neat" space with a concrete floor, faded green shades, a typewriter, three straight-backed chairs, and an army cot in a partitioned warehouse that served as Rickmer's office and home. "The corks are firm," McGowan recalled his host saying. "I suggest that we start with the light ones, then each heavier grade can be appreciated for itself and not be obscured by too much weight beforehand." McGowan regretted having been brought up during Prohibition. "My wine-tasting education was neglected." But he did appreciate them.

Oiled by fine wine, the conversation moved to the war. Herr Rickmers told Schnibbe and McGowan that shipbuilders, whose spies knew precisely how much less it was costing the Americans to build ships, realized the war was lost long before the German military did. As the evening progressed through a few more bottles, the host expressed his fears that the *Horst Wessel* job would be taken away from him because of the slow pace of the refit. "If they take this away from us it will be the end of the Rickmers line forever. I am the last of the line. I'm not going to fail." Rickmers pounded out the words on the desk top with his fist, then apologized, saying, "I care too much." At the end of the evening the host joined his guests as they waited for a car in the warmth of a guardhouse. Herr Rickmers glanced at the headlines of a late-edition newspaper. McGowan recalled his surprise when Rickmers began to tremble with rage. He put his head down on his crossed arms on the tabletop and broke into hard, convulsive sobs. McGowan wrote: "I caught Ka-Leut's eye and nodded toward the door. We tiptoed out. As I gently closed the door, I caught the words: 'These damn people will never learn! Time after time Germany tries to destroy herself.'" Schnibbe explained that the newspaper story was about a group of people trying to resurrect the Nazi party. Not long after, Rickmers presented Captain McGowan with a carefully wrapped package. Inside was the Coast Guard shield hand-carved from a piece of teak. It was exactly the size to replace the swastika that had been held in the German eagle's talons.

McGowan and his men were amazed at the differences in German and American military culture:

The first time a German sailor passed me on deck, he snapped to a rigid brace as he walked by, and followed me with his eyes until his neck was craned over his shoulder as though his head were on a swivel. Upon meeting a man in a passageway, he flung his body flat against the bulkhead, standing stiffly, with his chin pointing almost to the overhead, and remained in this position while I passed. When on duty, the crew quick-marched about the ship in a parade ground manner. There was nothing of the relaxed atmosphere of American shipboard life. At the same time they appeared to be cheerful and there were no signs of discontent. The general bearing of the crew made it clear that morale was high. This struck me as strange. Never having seen the aftermath of a war, I had not until now given a thought to how defeated men behaved. Of one thing I was sure — my great granddaddy in Mississippi could not have had this attitude when he came in contact with Yankees after 1865, if my grandmother's yarns were to be believed.

MAY 16, 1999, 1600

Weather update in the wardroom. Motisola Howard says the wind will decrease once we're in the lee of Colombia, but we can expect thundershowers and winds up to 30 knots in the storms. Sail stations are scheduled for 1815. I suspect we'll wear ship because we're close to our destination, too early for *Eagle*'s appointment with the canal. We will sail tomorrow and head for it the next day.

The ship is rolling easy, making 5 knots. A lazy, hazy day. Waiting for chow and talking to Tracy Allen, with the South in his mouth, and Petty Officer Matt Welsh, who speaks Cape Cod. Tracy says he's been through the canal fourteen times, the first time right after boot camp; he was on an icebreaker with a scientist on board en route to the Arctic and then to the Antarctic to study plankton. And he's gone through at various other times during the eight and a half years he has spent at sea in his sixteen years in the Coast Guard. He worked Haitian ops out of Mobile on the *West Wind*, a 270-foot "wind class" icebreaker, then search and rescue aboard the *Point Heron*, an 82-footer out of Fire Island. In Houston he worked pollution response and vessel safety inspection. "Pollution stuff was the cocky thing to do — tracking down 'Whose oil is this?'" After that he was with a law enforcement detachment out of Galveston. "We were assigned to Sabine Pass, Texas, on the Louisiana-Texas border." He moved on to another search and rescue station — "half the time at the station, the other half on drug ops in the Caribbean. Our biggest bust was sixty keys, and we assisted in the seizure of six tons of cocaine, the largest marine bust at the time. It coincided with some big ones in cities, so it got lost in the media. A Coast Guard patrol boat made the seizure. We met them and acted as security. Brought it to New Orleans. The manifest said the container was filled with concrete. We never would have looked, but a few of the containers had locks on them. Locks for cement?" Tracy recalls sleeping on the seized vessel in sleeping bags, with the sound of flying fish thumping onto the deck throughout the night. "We rode navy platforms. They would be playing war games, and we'd be on the ships for forty-five days and board suspicious boats."

Tracy misses Lorlene and Zack, his kids. He and his wife, Earlene, love to dance. Tracy's parents were ballroom dance instructors. I watched Tracy and Earlene at one of *Eagle*'s Christmas parties, she in a full-length gown, he in a vest that matched it. Earlene, a nurse who works at the Coast Guard Academy, is a seamstress and makes their dance outfits. "I can make the things I want," Karl once told me, "but Earlene can sew really well."

Matt Welsh was a fisherman before joining the Coast Guard. He joined after the federal government began managing fish stocks by limiting a fisherman's days at sea. How times have changed. The Coast Guard's enforcing the number of days that a U.S. fisherman can be at sea is a far cry from the hero's welcome Captain Paul Welling and the *Vigorous* got from fishermen in Boston for bringing rapacious foreign trawlers to bay around the time the 200-mile limit was drawn. Matt says he fished for flats (flounder) in the summer, tuna in the fall, and cod — he pronounces it "cawd" — in the winter. He tells us about handlining a big cod, to the amazement of fellow Coasties, using somebody's freshwater gear and bait. "I've been doing it my whole life."

The fish stories have started, and they're not likely to stop soon. Matt once saw the purse-seine boat *White Dove* haul up a small whale in its net, and he knows a superstitious purse-seiner who saves a small piece of wood he once found floating. The man set his net around the flotsam and found a huge school of tuna underneath. It was the biggest tuna catch he'd ever made. Matt himself once caught a 925-pound bluefin tuna using a standup harness. The fish, full of fat, prime for the sushi trade, sold for $12.50 per pound. He said that in his small Cape Cod town he wasn't considered a turncoat for joining the Coast Guard; the seamen's bond between fisherman and the fish police was greater than any differences over fishing regulations. Welsh's eyes reveal a deep affection for the place. He smiles and breaks into song: "Cape Cod girls ain't got no combs, they comb their hair with cawdfish bones."

Dan Reynolds, the engineering officer, appears on deck. He is nearly always in good humor, a heavy man with a center of balance more at home in the nether regions of the ship. One of the OCS candidates asks him if he ever goes aloft. He chuckles. "Me and the bosun have an agreement: he keeps out of my engine room, I stay out of his rigging."

⟜

"*FIRST* no sails, now no engine," was how McGowan recalled his frustration after being taken below by his chief machinist's mate to share a discouraging discovery. "With the feeling of finding a snake coiled in tangled underbrush, I made out a spidery, almost invisible crack extending from the wall of number two cylinder to number three, skipping to the other wall of number three through four and from four to five, five to six, and six to seven. This hunk of steel was being held together by the bolts which fastened down the cylinder head assemblies. Without a word, I turned and left the engine room." Von Burske was sent off to the Maschinenfabrik Augsburg-Nürnberg factory, which he found was under British control and supporting a tremendous effort to rid the North Sea of mines. McGowan headed for Royal Navy headquarters in Hamburg, where he met a sympathetic officer, who said, "The Coast Guard's no stranger to me, y'know. I rode one of your stout little craft here and there in the Channel on D-day. Picked up dozens of flyers swimming about. Coast Guard chap got decorated. Damn fine show. They were smart vessels. Glad to help with the *Horst Wessel* if she's for your branch."

Horst Wessel's 800-horsepower diesel was a standard engine, the same one that had driven Zimmermann's U-boat, the Kriegsmarine's formidable Seven Seas model. A new block was snatched from the assembly line and lowered into place through a skylighted shaft located just before the quarterdeck and cleverly designed for just such an eventuality. But the holes for the bolts that fastened the engine to its mounting did not line up; serial numbers had changed during the war. The correct block was found, and again the Rickmers *Schwenkkran* came alongside and lowered it into place. The crew named the new engine Elmer.

With much of the heavy interior work done, and with the test and repair of the stays and shrouds completed in kinder weather, the barque was ready for dry dock and a new coat of paint. "As she settled on the keel blocks and the water receded, her beautiful body was slowly unveiled. She had the underwater lines of a racing yacht, the delicate curving contours of her hull sweeping aft with poetic grace. The Germans beamed with pride, and the Americans' eyes lit up with admiration. This charmer had captured our hearts," McGowan gushed in his book.

To see *Eagle* in dry dock is to see her undressed, and it is impossible to avert one's eyes. I've had the pleasure of that sight at the Coast Guard yard in Baltimore. As Karl put it, "You know how a parent never tires of admiring his child. Well, every morning when we were at the yard, when I'd come down to work, no matter what mood I was in, I'd look at this ship up on the ways and say, Damn, that's a good-lookin' boat. Isn't she gorgeous? Like a yacht. The shape. The lines. There's so many lines moving together, lines sweeping down this way, and sweeping that way, and curving under."

The only major problem left at the Rickmers yard was the rudder post, which had been shocked out of alignment by a bomb that exploded close to the ship a few days before the war's end. It was quickly fixed. What worried McGowan now was his lack of crew, as well as a more distant concern: because the refitting had taken longer than expected, *Eagle* would be crossing the Atlantic during hurricane season.

The barque required a minimum of sixty or seventy people to lift anchor and handle the sails. She was intentionally built to put more than two hundred people to hard work. Again, McGowan's scavenging instincts paid off. He said that a British officer must have seen the worry written on his face when he sank into the chair next to him at the officers' club one evening. "What ho, Mac. Why the tears in the beer?" McGowan laid out his problem. He had only about fifty hands and had just received word that the cadets from the States that had been promised would not be coming.

"How many do you need?" the officer inquired.

"I'd love to have two hundred, but I'm willing to gamble with a bare minimum of fifty more." As luck would have it, the Brit was in charge of a major minesweeping operation. "Germans, man, Germans — some of the best. I've got tons of 'em. Not POWs, but ex-navy volunteers. For that matter, why don't you take those boys you have on the

Horst Wessel, if you like 'em. Tell their captain to come see me tomorrow and I'll sign 'em on as mine swipes and put them on my payroll. When you get to America just dump 'em in a POW camp and they'll find their way back to me."

The German crew living on the ship helping to refit her was the same noncadet crew that had manned her at the end of the war. Schnibbe now tried to contact members of his last class of cadets. In the final months of the war, Peter Herger Jepsen, like his classmate Tido Holtkamp, had been transferred from *Horst Wessel* to a ground troop unit making a last stand, "the last defense of German soil," as it was called. Jepsen was wounded in January of 1945 and spent the last terrible weeks of the war in a hospital, "which, I feel, was my luck," he told me. "I was home in May of 1945. Telephone and mail service were slowly restored. There were hardly any communications, but the news spread fast that the Americans were looking for experienced square-rigger sailors to sail *Horst Wessel* to the United States. We were without work, hungry, but lucky and grateful to have survived the war. Now we had an opportunity to sail across the Atlantic to America."

McGowan had his crew by mid-April: forty-eight Germans, seventy-two Americans; Knud Langvard, the former executive officer of *Danmark*, who had agreed to come along, much to McGowan's relief, plus a navy dentist, a German physician friend of Captain Schnibbe's, two wire-haired terriers, and twin dachshund puppies.

Until the day the ship sailed, the crew also included a fourteen-year-old boy who had materialized on the dock one day and attached himself to the ship. He spoke English without any accent that might hint at his origins. He identified himself as Eddie Didion and said he had been born in France, near Normandy. Orphaned when the war began, he had joined up with a U.S. Army Military Police battalion after the Normandy invasion and had stayed with the MPs until they were shipped back to the States from Bremerhaven. He had attempted to stow away on the transport but had been discovered and put off. His story seemed credible. He did things in a military manner; he painted, and scrubbed, and he quickly ingratiated himself with the crew. A uniform suit of blues was sewn up for him, and a flat cap was found that fit over his curly blond hair. As the *Eagle*'s fitting-out moved toward completion, an effort was made by a member of the Coast Guard crew to adopt Eddie legally. The Red Cross discouraged it.

The commissioning was scheduled for May 15. An engineer, formerly with the North German Lloyd Line, was put to work translating nomenclature for the hundreds of machine parts, electric lines, blueprint legends, and name plates that the Germans had placed throughout the ship. Captain Schnibbe inquired about the ship's name. What would she be called on commissioning day? *"Eagle,"* McGowan told him.

> Schnibbe seemed surprised, and chuckled as though I had told a joke. I was puzzled and a little irritated. "Igel?" he said, and placing his hands about twelve inches apart as if measuring fisherman style, he repeated, "Igel? In German that word means little animal, what you call groundhog."
>
> Groundhog! From my small store of German words I found the one we wanted. "Oh no, not *igel*. Eagle is the English word, meaning *Adler.* Comprehension dawned. "That is a fine name, Captain. It could not be better."

On May 15, the barque's new covering of "snowy white" paint, not all of it dry, covered the formerly grayer shade. The masts wore a new coat of spar varnish. The yards were squared. The commodore from the U.S. Naval Command arrived. The men were piped to general muster just forward of the mainmast. The American enlisted men stood at attention on the starboard side, their German counterparts stood beside them but farther forward and along the port side. A double rank of American officers was lined up athwartships, the German officers behind them. McGowan, the navy chaplain, and the commodore faced the crew. McGowan recalled that a short prayer by the chaplain coincided with the sun's bursting from the morning clouds. "Surely a good omen," he said.

> I read my orders, and assumed command. With this, we faced aft at hand salute, and to the accompaniment of shrilling pipes, our national ensign was hauled smartly to the gaff. I directed the executive officer to set the watch. Sideboys fell in at the gangway and the Commodore left the ship. As the formation was dismissed, I glanced at the ranks of the Germans.

They were standing stiff as ramrods, tears coursing down their cheeks. Ka-Leut came over to me and offered his hand in congratulation, and with a forced smile, disappeared into the cabin area. Up to this time he had been living in the captain's cabin. I had been dreading the day when I would have to move him out of the quarters which had been his home for so long. I looked for him to thank him for his courtesy, and discovered his newly selected room. His head was on the desk, his arms outstretched. His shoulders were shaking silently. Seeing that he had not noticed my intrusion, I tiptoed quietly away.

Seeing the American flag flying at the gaff was no less traumatic for the German sailors. Willy Starck was a former cadet who kept a log during the trip across.

30 MAY 1946: While I write these lines, we have already said farewell to Germany. Bremerhaven lies several miles behind us. We are steaming down the Weser River toward our first goal, Falmouth in the southwest of England. Now it will be our task to introduce the Americans to sailing and familiarize them with all aspects of it. None of us, when we departed this ship two years ago, would have thought we would ever return. But things always take unexpected turns! The Americans asked us to join them, and we followed this ray of hope. We can only call it a ray of hope, this offer, which promises to take us out of the misery of our homeland for some time, perhaps forever. Of course we were also troubled: Is it the right thing to do? It is certainly not simple to make our own ship ready for the victor, and then sail it across the big pond. But if we decided not to do it, others would, and under the circumstances we are most qualified to prove our seamanship, attitude, and ability. Perhaps it is the last duty we can do for our navy. We do not want to take this duty lightly. On May 15, our ship was officially turned over to the Americans. As of now the good old *Horst Wessel* has become the U.S.C.G. cutter *Eagle*. I spoke before of a difficult time. But if I want to speak of a really difficult time, then I must not forget the 15th of May, when the Stars and Stripes went up over the ship, and we stood by saluting. We have lived through this hour, which stirred up so many feelings in us and the old question — should we really go on this trip?

31 MAY 1946: A stiff northwester drives dark clouds across the sky. The short waves of the North Sea play mightily on our little ship. We

cannot set sails yet. Because of the danger of mines, we have to follow a narrow course through the North Sea to the English Channel. The captain goes up and down the bridge with sadness in his eyes, for the major part of the American crew is seasick. We are furious that some of us — not having been to sea for a while — are also hanging on the outside rail and returning those fried eggs that we wolfed down with such a huge appetite this morning. This will change in the next days.

1 JUNE: Now we have set staysails and are making 10 knots. The tug has trouble keeping up. This afternoon we passed the Dover-Calais narrows and are keeping close to the English coast. At lunch Kurt appeared with a well-filled tray in one hand and an empty pail in the other. He sat down at the table and put the pail behind him. The first sausage went down well, but when he followed Rolf's advice to add some potatoes to the fatty sausage, he turned around, picked up the pail, and dropped the sausage and potatoes into it with a bow. Then he quietly proceeded to polish all but the potatoes from his plate.

2 JUNE: Tonight we passed Brighton. For us it was a peculiar, yet moving view. After the destroyed Bremerhaven, with its tired and hopeless people, we suddenly saw a well-lit city with bright advertisements before us. A city in the land of the victor. We really felt lost. But the camaraderie on board is wonderful, and we get along well with the Americans. It is like everywhere: if the little man from one side has the opportunity to get to know the little man from the other side, then all hatred and enmity are quickly buried. Because of their strangeness and their proverbial good-naturedness, our two black American comrades seem especially attractive to us and they enjoy general esteem. There is Mr. Goins, our cook, who shows us his affection by putting not three but four beefsteaks on our food tray. The other Negro is Mr. White, the steward. I always have to be careful not to call him "Mr. Black," for that would certainly insult him. Today I made a good deal with him. For an old Kaiser Wilhelm memorial plate, which shines like gold but otherwise is not worth much, I received a large chocolate bar and quite a bit of chewing gum. The tug will take these back to Germany as farewell presents.

Also back in Germany somewhere was Eddie Didion. McGowan noticed that he was suspiciously absent the day before the ship was to leave. "On sailing day, Eddie was nowhere in sight. I called the crew together and told all hands that Eddie must be produced forthwith. No Eddie — no sail. Their faces showed plainly that they had hoped to 'discover' the stowaway after the ship was well out at sea. It took about half an hour, but they dragged him kicking and biting to the ship's side. He had been hiding in a locker. The pilot boat swung away with Eddie, a tiny bit of human misery in the cockpit. He never looked back."

At the end of a nervous passage across the English Channel, most of it under tow, past the wreckage of half-sunken ships and through old minefields marked "swept but doubtful" on the charts, *Eagle* touched in Falmouth for fuel and water. There she waited for three days to let a southwest gale blow itself out. At 1130 on June 6, without the aid of motorized winches, which McGowan's scroungers had been unable to find to replace the capstans, *Eagle* weighed anchor and stood out with the tide, bound for the island of Madeira.

∼

MAY 17, 1999, 0730
Earlier today, when I approached the bow stander, who's from Dallas, he was looking forward and playing one of the jib sheets like a bass guitar to a tune rocking away in his head. He said the littler flying fish reminded him of grasshoppers in a pasture. I have been rereading McGowan's book at night. My stateroom offers the sound of the sea brushing old steel, like a big bell. The sound reminds me of something wonderful I've learned about the ship's 12-inch bell — and about *Eagle* herself, by extension of her sounding like one as the waves brush and pound upon the old Krupp. From time to time, the bell is removed from its stand, located forward of the windlass on the fo'c'sle deck, where the bow watchman strikes it to mark the progress of the watch by the half-hour. If a crewman requests it, the bell is taken down, filled with water, and used as a baptismal font for a crewman's baby. After the child is thus cleansed of original sin, its name is inscribed on the inside of the bell. According to the tradition, which originated in the Royal Navy, the child is then forever linked to God and country.

In the spring of 1946, *Eagle* was sailing west toward Madeira en route to Bermuda. This spring she is sailing west with pretty much the same sails set, trimmed the same way, to receive a similar wind. She is making the same graceful bow amid the same symphony of sounds: a cry aloft, the pounding of feet on the deck above, and the constant rush of the sea. Where, I wonder, have the intervening years gone? Or have they?

⌒

THE 1,400-mile passage to Madeira was uneventful, even though two groups of men were struggling to learn each other's language while sailing a ship. A shackle left aloft fell to the deck when *Eagle* first met ocean waves, nearly hitting a crewman's head on the way down. McGowan wrote: "All day long, I was plagued with a premonition of impending disaster. Faith in our ability to negotiate the next 5,000 miles melted away. The falling shackle seemed a bad omen. This pessimism is nothing new. It is the only form of seasickness I have ever known. Throughout my career I have been plagued with the first-day-at-sea blues." But on the morning of the second day, McGowan mellowed as he sipped coffee and "watched the stars fade. The coming of day on a clear, calm morning is a quiet, still thing. To the east the deep blue gently fades to pale violet, and gives way to delicate rosy opalescence." Later that morning, the mixed crew set sails for the first time. The initial excitement was doused quickly when the new manila line, remembering its curled-up lazy days, recoiled from work. "The parallel purchases of the tackles twisted and writhed like a family of snakes. Aloft, all the line we had been renewing in the past weeks was busily knotting itself into rats' nests as though it had a will of its own," McGowan recalled. The unreeving and rerigging lasted nearly all day.

On the third day, McGowan was informed by the navy dentist that one of the young Germans had an unhealed wound in his side that bore watching. The nineteen-year-old had hidden his condition in hopes of getting better treatment in the States. He'd been injured eighteen months earlier when the Messerschmitt he was flying was shot down by Russians. The young combat veteran's plight caused McGowan to meditate on the enmity of the recent past and to recall the disturbing fantasy he'd had when he first arrived in Germany, that the Germans would come at the crew as they slept, slit their throats, and sail the ship to a deserted island to live out their lives as "forgotten men." Much had changed in the five months they had worked together.

Eagle arrived in Madeira at 2330 on June 11 to a spectacular fireworks display in honor of a local saint. Funchal, Madeira, had been a popular stop for cruise ships before the war, but in June of 1946, holiday ships were scarce. As a result, the bumboats selling fruit, canaries, fine linen, wine, and souvenirs surrounded *Eagle* almost constantly during her three days at anchor. As day broke on the first morning, the sight of the mountainous tropical island, with its tile-roofed houses, lush greenery, and fiery bougainvillea, made the crew itchy for shore leave.

Ed Lowe recalled returning to the ship after a day in Funchal. "We had been ashore and had wine in those baskets. That whole day we sampled the Madeira. We decided that it was about time to get back, have supper, and sober up. One of the guys had a bottle with a broken neck. We had a couple of drinks on the way back to *Eagle*. The guy with the bottle turned around and looked at the two civilians in the boat. 'You ought to have a drink,' he said. One of the men said, 'Thanks a lot, best if I don't. I'm going aboard to meet your people. I live here, so I know the vintages.' Nothing more was said. When we reached the ship, the sideboys were out, and the U.S. ambassador and the governor of Madeira climbed up the ladder and were piped aboard. I wondered, What's the old man going to say if he hears about this?"

The Germans were not granted liberty on shore; they had been told they would be given two postage stamps and an afternoon swim instead. It was only after *Eagle* left for Bermuda that the American crew learned that five of the Germans, one of whom was Willy Starck, had decided to go ashore anyway. After sunset, they slid down the anchor chain and swam to shore with their clothes in waterproof bags that turned out to be not quite waterproof. Once ashore, after a swim that was far longer than anticipated, they put on their very damp street clothes. They told people they were Americans. Though they had no money, they were invited into a bar, and from there they went on to the Royal Dance Club, where "dreamed-of beauties" lined the bar. The girls came over, and the Germans danced one rhumba after another. Starck said that before the night was over, every girl's chest was wet from her partner's soaked shirt. As the men headed back through the streets of Funchal, two in the party had "hot pants," Starck said, and ventured on to a "little house." When they finally left for the boat, it was nearly dawn. The sailors were too tired to swim back to the ship.

According to one version of the story, there was some urgency in their return, for a few townspeople felt undercompensated by the chocolate offered for services rendered. In any case, the sailors were able to convince a fisherman to take them out to the ship for 200 cigarettes. En route, they stuffed their white shirts back into the bags so as not to be spotted in the moonlight. It wasn't easy to climb back up the six meters of anchor chain, but they did it and were lying low in the netting under the bowsprit when one of the four-to-eight watch found them. "We told him we had just done business with a bumboat. Whether he believed us or not, I don't know," Starck said. Belowdecks their comrades greeted them with freshly made potato salad and a little wine. "We'd hardly slept an hour when the reveille pipe woke us. We didn't want to hear it, but the boatswain came and dumped us from our hammocks."

Eagle left for Bermuda on Friday, June 14, a bit behind schedule, because McGowan had underestimated the time it took to march the miles around the capstan hoisting 50 fathoms of anchor chain and a 3,000-pound anchor. Seeing McGowan's frustration, Schnibbe suggested that he have an accordion player sit on the capstan, as was the German custom. The suggestion was not taken. *Eagle* left Funchal under power but quickly found the trade winds that would carry her along the old sailing-ship route to the Americas. The first part of the sixteen-day passage would be filled with the routine ship work meant to return *Eagle* to her original splendor. Paint was stripped from the brasswork, and the decks were scraped clean of stains, using the pumice stones the Germans knew as "prayer books" and the Americans as "holystones." In all navies the work is done on one's knees, as though in supplication. In the early '90s, an attempt was made on *Eagle* to replace holystoning with a chemical cleaner. The deck resisted, and it was back to holystones.

Using pidgin English, the German hands taught their American counterparts the intricacies of sailing the barque. Except for *Danmark*, which was sailed by her Danish officers and mates, the last square-rigger used by Americans for training was the *Alexander Hamilton*, formerly the naval gunboat *Vicksburg*, twenty-five years earlier. If there had been an actual ship-handling baton to pass, it would have happened during this 1946 crossing from Bootsmann Erich Schultz to Chief Boatswain Michael Pasko and Lieutenant Fred Goettel. The science did not have many practitioners in the early years under the U.S. flag.

About a week and a half out, *Eagle* found herself in the horse latitudes, areas of light finicky winds approximately 30 degrees off the equator. Ed Lowe recalled that lack of wind was not the only problem. "We were having a hell of a time because the water we received in Madeira was polluted. Chlorine had to be added to everything — potatoes, coffee, everything. The water was rotten. The fuel was contaminated too. We didn't know that until it started plugging up the generators, and that became a real concern. It got to the point where just about every hour we took the filters out, flushed them, and put them back. They would last a little bit, then the power would drop down, the lights would flutter. It all happened at once. The ocean was flat calm, with a lot of seaweed and lots of things floating around. The engine wasn't running good, the water was not good, and morale was getting pretty rough.

"Around this time we came up with an idea for some recreation. It wasn't like when the cadets came later, when we had a band and showed movies. I said, 'I'll organize a boxing team.' I put out a feeler. The Germans thought it was a good idea. The one thing we didn't think about was that the Germans were just beginning to recover. They had been starving a long while. We tried to get five bouts, but we realized too late that the Germans had no stamina. They could put a flurry on, but then they were done. I was the referee. I told the Americans, 'Look, for crying out loud, you got 'em beat. Take it easy. They're not in condition.' The word got around. I had an American and a German winner after the first bout and, man, did everybody cheer. And that's the way it went. Each bout was a tie. When it was over, that was the end of it, and we went and got coffee, cocoa, and cookies. That was a hell of a big day."

There were a few books to occupy the crew. David Ruley, the Coast Guard photographer assigned to document the return of *Eagle*, was also made ship's librarian after the Red Cross donated a box of paperbacks for the trip. But all the books were in English. Ruley said several of the Germans could read English well enough to translate for their mates during off hours. "Our most popular book was *Forever Amber*, which, although it would scarcely raise an eyebrow today, was considered rather racy reading in 1946. I believe the English of quite a number of our German crew improved considerably because of that book."

Meanwhile, the chief engineer tended some plants he had purchased in Madeira. The chief was about to retire, and McGowan thought that his passion for growing plants was a symptom of the not-uncommon dream of old salts to take up a life of farming. The Germans sang songs. The sun beat down. The monotony was broken by a case of appendicitis, which prompted the German doctor and the American dentist to sharpen their tools, but penicillin made it possible to postpone surgery. The former pilot's war wound healed completely. McGowan figured it was the fine weather and a regular diet that did it. One day out of Bermuda, *Eagle* was passing through long patches of yellow sargasso weed. Knowing that fish hide beneath sargasso, McGowan took the opportunity to troll a Japanese feather off the fantail. He was rewarded with a 25-pound wahoo and a smaller mahi-mahi. On June 30, the barque entered Hamilton Harbor, where Captain Thiele had anchored her seven years, eleven months, and countless lives earlier.

15 *P*ASSAGE *H*OME

Latitude 9 degrees, 41 minutes north; longitude 79 degrees, 46 minutes west, which means we are fast approaching Panama. It is hot, humid, and misty. Wade Smith is working aloft on the main t'gallant yard. I wonder how he would explain all this to his counterpart on the *Constitution* in 1812. The nineteenth-century man would understand a steel sailing ship, because the wood of *Constitution*'s hull was said to be as hard as iron. Cannonballs had bounced off it. And he would appreciate that a canal had been cut through the isthmus of Panama to avoid rounding the Horn. But navigating by satellite would be puzzling, and the heavy metal banging away on the CD player in the galley would scare him for sure. We have about 10 knots of wind, despite being in the lee of northern South America. Mountains are visible off the port bow. The ship is rolling in a following sea.

Karl Dillmann is in high spirits as he again takes his foremast

Karl Dillmann approaches the helm.
(Russell Drumm)

hands through the process of stacking the yards. He is an expert whis-
tler, and in this light breeze he clearly feels no qualms about breaking
the seagoing taboo against it. He whistles the regimental march of the
Royal Marines, then sings a verse, in Dutch, of a Boer song about the
"Khakis" — the Brits — rounding up Dutch civilians. He tells those
within earshot that the word "commando" comes from Afrikaans —
South African Dutch — a Boer word for tactics used against the British. He switches to Cockney to growl at the hands heaving round on
the lower-topsail brace: "Belay! — belay, or I'll 'ave yer guts for gar-
ters!" They've anticipated his order by lining up at the correct belaying pin ready to heave on the correct line, and he's pleased. They know
he's pleased because he's now singing in German, the St. Pauli song
about the girls on the Reeperbahn. The hands are pleased in turn because yesterday Bosun Ramos passed the word that knowing the pin
and fife rails by heart, as most of them do, will be the ticket to liberty in
Panama.

Last night on deck after the evening meal, I overheard Captain
Luke, speaking about leadership in general, observe that "liberty was
the great motivator." He was addressing a small, amused audience on
the poop deck about an angry boatswain on another boat who was
pitching a fit, as bosuns will. Or as he put it, the man was "in the-
asshole-puckered-up-so-tight-you-couldn't-pull-a-ten-penny nail-out-
of-it-with-a-John-Deere-tractor mode." Was it true? "Are they really
thinking of mixing boatswains and skivvy wavers?" he asks his audience
rhetorically (skivvy wavers being quartermasters). He was clearly taking
a stand against a new quartermaster–boatswain's mate hybrid position,
to be called something like "operational navigation specialist," rumored
to be in the offing.

Luke said he liked the new leadership model, the Total Quality
Management system. It had been borrowed from the corporate world
in the early '90s as a response to the highly efficient Japanese approach.
The system's steering committees and feedback symposiums were imposed upon the less cushioned military methods with some success, although Captain Luke bemoaned the fact that "chewing butt is becoming a lost art. Yelling is good for stress," he said, "like puking is good for
seasickness," although I sense that Ivan Luke is not a yeller himself.

But, he added, the occasional butt-chewing should not be confused with the much more dangerous elitism, a vestige of which could still be found at the academy. "Ring-knocking," as he called it, did not stand up to experience. "In the '50s, I doubt you'd see an officer falling into conversation with the enlisted on this ship. That attitude lasted way past its time." His audience, comprising a lieutenant, two petty officers, and two seaman who were within earshot at the helm, were getting the measure of their skipper-to-be. Like Captain Papp, Luke likes diversity in the wardroom. "It's hard to buy in if, when you're coming up, nobody likes you. We're ahead of our sister services assimilating females into the culture. It's hard to retain a prejudice when you work with them and see the job getting done." It turns out his mom was a SPAR, the World War II Coast Guard equivalent of a WAC or a WAVE. His father was a merchant seaman then, sailing on Liberty ships.

His parents met at a USO dance, "where my father had gone so he could dance with girls," Luke said, his audience snickering with him at the euphemism. "My mother's heart was set on my being in the Coast Guard. We went to see Annapolis, but it was too big. Then we went to West Point, and it was even bigger. When we got to the Coast Guard Academy, I saw a sign on a building that said 'Billiards,' and I said to myself, 'This is for me.' Later I realized it was Billard Hall, named for Frederick Chamberlayne Billard, commandant of the Coast Guard in the '20s." Laughter. "When people ask me why I joined, I say, My mother told me to." More laughter. Then he admitted to having had a red, white, and blue Fiat Spider with flames when he was at the academy. Appreciative smiles in the gathering dark. His father played baseball with the Cardinals organization after he left the merchant marine but never made it out of the minors. He sold insurance for the rest of his life and became a hero in his son's eyes because he stayed the course after his dream was broken. He said his ancestors were among the original English settlers in Georgia. "There are records of Lukes going off to fight in the Revolution from Columbia County." I wondered what those old Lukes would think about this one, who had driven a red, white, and blue Fiat Spider with flames. Captain Luke was taking shape. His stories would be conveyed throughout the ship within a few hours and remain on board forever.

So many stories, especially now that the work has eased. Tom Dickey, the OCS instructor, tells me he was on search and rescue patrol in Alaska and responded to a call from a dismasted sailboat. It took twenty-four hours to tow the boat and its owners to shore. In appreciation they gave Dickey a sourdough bread starter that came from a seventy-five-year-old recipe given them by a gold miner. Dickey has kept the starter alive. I've tried to estimate how many people have trained and served on this barque in her sixty-three years. More than a hundred thousand, all bringing individual stories aboard and creating new, terrifying, ecstatic, sad, and proud ones once on board. The stories are all spliced together into a long, interwoven coil that never leaves the ship. A few splices stand out, Captain McGowan's in particular, because it was there the line nearly parted in a hurricane. No one on the 1946 crossing would have been saved, and those they might have rescued in the future wouldn't have been saved either, and on and on. McGowan's story of the crossing remains fresh in my mind.

During his courtesy call on Bermuda's consul general, he asked if he could allow the German sailors to go ashore. He hadn't heard about, or had refused to acknowledge, their surreptitious landing at Funchal. "The poor devils had served faithfully," he wrote, "without once setting foot on the beach." None was a POW, each was a volunteer, he told the consul general, and each had been cleared by naval intelligence. But his entreaties were ignored. McGowan did show off the Teutonic side of his crew, however, by using Captain Schnibbe's picked boat crew, in their flat hats with two trailing ribbons, snug-fitting jackets with brass buttons, British-style broad collars, and bell-bottom trousers, to pay a call on Admiral James Pine's flag cutter *Sebago*. Admiral Pine was the academy commandant. The *Sebago* had just arrived in Bermuda with academy cadets on their summer cruise. With her decks spotless and her sexy hull gleaming white, *Eagle* drew officers, friends of officers, cadets, and yachties like flies. The yachtsmen were fresh from the finish of the annual Newport to Bermuda Race. There was a Fourth of July celebration at the consul general's house, then an academy reception on *Eagle*, during which the German crew sang on the fo'c'sle deck. McGowan recorded the moment: "Floating out of the darkness came the rich chords of classic German music. As the music rose, a hush fell over the guests. I thought of a Sunday in the streets of Bremerhaven when I had paused before a German church and heard the same music through the open door."

The celebrations, and a constant flow of visitors to and from the new training ship, kept McGowan in Bermuda four days longer than he'd intended. *Eagle* left on the morning of July 5 with the envious Admiral Pine on board, insisting that sails be set despite the lack of wind. Much to McGowan's relief, the admiral soon moved back to *Sebago*. *Eagle* doused the useless sails and proceeded under power on a mirror-flat sea. McGowan wrote that "just before sunset a refreshing breeze came sweeping in, heralding its approach with a dark line marking the ruffled surface from horizon to horizon. We set lower courses and topsails and settled down for another night at sea, happy in the prospect that only a few hours separated us from the end of our trip." But then, "as darkness approached, I felt a small twinge of uneasiness — a vague wordless worry that I could not identify. I was overlooking something important."

᠆

THERE IS an uneasiness of a different sort as *Eagle* closes in on the small city of Colón and its big harbor outside the Atlantic entrance to the Panama Canal. Ships can be seen queued up in the distance. The mood on board has changed. Small clusters of seamen are studying the pin rail assiduously to win liberty. The sound of the tops slamming on the wooden chests that hold the climbing belts, at the base of the fore- and mainmasts, means that the order has been passed to begin the long hot job of dousing and harbor-furling the sails. The heat has sucked the good humor from the crew. Max, the main engine, has been lit. I can only imagine the heat down there.

Karl's mood has changed, too. He's pointing out to Greg Giggi how the previous foremast captain had mismarked the lift blocks and used different shackles so that although the yards were square, parallel to the horizon, not acockbill, the blocks themselves were at different heights off the deck, unsymmetrical. And he also would like to point out — his voice rising — that "someone painted the goddamned pad eye again. They are never to be painted. Some of those people on those ships," he says, pointing to the huge tankers, container ships, and smaller fishing trawlers waiting to enter the canal, "trained on square-riggers. Sail training used to be the law in Europe for merchant seamen. They know the difference. You want them to go home and say the Americans are squared away." He barks at one of his crewmen who again has walked too close to the widow-maker blocks, which swing with each breath of the sails. "It'll explode your brains."

The bosun too is suddenly pissed off as land approaches. He growls at one of the officer candidates aloft on the main yard, tells him to lay in and down. "I want my crew, not the OCS folks, doing the work today to speed up their training." He is under pressure to develop a seasoned "permanent" crew, which will be anything but permanent. He is faced with the imminent departure of Petty Officer Tracy Allen and the possible retirement of Karl Dillmann, both with skills honed to instinct.

Eagle drops anchor at a prearranged spot inside the Colón breakwater. We will enter the canal in the morning. As the sun begins to set, binoculars on the quarterdeck discover that one of the ships lying at anchor is on the Coast Guard's list of suspected drug runners. The information will be passed along to another cutter. The Panamanians have invited the Coast Guard to remain after the canal is officially handed over on January 1, 2000, to continue its drug interdiction work. At a navigation briefing in the crew mess, Greg Weisner, the operations boss, goes over the charts showing the approach to the canal. He tells fellow officers, petty officers, and officer candidates that tomorrow command of *Eagle* will be relinquished to the Canal pilot. "It most certainly will not," Captain Papp snaps, his response melting his operations officer and drawing grins from the others, who understand that such a suggestion is just shy of mutinous.

At quarters in the gathering dark after the nav briefing, the captain encourages the OCS people to remember their *Eagle* shipmates and all the people who work hard every day throughout the Coast Guard. He recognizes young Kehoe, the Nova Scotian Sea Scout, for the superb job he's done. With mock ferocity, he orders the armorer to take the valuable seaman and lock him in the bosun's hole until the ship is well out in the Pacific. The crew laughs. Kehoe blushes and looks at his feet. The captain speaks of Panama and Panamanian pride and reminds the crew of their diplomatic mission. He means, Mind your pints and quarts ashore. He bids goodbye to those who will leave the ship when we reach the former U.S. Navy base at Rodman on the Pacific side. He thanks the contingent from the *Constitution;* he thanks his civilian guests for helping in the scullery. He thanks me for hauling lines. He asks Greg Giggi to lead three cheers for the departing OCS class. "Hip, Hip . . ."

∽

McGOWAN didn't like the look of a fanlike cirrus formation in the west just before sunset on the evening *Eagle* left Bermuda. Nor did he like the barograph record, a paper tape marked by an ink stylus to show the pressure trends over time. In the tropics there is a pronounced semidiurnal variation in barometric pressure, but on the evening of July 5 the tape showed a horizontal line for the previous ten hours. McGowan said his instincts told him to turn west to allow whatever was coming to pass by. There was, of course, no satellite view to help with the decision. After huddling with his executive officer, he decided to stay on course. As the XO said, New York was only two days away if the wind held. McGowan turned in at midnight, noticing on his way to bed that the high clouds had thickened.

"Suddenly I was wide awake. It was still dark. I became aware of sound — W I N D! The soft monotone of the steady breeze was gone. A gusty, uneven moaning had taken its place. The ship was lurching in an uneasy fashion as though in a resentful mood. The air felt wet and sticky." Then he remembered the telltale sign he had seen but not recognized the day before: the long, low, even swells on the horizon that telegraph an approaching storm, often days in advance.

∽

MAY 19, 1999
Reveille is early today. "Heave out, trice up, lash and stow, lash and stow. It is now 0400." The anchor detail forms up on the fo'c'sle deck. Kelly Nixon looks shoreward at first light. She knows the area well, having done joint boardings with the Panamanian Coast Guard. I will

be leaving the ship soon, so I offer her congratulations. She is about to be promoted to mainmast captain, *Eagle*'s first female mast captain. She looks at me curiously: "What for?" When I explain, she shrugs her shoulders and says, "Oh."

Eagle is under way, passing palms and brilliant orange flamboyant trees en route to the Gatún locks, the first of three that will eventually put *Eagle* in Gatún Lake, 74 feet above sea level. The pilot boat *Remora* comes alongside with the canal pilot and a half dozen line handlers. Bosun Ramos is freaking at the thought of outside line handlers. I'm at the port railing on the fo'c'sle deck, watching our approach. The entrance both underscores and belies the importance of the canal. Twelve thousand ships per year pass through here — that's forty per day — but the canal itself, like *Eagle*, is from another age. Two rowboats, one on either side, bring the four cables that will be tied off, two at the bow, port and starboard, and two at the stern. They hold the ship in a kind of cat's cradle. Each cable runs to a small railroad train engine, two on either side of the canal. They will pull *Eagle* through the locks to the lake. Karl is behind me speaking French to Lambert, the officer candidate from the Haitian Coast Guard. French was the language that built the canal until debt, scandal, and the fevered deaths of tens of thousands of workers put the project in American hands for completion. Not everyone is happy at the pace of the turnover to the Panamanians; there are Colombian insurgents, funded by the drug trade, who would like to see Panama returned to Colombia, from which it was carved when the canal was built.

Most of the crew is idle, watching the scenery and telling stories. A few recall the pitiful *yolas*, boats built on the north coast of the Dominican Republic, built in one day, painted Caribbean blue with a blue tarp for camouflage. People pay a year's salary just to get on a *yola*. Dominicans are more aggressive than Haitians in their attempts to get to the States. The Chinese try to get in through Puerto Rico. Cubans and Haitians go through Florida, Dom Reps through San Juan, which has a big Dominican community. Candidate Williamee is in the middle of a tale about taking Haitians off a boat between the Dom Rep and Puerto Rico in '91 in heavy seas. The ribbed inflatable boat was sinking because of the number of people being ferried to the 270-foot *Harriet Lane*. "We lost an M-16 and a motor surf boat in the process." Candidate Howell chimes in and says that when he was on the 110-foot *Matinicus* out of Cape May he saw an enforcer, one of the people paid to sneak people into the States, hitting a kid with the backside of a machete. "The kid was puking, seasick, and he signaled us that he wanted to be rescued. He was bleeding into the boat. The Coast Guard is emasculated because it can't really stop the migrants." The painful irony of being able to rescue these people but not save their lives in a larger sense clearly weighs on the Coasties.

The small trains pulling *Eagle* ring bells to mark their place on their respective tracks so the port and starboard tow lines stay even. High fences with razor wire separate the canal itself from the jungle. Dozens of black frigate birds circle overhead. Karl, looking at the jungle, says we are at the same latitude as the Philippines. "And this isn't just any ship," he says, still staring into the bush, into potential danger. Once in the lake, we are to rendezvous with small boats carrying Admiral Roger Rufe, vice admiral in charge of Atlantic Area operations, and Simon Ferro, the U.S. ambassador to Panama, and his wife, as well as other dignitaries. They will board *Eagle* for the rest of the passage through the canal.

⌒

BY THE morning of July 6, 1946, *Eagle*'s barometer had begun a precipitous plunge. "As the clock indicated sunrise, the thickening overcast absorbed the growing light, leaving us in a pre-dawn gloom," McGowan wrote. "Spitting rain squalls gradually increased in frequency and intensity." The barque was sailing under courses and upper and lower topsails. McGowan reckoned that if the storm was a true hurricane, then at *Eagle*'s latitude — halfway between Bermuda and New York — its path should already have begun to curve to the northeast, away from the ship. The gusts coming out of the northeast meant the storm was southeast of *Eagle*. Or they might be in an isolated outlying squall whose wind did not provide an accurate picture of the storm. At this point the captain decided on a strategy he knew had been used successfully by some square-rigger skippers. He would run before the weather while bearing west, away from what he figured was the storm track. "All hands were engaged in putting extra lashings on the boats, rigging lifelines, securing air ports, dogging down hatches, and closing watertight doors. I resolved to keep the wind nearly astern, favoring starboard over port. As long as the wind stayed northeast it would take us toward the New Jersey coast" — and away from the system.

Eagle plowed along until "the sea began to build to impressive size." The two helmsmen struggled with the wheel. The following sea had begun to outpace the ship. Waves were hammering the champagne counter and the rudder below. Two more helmsmen were ordered to take their place at the second of the barque's three wheels. In short order,

> eight men were gathered around toiling at the spokes. When I first saw this rig I was curious about the need for the multiple positions. I was now learning the hard way why the Germans had been so generous. My helmsmen and I were a tight little island of humanity on the broad quarterdeck. There had been no morning coffee and no breakfast, but I gave this not a thought. A strange feeling of elation gripped me as I watched the drama unfold. I was living in the moment, and time was standing still. If the quartermaster was marking time with the ship's bell, it was a futile gesture, since the ding-dinging would not have registered on our consciousness.
>
> "Whitecaps had long since disappeared and been replaced by angry streaks gouged on the breast of the waves by the claws of the wind. Puffs became roaring blasts of wind. The average velocity rose above 50 knots. The streaks on the surface vanished, giving way to clouds of spray as wavetops were sheared off by the wind. When this occurs there is a momentary period of deceptive smoothness. The stinging pellets of water fly horizontally downwind, knocking down the waves as they try to rise. It gives a false sense of calm, but experience tells the seaman that this will quickly pass. At this point a really big sea begins building. I was fully aware that this was only the beginning, and as awesome as the weather looked, it was bound to get worse.

Another hour passed, and McGowan said that the distance between wave crests appeared to be eight to ten ship lengths. The wind was over 60 knots and the barometer continued to fall.

As the ship began to plunge and wallow as each crest overtook us and went roaring by, it became hard to retain a footing. All hands were directed to remain where they were until further notice, and there would be no relieving of watches except for the relays of eight men at a time at the wheels. They tired rapidly and had to be relieved at fifteen- to twenty-minute intervals. The pool of manpower for the task was clustered about the quarterdeck, hanging on to lifelines and railings. The earlier skirling and piping of the fresh gale through the rigging had risen in volume and tone to bellowing and shrieking. The vast sound seemed to fill the world. Voices of men died away and became inaudible. Each man found himself suddenly alone with the wind. Lips moving, neck cords and veins standing out recalled the silent movie days. Here were faces transmitting thoughts by expression alone. Here was sound without sound. It pressed upon eardrums and bodies as a solid thing. The singleness of this mighty roar brought about a solitude. The weight of wind and sound tightened our isolated worlds about us.

The massiveness of the sea, dwarfing the ship, created an illusion of slow motion. The illusion was shattered into hard reality as we dove into each trough and felt the shock of the solid wall of water. As each wave front approached from astern, the advancing face of the wave seemed to steepen and bear down upon us with a rolling motion that is seen in miniature when breakers curl in on a beach. Each time we were overtaken, our stern rose high in the air. As the wave moved forward, the stern would begin to settle on the back of the wave, and momentarily the ship would be suspended at her midpoint with bow and stern protruding, each from its own side of the watery edge. At this moment tons of water plunged in from port and starboard, filling the welldeck. The voice of the storm was more than a roar. There was a sharp tearing sound — the ripping of the fabric of the gates of hell. The bellowing blasts, born of the heat of the tropics, slowly accumulated during months of gestation at the edge of the Doldrums, were the main theme. This tapestry of sound bore the pattern of maniacal majesty. The fore upper and lower topsails were the first to go. One moment they were there; a second later they had vanished. All that remained of the broad spread of sail were these ragged little ribbons.

The wind was now blowing 80 knots.

The ship had begun to dive and wallow like a wounded thing. Each time a wave overtook us I looked apprehensively astern. As the stern began to lift on the face of a wave, the bowsprit dipped deeper and deeper until it disappeared from sight. When each crest swept from aft forward, the stern settled deeply upon the back of the wave, and the bowsprit pointed toward the sky. The water that had been scooped up by the fo'c'sle would come thundering aft, burying everything in the welldeck under a foamy green burden. As the *Eagle* shook herself like a giant dog, tons of water tore out through the freeing ports.

The time had come to heave to. Schnibbe and Knud Langvard were by McGowan's side, but protocol dictated that it was McGowan's decision alone. It was a terrifying one. Heaving to — putting *Eagle*'s bow into the wind and waves — meant turning her 90 degrees in the trough of a wave and timing it so the following wave would not broach her. If the attempt was not made, the ship would likely broach anyway after surfing down the face of a wave and burying her bowsprit. She would sail under.

At this moment *Eagle* received a radio message from an American freighter somewhere close by, warning all vessels that it was unable to maneuver, to steer clear. Langvard asked McGowan, Didn't he think it was time to heave to? Ed Lowe was belowdecks. He said, "I was on the port side, where a porthole gasket was leaking, and I had water all over the place. The room was flooded and the water was swishing back and forth. We had lost communication with the bridge, and no one was going visiting, although we had people going up there to see what was what. They were going to have to make a decision. The storm was so bad we couldn't continue. We thought we might not make it another time because we had no keel, just the ballast. She'd go over so far, and there was a feeling. We'd roll over and you'd think it wasn't going to stop and there'd be a shudder, like the ship was fighting. It was a funny feeling to go over and then right yourself and wait for the next one and wonder what was going to happen. The staysails were the only thing that kept us going."

One of the main's topsails could not be doused. The rest of the square sails had blown out. The clewline might have been jammed in its block. The sail posed a great danger, because it was exaggerating *Eagle*'s roll. McGowan doesn't record the incident in his book, but both German and American members of the crew recall one of the German hands climbing into the rigging to cut the sail loose.

McGowan wrote,

> My next visitor was the Exec, who indicated through sign language that he wanted to know my decision about heaving to. Moments before he asked, something happened which removed all doubt from my mind about our course of action. Along came a sea that was the daddy of them all, and caught us at a slight angle, the very thing I had been trying to avoid. The ship partially broached, and with a thunderous BANG! literally dove into the ocean. The bowsprit and entire fo'c'sle disappeared under green water all the way to the base of the foremast. The mainsail exploded like a child's balloon. We rolled deeply to starboard. We hung momentarily at the bottom of the roll, while I stared across the quarterdeck, looking almost straight down at the boiling surface of the ocean.

Joseph Terrels, a radioman third class, was belowdecks when *Eagle* rolled to 49 degrees. He said there was a man locked in a makeshift brig in one of the spaces two decks down by the sail locker and the bosun's hole. He had been transferred from the *Sebago* shortly before sailing and was to be delivered to a court-martial in New London. Terrels said, "He was thrashing his arms and snorting, pacing back and forth like a madman. I wished I was at St. Agnes Church. I never thought we would survive."

∾

PANAMA, 0945
We're in the lake now, moving slowly in the tropical heat. The lake is dotted with small islands, which were actually hilltops before the Chagres River was dammed. Ospreys cry and search for fish. Karl says the hummock hills remind him of the islands off Bataan, where he took his Marines on patrols with night scopes. The small boats bring Admiral Rufe and his guests alongside *Eagle*. Charlie Wilkens, who has been asked to pipe the guests aboard, asks Karl if he can borrow his bosun's pipe, which is closer at hand. Chief Boatswain's Mate Vaught tells me he has a bosun's pipe, a sterling silver beauty, which he goes to get. It once

belonged to a Chief Moore, one of two survivors from the crew of the cutter *Escabana*, sunk by a U-boat in 1943 with the loss of 101 lives. Vaught had met the bosun's aged father at an Elks' lodge in California. The man said the pipe had been sitting on the mantel next to his son's picture. He gave it to Vaught, saying he wanted it to stay in the Coast Guard. Vaught intends to give it to the bosun of the current *Escabana*. He says another cutter, *Campbell*, was named after the cutter that sank a U-boat by ramming it.

Sideboys are formed up, and Wilkens pipes the dignitaries aboard.

Mrs. Dillmann has joined the large group of people on the fo'c'sle and boat decks. Karl takes a seat beside her on one of the lifeboats. *Eagle* is approaching the west end of the lake, where it narrows into Culebra Cut, whose sides are steep. The jungle is close again. Someone shouts: "Monkeys in the trees!"

Kelly Nixon is standing behind Karl, talking and chewing gum. She snaps her gum the way some girls learn to do in high school, and the sudden *pop* causes Karl to flinch, a quick duck. I'm the only one who seems to notice. His mother is facing the other direction, talking to the person next to her. I look back at Karl, and he's wiping a tear away with his sleeve, a drop of brine from the ocean within.

～

McGowan wrote:

My ship quivered and fought her way upright with laboring effort. We couldn't take many repetitions of this. The time to heave to was right now. We rehearsed the maneuver in pantomime. I whistled the engine room, ordered the [propeller] shaft connected, and told them to stand by the engine telegraph for a short "ahead" bell. We had agreed that we would heave to on the port tack with our remaining main lower topsail still set, provided the wind didn't blow it away. At the same time, we would set the small lower mizzensail in order to strike a balance with the forward sail. Immediately after the next and largest wave bore down upon us and swept by the ship on a fairly normal angle to the sea, I gave the Exec a wave of the hand, and ordered my toiling helmsmen to put the wheel over to left full rudder, at the same time ringing ahead two-thirds on the engine telegraph. As the ship's head began to swing, I stopped the engine and began to pray. The next thirty seconds were critical. The boys on the braces and those on the mizzensail sensed our dangerous situation. They worked in desperate haste. The ship snapped around to her new heading as though mounted on a pivot; the yards braced around, lines set taut. The mizzensail zipped into place. It was as though the whole operation had been performed by one pair of giant hands.

To those who experienced it, the great storm, the fifth and largest to have threatened the barque, must have seemed like the final exhalation of a dying beast. *Eagle* rode it out, then resumed her course to New York harbor, where she anchored, on July 10, her sails hanging in tatters. Orders were received by telegraph to proceed up the Hudson River about 20 miles to Camp Shanks. Not long before, *Prinz Eugen* had cruised into Philadelphia with a half-German crew. Unfortunately for their counterparts on *Eagle,* the rowdy welcoming party aboard *Prinz Eugen,* which had been joined by American relatives of the Germans, was roundly criticized in the press. The Coasties aboard *Eagle* wanted to show the Germans New York City, but it was not to be. The graves were still fresh from the war fought to save the city and the world.

The critical battle for the Atlantic had been a closer call than seems possible today, but not as close as some of *Eagle*'s German crew believed. As she passed the Statue of Liberty for the first time, Emil Babich, a Coast Guard machinist's mate on the mixed crew, heard a few of the younger Germans voice surprise — he was not certain if the expression was heartfelt or sardonic — at how quickly New York had been rebuilt after its destruction by German bombs.

The Germans were taken from the ship by military police to Camp Shanks, where they were dressed in POW uniforms and assigned numbers. One of the Coast Guard crewmen said that when the Americans entered the Germans' berthing area after their departure, they found graffiti on the bulkheads: a swastika and bitter words about being treated as POWs. But others didn't remember any swastikas, and surviving members of the German crew said no, that while they were disappointed to be thus treated, they understood the situation. They sailed for Le Havre on July 21. Once they arrived in France, their German navy uniforms were returned. They sailed to Bremerhaven aboard the *Texarcana Victory* and were greeted by Commander Lord of the U.S. Navy, who thanked them for their service.

Soon after, Captain McGowan was given his next assignment: to take a group of men to Korea to set up a Coast Guard flotilla.

⌒

PANAMA, 1100

Eagle is brought back to sea level in two stages, at the Pedro Miguel and the Miraflores locks, respectively. The deck force has donned orange flotation vests in preparation for docking at Rodman. Karl is again in high spirits, alternately whistling and chatting up Captain Luke for the first time. He also talks with Admiral Rufe, who sailed on *Eagle* when John F. Kennedy was chief boatswain's mate from 1961 through 1964 under Captain Robert Schultz. Rufe tells Karl that his reputation has preceded their meeting.

The class of 2000 will arrive tomorrow aboard a C-130 transport plane. I will be gone by the time the captain musters them in welcome and in warning. One hundred and twenty new souls will form up in the waist of the ship whose deck their predecessors have heaved miles and miles of line upon, slept on in the sun, fallen on from above, died upon, been buried from — the same deck that Hitler strode. It's been washed clean by the waves of the storms that the ship has survived. In the end, absolution is the sea's to give. Now, *Eagle*'s deck is where saviors are born — Baywatched and television-wrestled, perhaps — but proudly yoked by a sense of higher purpose, the best kind of people.

Bosun Ramos is on the bridge yelling directions in Spanish to the line handlers on the dock. Kelly Nixon is directing operations midships. Karl is at the bow. *Eagle*'s heavy, white-braided hawsers are pulled onto the dock by the smaller throwing lines attached to their bitter ends and brought to their respective cleats by the shore crew. The deck force will snug *Eagle* up to where the bosun wants her. "Haul around!" Dillmann barks, his voice having risen in volume and deepened to fit the purpose. Off the opposite — port — bow, two sleek patrol boats of the Panama-

*The bow watch applies his binocu-
lars to the horizon.* (Collection of
Herbert Böhm)

nian Coast Guard rest at their moorings. The swirling design of Caribbean blues, black, and gray on their hulls is meant to make them invisible at a distance. Karl declares, "It's an old-pattern camouflage."

I'm not surprised that Karl recognizes old-pattern camouflage nor
that such patterns change over time. Why not? If the years alter the way
we see the world, they must also change the way we don't see it. This
explains how, once the crew has furled her sails and tethered her to
land, *Eagle* can be hidden on a bright sunny day, cocooned in stately
anachronism, dismissed as a beautiful thing. She shows her true colors
only in midocean under sail, when she charges through swells sent over
time from distant, dangerous storms. When orders are passed along the
deck to brace the yards sharper — "Handsomely there" — and passed
up to the highest yards — "Let fall the royals" — *Eagle* sloughs every
inanimate posture. Now, if I'm asked how people can attempt a rescue
through mountainous waves or approach a sea of burning jet fuel and its
burden of death, I will say that they, or those who lead them, must first
have accepted that sailing ships are alive, that they are the only living
things ever created by mankind outside our image from whole cloth,

rope, wood, and then steel. And that sailing ships do not exist apart from sailors. Nor do sailors fully exist apart from their ships, once they have breathed and pulled together — married to outwit a mercurial sea. If you allow this, you might also entertain the immortality of certain seamen.

POSTSCRIPT

Karl Dillmann was promoted to chief boatswain's mate in the late fall of 2000. Just before Christmas, Captain Ivan Luke canceled the scheduled late-winter OCS cruise and moved *Eagle* across the Thames River from the Coast Guard Academy to the Groton submarine base for repairs. At his insistence, the deck force has been increased by ten nonrates and three petty officers to reduce fatigue. *Eagle* leaves for Halifax, Nova Scotia, on May 1, 2001, en route to Cork, Ireland; Brest, France; and Gibraltar. She is to sail home via Bermuda and ports of call along the northeast coast. I wish her "royals all the way."

Glossary

ABACK. The position of a sail when the wind strikes it on the forward side.

AMIDSHIPS. Midway between the bow and stern of a vessel or midway between the port and starboard sides.

ASTERN. Behind a vessel (180 degrees from its heading).

ATHWARTSHIPS. Across the vessel from one side to the other.

"AVAST" or *"'VAST."* A command to immediately stop doing something. Used only when continuing will endanger gear or personnel. The normal, less urgent, command is "That's well."

BACK. 1. In the Northern Hemisphere, to experience a counterclockwise change in wind direction. 2. To intentionally cause the sails to be aback, as when tacking.

BACK EASY. To slowly ease a line, either to check a stopper or to turn the line on or off a belaying pin.

BARQUE. A sailing vessel with three or more masts whose aftermast is fore-and-aft rigged. *Eagle*, a barque, is called a ship only for convenience; a ship, technically, is square-rigged on all masts.

BELAY. To secure a line to a belaying pin, cleat, or other point.

BOLTROPE. Roping around the edges of a sail.

BOWSPRIT. The large spar extending forward from the bow of a sailing vessel. The stays that support the foremast and headsails (jibs) are fastened to it.

BRACED SQUARE. Of yards, perpendicular to the ship's heading.

BRACE. A line used to move a yard in a horizontal plane.

BROACH. To move broadside to a heavy surf or sea.

BUNTLINE. A line used to haul the foot of a square sail up to the yard to douse the sail.

CATENARY. The natural downward curve of a line or chain caused by the weight of the line. It provides a spring or elastic effect.

CAUGHT ABACK. The position of a ship when, because of a wind shift or a helmsman's error, the wind strikes the forward rather than the after side of the square sails.

CHEEK BLOCK. A block attached to a yardarm through which a square sail's sheet is led.

CLEW. A lower corner of a square sail or the after lower corner of a fore-and-aft sail.

"CLEW DOWN." A command to haul on the clewlines while holding the sheets to settle a yard into its fixed lifts.

"CLEW UP." A command to haul a sail up into its gear by easing the sheets and hauling on the clewlines, buntlines, and leechlines.

CLOSE-HAULED. Point of sail at which a vessel is as near to the wind as possible.

COCKBILL or *ACOCKBILL.* Slanted, not horizontal, position of the yards.

COURSES: Collective term for the mainsail and foresail, the biggest square sails, which are closest to the deck.

CROSSTREES. Horizontal crosspieces at the point where the topmast and topgallant mast come together.

DOUSE. To take in a sail.

"EASE." A command to pay out a line slowly and with care or to reduce strain on a line.

FAIRLEAD. A block or fitting that changes the direction of a line or that allows it to run free without chafing.

FALL OFF. To change course in a direction away from the wind.

FANNING. Bracing each higher weather yardarm slightly more aft to take advantage of differences in relative wind speeds at different heights.

FID. A wooden marlinespike used primarily to splice line.

FIFE RAIL. A rail around three sides of each mast used to belay running rigging.

FOLLOWING SEA. A sea running in the direction of the ship's course.

FOOTROPE. One of the ropes that hang below a yard to provide footing for climbing out on the yard and handling sail.

FULL AND BY. Sailing as close to the wind as possible, with all sails drawing full and course changes being made to adjust for wind shifts. With all sails set, *Eagle* can sail about 75 degrees off the true wind when sailing full and by.

FURL. To take in a sail and secure it.

FUTTOCK SHROUDS. A steel rod leading from the futtock band below the top to the edge of the top, providing a foundation for the topmast shrouds.

GASKET. A canvas strap used to secure a sail when furled.

HALYARD. A line used for hoisting and lowering sails and yards.

"HANDSOMELY." A command to proceed deliberately and carefully but not necessarily slowly.

HANK. A metal ring that rides on a stay and to which the luff of a staysail is seized.

HAWSEHOLE. A heavy casting through which an anchor chain runs from the deck to the anchor.

HEAVE TO. To stop the ship's headway by turning into the wind or by backing the sails on one or more masts.

HOUSE. To lower the fore and main topgallant masts so that a vessel can pass safely under a bridge. *Eagle*'s topgallant masts can be lowered approximately fifteen feet.

IN ITS GEAR. The position of a sail that has been taken in and is being held by its buntlines, leechlines, buntleechlines, and clewlines all two-blocked and belayed.

IN ITS LIFTS: The position of a yard after the halyard has been eased and the yard's entire weight is supported by the fixed lifts.

JIBE. To change tack by bringing a vessel's stern through the wind. Fore-and-aft vessels jibe, while square-riggers wear (another term for a controlled jibe).

KNOCKDOWN. A sudden and extreme heeling caused by a strong gust of wind.

LEECH. The after edge of a fore-and-aft sail or the sides of a square sail.

LEECHLINE. In general, a line leading to the leech of a square sail that hauls it up to the yard for furling.

LEEWARD. Away from the wind, downwind.

LINE. In general, a fiber rope. Wire rope is called rope, wire rope, or wire.

"LIVELY." A command to proceed quickly, either easing or hauling at a faster pace.

LUFF. 1. The leading edge of a fore-and-aft sail. 2. The shaking of a sail when the sheet is too slack or the vessel is too close to the wind.

MARLINESPIKE. A pointed tool used to separate strands of rope.

OFF THE WIND. A vessel's position when it is not sailing close-hauled and the true wind is abaft the beam.

PAD EYE. A steel ring welded to a deck or bulkhead to which gear is rigged.

POINT. One of the thirty-two divisions of a compass card, corresponding to 11.25 degrees. "Pointing" refers to a vessel's course and its ability to steer close to the wind.

POOP. To take a heavy sea over a vessel's stern or quarter. This may occur when the vessel is running before the wind in a gale.

QUARTER. A position 45 degrees abaft either beam; directly between abeam and astern.

QUARTERS. A muster of officers and enlisted personnel.

RATLINES. Lines fastened horizontally to the shrouds, upon which sailors climb aloft.

REACH. The point of sail at which a vessel is neither beating to windward nor running before the wind.

RUNNING RIGGING. The movable lines and blocks used for handling sails and yards.

SCUPPER. A drain in the deck that carries off rain or seawater from the waterways.

SHEET. Running rigging attached to the clew of a sail.

"SHEET HOME." A command to ease the clewlines, buntlines, and leechlines and haul on the sheets to put the square sails in position. Also, a command to haul the sheet in and trim the headsails and staysails to best advantage when setting them.

SHROUD. One of the cables or lines that support a mast laterally, running from the masthead to the deck.

STANDING RIGGING. The fixed cable stays and shrouds that support the masts.

STAY. 1. One of the supports for the masts. Some stays carry staysails. 2. To tack. The ship is said to be in stays when she is coming through the wind and to miss stays when she does not make it through.

STOPPER. A short line fixed to the deck that holds a line under strain while it is being belayed.

TABLING. A broad hem of canvas or Dacron sewn into the edge of a sail to reinforce it. It has the same purpose as the boltrope used on sails in earlier times.

TACK. To change direction by bringing the ship's bow through the wind.

TELLTALE. A flag or pennant that indicates the relative wind.

"THAT'S WELL." A command indicating that a line has been hauled enough. A less emphatic form of "Avast."

TOP. A platform at the top of a mast, such as a foretop or maintop. It is not the uppermost point of the mast. On *Eagle*, the tops are the platforms on the fore- and mainmasts below the crosstrees.

UNFURL. To cast loose a sail by throwing off the gaskets.

"UP BEHIND." A command indicating that a line being belayed has enough turns on the pin so that one person can hold it. Also a command to those behind a line to drop it so it can be belayed quickly.

VEER. 1. In the Northern Hemisphere, to experience a clockwise shift in wind direction.

WAIST. The portion of the main weather deck between the raised fo'c'sle deck and the poop deck.

"WALK AWAY WITH IT." A command to grasp a line, usually a halyard, with both hands and haul on it.

WEAR. To change direction by bringing the ship's stern through the wind. Compare *Jibe*.

WEATHER. On the side toward the wind. Objects on the ship's weather side are said to be "to windward" or "to weather."

WEATHER DECK. The uppermost deck exposed to the weather.

WEATHER HELM. A condition in which lee rudder must be used to keep the vessel on a steady course, occurring when force aft of the ship's pivot point turns the bow to windward. Although excessive weather helm is undesirable, *Eagle*, like most sailing vessels, is designed to sail with some weather helm.

WORM, PARCEL, AND SERVE. A procedure for protecting standing rigging. To worm is to fill the spaces between a rope's strands with small cordage wound spirally. To parcel is to wind tarred canvas around a rope. To serve is to wind small cordage tightly around a rope to hold the worming and parceling in position.

YARD. A spar rigged horizontally on a mast to which the head of a square sail is bent (made fast).

YARDARM. Outboard end of a yard.